HEART

of a

LIONESS

SACRIFICE, COURAGE AND RELENTLESS LOVE
AMONG THE CHILDREN OF UGANDA

IRENE GLEESON

with NICOLE PARTRIDGE

Authentic

Cover design by Peter Gloege | LOOK Design Studio
Cover photo of author from the 2002 IGF documentary by David Vernon, SDTV, Sydney.
Cover photo of children by Jon Love Photography, jonlove.com
Internal photos by Jon Love

Published by Authentic Publishers
188 Front Street, suite 116-44
Franklin, TN 37064
USA

28 West Parade
West Ryde NSW 2114
Australia

Authentic Publishers is a division of Authentic Media, Inc.

Library of Congress Cataloguing-in-Publication Data

Gleeson, Irene
    Heart of a Lioness: Sacrifice, courage and relentless love among
    the children of uganda / Irene Gleeson
p. cm.

ISBN 978-1-78078-047-4
    978-1-78078-249-2 (e-book)

Printed in the United States of America
20 19 18 17 16 15 14   10 9 8 7 6 5 4 3 2 1

This book is dedicated to Papa God,
my Australian family, and
my Acholi family in northern Uganda.

CONTENTS

ACKNOWLEDGEMENTS

THERE ARE SO MANY good friends who have been inextricably woven into the tapestry of my life. These people have added colour, depth and texture to my story, and for that I am truly grateful.

To my four children Maree, Gregory, Shelley and Heidi, and my fifteen grandchildren—thank you for sacrificing all the care and love that a mother and grandmother is supposed to give by allowing me to follow God's call to Africa.

Thank you C3 Church, Australia—the church family who welcomed, inspired and championed my walk with Christ and who were central to my life story and calling.

My heartfelt thanks go to John Paul Kiffasi, my gifted administrator, who now carries the mantle of the Irene Gleeson Foundation (IGF) along with all my African sons.

I thank God daily for Alice and Paul Zagorski for their enduring friendship and loyalty and for upholding the Australian end of my ministry. Thank you for your faithfulness.

Thank you David Loxley for your tireless commitment to the ministry of IGF for so many years, and David Welsh for your leadership and guidance in helping me navigate my course.

Thank you to my faithful friends, Jacky Martin, Julie Worsley, Terri Irvin and others who stood by me in good times and in bad.

To my "adopted son" George Timothy Lubega (Exodus Ug) who added life and vitality and who introduced me to the world of Hip Hop music—thank you.

Grateful thanks to all our faithful supporters including Kenneth Copeland Ministries, Crossroads, Feed the Hungry and Global Development Group whose financial commitment made the work at IGF possible.

My sincerest appreciation to Daystar TV, especially Marcus, Joni and Rebecca Lamb, for allowing me to share my vision with a global audience and to Grant Windle for paving the way with the award-winning documentary, *Cinderella Children*.

I am eternally grateful to my good friend and fellow writer Nicole Partridge, who has invested her life into the making of this book.

Thanks go to Authentic Publishers and Koorong for championing this book right from the outset, and in particular Gavin Shume, Paul Bootes and Rob Bootes for persevering and for believing in the power of one woman's story and the impact it could have. *Heart of a Lioness* has been enriched by the skills of our truly gifted editors Julia Evans and Liz Williams and the writing skills of Susannah McDonald. My sincere thanks to my "American grandson," Trent Fuenmayor, for taking care of the day-to-day details in the lead up to the publishing of this book.

Special thanks to my good friend Valerie Schache for bringing to life my first memoir, *Dance of the Tragic Heroines*.

I am indebted to Drayton Nabers Jr. and the staff in the USA for taking on this little Aussie woman and for helping to spread the word about the work of IGF. My deepest appreciation to Ben Okello Luwum and Henry Okello Oryem for standing by me and the ministry of IGF.

To my African staff, many of whom are rescued children—I am so thankful for your personal sacrifice, devotion and commitment to the work of IGF over so many years.

Thank you to the scores of visitors and volunteers who have travelled to Uganda over the past twenty years, sometimes putting their own lives on the line working shoulder to shoulder with me in order to put a smile on the faces of beautiful African children.

Most of all, I'd like to applaud the real heroes in this book—the Acholi people of northern Uganda whose courage, faith and spirit have been a constant inspiration to me.

Finally, thank You to my sweetheart Jesus, who was my husband and my writing companion—this is His story.

ON A HOT SUMMER'S DAY in January 2009, I met Irene
Gleeson for the very first time after having been commissioned
by *Charisma* magazine to write a feature story on her. The interview took place at her daughter's home in suburban Sydney.
It was very informal. We sat on deckchairs in the shade looking
out onto the backyard, while two of her grandchildren bounced
happily on the trampoline.

As we munched on grilled cheese sandwiches and drank tea,
Irene shared her extraordinary story with me, beginning with
her traumatic childhood, sexual abuse and early marriage at the
age of 16. She spoke of the wrong choices she had made and her
continual search for love and acceptance, which took her to all
manner of places, including a small beachside church where she
had an encounter with God.

A decade later, she was called to work with the Acholi people
of northern Uganda where for the next twenty years she carved
out the most impressive project I have ever seen. I remember
thinking Irene was an unlikely missionary. For a start, she was 47
when she left for Africa, she didn't grow up in church or with a
call to mission, and for many years her life was a mess. By her own
admission, at 37 she was "washed-up." But in God's vernacular,
there's no such thing as being washed-up. He wasn't concerned
about her flaws or insecurities. Instead he saw her heart—a heart

that was moved by injustice and willing to leave a comfortable middle-class life and relocate to an isolated, war-ravaged region in order to rescue destitute children.

"But didn't you ever get scared?" I asked her after hearing about one of the many late-night rebel attacks on her caravan.

Irene grimaced.

"NO!" she replied, almost defiantly. "I never get scared."

"Really?" I probed. "But what about . . ." as I presented a number of scenarios that might unnerve even the bravest and most spiritual among us.

"Okay," she finally said, surrendering her mock bravado. "I sometimes sleep with my boots on." Later on, it struck me that this might be a fitting metaphor for Irene's life—always dressed and ready for combat, both physically and spiritually. That's not to say she didn't falter—because at times she did. Nevertheless, she overcame every obstacle, proving she was an indomitable force for good against the powers of evil working in northern Uganda.

At the end of our two-hour interview I asked one final question: "Irene, what makes you cry?"

"Nothing," she said indignantly (there was that mock bravado again).

"Come on Irene," I challenged, "there must be something that makes you tear up. What about leaving your family?"

"No!"

"Your husband leaving you?"

"No," she said, looking at me like I was a crazy woman.

And then I hit a nerve.

"What about the plight of the children in Uganda?"

After a moment of silence she looked down, seemingly unable to speak, her eyes moist.

"Why the tears Irene?" I probed gently.

"I don't know," she whispered. "Perhaps it's the heart of God for these children."

In that moment, I knew that something miraculous had taken place in Irene's heart—a heart that in many ways was like that of a lioness. For years Irene had seen herself as a lioness in Uganda. This imagery only became clear to me after some research. Lionesses are protectors, defenders and nurturers—moreover, they'll stop at nothing to ensure the wellbeing of their pride. This was Irene. During this interview and the ensuing friendship that developed between us, I discovered how self-sacrificing she really was. Never elevating herself above the locals, she ate what they ate, lived as they lived and for many years did without creature comforts such as hot and cold running water. Her motto was, "If the locals don't have it (nicer food, running water, air-conditioning, etc.), why should I?"

In 2012, when Irene was diagnosed with cancer, the board decided to rename Childcare Kitgum Servants the Irene Gleeson Foundation (IGF). Irene wasn't altogether comfortable with this and preferred to call the organisation "In God's Favour." You see, it was never about Irene making a name for herself—it was all about the vulnerable and traumatised children of northern Uganda. Apart from Irene's own family, the Ugandan children were all that mattered. These were her cubs, who are growing up and becoming the lions of IGF.

The release of this book is bittersweet for me. Although I'm delighted to see Irene's book in print, I'm saddened that she isn't around to see the fulfilment of her dream. The pages crafted have been a "work in progress" for more than a decade. What began as a cathartic process during a period of grief for Irene has become the book you are about to read and one I know you will enjoy. Irene was a storyteller. She loved the drama and ongoing narrative. She spent many a night recording her African adventures, hammering away on an archaic typewriter under the dim light of a paraffin lamp in her caravan. I'm told that most days, after doing rounds of the project site, she could be found writing. This was a pastime she loved. Just recently I was in Uganda doing some research for her book and found reams of paper: manuscripts, screenplays, old diaries and journal after journal on Irene's long wooden work table. Perhaps the most exciting discovery was a prophetic word that was given to Irene back in 1983 stating that she would write a book that would connect the world to Jesus. I think this is it. I hope you find Jesus in the pages of *Heart of a Lioness*. I have, and trust you will also.

—Nicole Partridge

1

AMBUSHED

KITGUM, UGANDA, NOVEMBER 1992

IT WAS 2 A.M. and I was having trouble sleeping. I turned restlessly in my bed and thought about my new home near Kitgum Town, in the dusty north of Uganda. It seemed thousands of years as well as thousands of kilometres from my former beachside home in Sydney, Australia.

I reached for the iridescent shell next to my bed, and held it close to my ear. As the shell breathed out the sea's song, I imagined the surges of the waves lulling me to sleep.

THUMP! Something hit the side of the caravan with a loud thud.

I sat up, startled, then rose quickly and peered through the window only to see a man ducking out of sight.

Opening the small metal door, I stepped down onto the dirt. "What do you want?"

A man, ugly as a gargoyle, his face distorted with rage, was crouching at my feet. He sprang up, shoved a rifle barrel in my face and sneered.

Four other men closed in, waving AK-47s and sticks. One pointed a bayonet at my ribs.

I yelled out.

My husband, Jeff, appeared behind me muttering, "What's going on here?" He shone his torch in their faces.

A stocky man swung a cane stick against Jeff's head. His ear began to drip blood. Panic welled up in my throat as I watched blood trickle down onto Jeff's pyjamas.

Tonight we die, I thought. *Hmm, short career as missionaries. Okay, get ready. We're coming to see You, Jesus. I wonder if I'll feel the bayonet.*

I stood there with my eyes closed.

Ker-shunk. Ker-shunk. Bullets were dropped into a gun chamber.

"Dear Jesus," I said out loud, "Yours is the next face I will see."

I could hear Jeff praying loudly behind me.

Time stood still.

I opened my eyes. The men were prancing around me, wild-eyed, barking at each other, "Shut them up. Stop their mouths." They paced backwards and forwards.

Facing their macabre ballet, I screamed out repeatedly, "The blood of Jesus . . . the blood of Jesus."

The five armed thugs were in total confusion. One ran at me with a threatening expression and then scampered away like a frightened animal. Another watched him, puzzled, and then lunged at me menacingly. He too reeled backwards.

I pounded on my annex table to my war cry: "Jesus Christ . . . Jesus Christ." My throat grew hoarse, but I dared not stop.

It seemed as though there was an invisible shield of bullet-proof glass between us.

Our fear turned into anger at the men's intimidation. "In Jesus' name, go!" we commanded, pointing to the bush.

Without a word, each of the men dropped their weapons. As quickly as they came, they disappeared into the black night.

Standing out in the dark, still dressed in our pyjamas, Jeff and I danced and sang victory songs. We raised our hands to heaven and declared the miracle-working power of God over the forces of evil.

The next morning, shy villagers crept into our compound.

"Why didn't you come to help us?" I challenged them.

"We thought you were having a prayer meeting!" they responded, with smiles on their faces, wondering about the power of this God who had been introduced to their dusty African village.

The following day, still badly shaken from the attack, we were visited by a security official.

"You are a security risk living in that caravan in the bush without any guard," the thickset army officer explained. "You are inviting robbery . . . You see that army barracks?" he said, pointing to a nearby hill. We could distinguish some small grass huts. "One thousand men who have been retrenched will be processed there on their way back to their villages. Many have suffered and we can't be responsible for their actions once they leave the army."

Undeterred by this news, God gave us a plan of attack.

"We're not going to sit here, quivering in fear. Let's go to the camp and show them the healing power of God's Holy Spirit," I declared.

Like David, we ran towards Goliath.

❖ ❖ ❖

On a sweltering Saturday afternoon, Jeff and I loaded up our car with a generator, a TV screen, video player and the evangelistic movie *The Jesus Film*, and drove ten kilometres (approximately six miles) to Pajimo army barracks. With permission, we set up our equipment under a grove of mango trees.

Soon, a crowd of about 500 soldiers and village families gathered. They sat in the dirt in rapt attention as the life of Jesus unfolded on the screen. At the end of the movie, at least a hundred rugged khaki-clad soldiers knelt before us, weeping, and asked for the healing touch of Jesus.

A few weeks later, we drove to the army barracks to baptise them. Eighty soldiers and wives were gathered on the edge of a dam. It looked like a scene from the Bible with long-garbed church officials grumbling on the hillside. After sharing the benefits of water baptism, we carefully descended the slippery mud path to stand in the middle of the cloudy, weed-filled waters. I could feel huge African snails or eels nibbling at my toes. Nevertheless, we continued. A corporal called Darius helped each person kneel in the water. As they bowed under, we proclaimed them no longer slaves to sin (see Rom. 6:6). Rising in a shower of sparkling drops, surely Jesus now lived within them, giving them courage to withstand their clan's criticism.

The response was exhilarating, and in that moment I knew this was my mission. But it had been quite a journey getting to this point.

2

THE UNLIKELY
MISSIONARY

SYDNEY, AUSTRALIA, 1944-1961

FROM THE BEGINNING my childhood was unusual. I was conceived in a park blacked out by the wartime curfew, underneath the northern pylon of the Sydney Harbour Bridge. My father was a good-looking, blonde, Swedish-born American marine, and my mother a young woman who was desperate to become an American war bride.

When the young man heard the news of my impending arrival, he wrote a letter to my grandmother denying any responsibility and informing her that no amount of sobbing from my mother would change his mind. He thanked my grandmother, Jessie, for treating him "swell" during the year he had been billeted in her home and closed his letter by saying, "I'm so glad to get this off my chest." As far as he was concerned that was the end of it. He was gone.

Despite my mother, Cynthia's, emotional fragility and my biological father's rejection, I was on my way. Shortly after giving birth to me my mother considered having me adopted, but changed her mind and instead brought me back to her parents' house where she sat trembling, waiting for her father's reaction.

Of course, I have no memory of this time—my grandmother Jessie shared these details with me when I was a young child.

"Irene, I first saw you when you were ten days old, and I was just saying how much you looked like the Swedish side of your father, Herbert's, family when we heard the squeaking of the gate. We braced ourselves, because your grandfather had quite a temper. There was a rattling of keys and a banging of the door, and then suddenly your grandfather Jack stood there, looking at you. His face was ferocious and he twitched as he barked at your mother, 'What have you got there? What have you done? You've brought shame on the family. That's what you've done. You know better than to bring that thing under my roof!'

"He crossed the room, grabbed you and examined your face. 'Hmm, it doesn't look like any of us and it's a female to boot,' he said, as he shuffled into the kitchen. 'Little bastard thing, bringing shame to our family. It'd be a kindness to finish it off now. Dash its brains out.' He lifted you above the stone step, threatening to drop you. Your mother yelled, 'Dad! Dad, give me my baby!' But your grandfather was in a rage and held you higher.

"All of a sudden his body crumpled. Your mother reached out and took hold of you as he staggered backwards and fell to the floor. He was having a stroke . . . he never recovered. I took you to visit him in the hospital for four years, and he grew quite fond of you in the end.

"The neighbours weren't quite so forgiving. They considered you an embarrassment and would spit at your pram as I wheeled you past. You see, Irene, it wasn't your fault, but local girls were supposed to wait faithfully for the Australian soldiers to come home from the war. It was shameful to sell your young body for silk stockings or chocolate. That's how it seemed anyway."

❖ ❖ ❖

One of the earliest memories I have of my childhood is of me as a little girl drawing pictures and patterns with a wet matchstick on clay pots that stood in saucers of water on my grandmother's tiled verandah. There was always a sense of urgency to complete the pictures before the water evaporated. Racing against time, I would dip the matchstick in the water and scroll my childhood images in a circle around the pot. Not surprisingly, the images would evaporate before I reached the end. Then I would look up from my creation and feel a greater sense of defeat as I'd watch my mother, who looked like a movie star, clack across the tiles in her high heels, clank the gate shut and disappear around the corner to meet up with one of her many suitors. Evaporating picture, evaporating mother—or that's how it felt at the time. How I longed for the attention my mother gave to the men she hoped would become my new daddy.

I suffered two stepfathers. The first was an adulterous alcoholic who fathered my sister and two brothers. The second was sadistic and secretive—a beady-eyed, bespeckled man who took great pleasure in exacting punishment on us children with his long leather belt, then skulking into my dimly lit room, sliding beside me and proceeding to show me "where babies came from."

"It's our little secret," he'd whisper, his voice dripping like treacle.

Together, he and my mother had four more children.

My mother didn't cope well with either of these relationships or with the demands of caring for eight children, so the job of keeping house and helping to care for my siblings fell to me. Every afternoon after school I'd help cook dinner, wash up, clean, and put the children to bed. Once the house was quiet, I'd curl up under my threadbare blanket with a small torch and read the *Pollyanna* books that were given to me by my grandma. Here in my makeshift cocoon, I would imagine a different life. Every now and then, my imaginings were taken to the big screen.

Saturday night was the big picture show at the Orpheum Cinema in Cremorne. As a family, we would stroll wide-eyed underneath the gilded portico and climb into one of the 500 cloth seats, then nestle into a world of fantasy. All the adventure, all the love and all the happily ever after would be mine for several hours: *Looney Tunes* and *Movietone News* featuring travelogues of the Queen as she toured the colonies. One time I watched with amazement as tribal people danced before the royal party, who were sheltered from the African sun by a large umbrella. I was mesmerised by their exotica: feathered headdresses, hypnotic drumming and half-naked babies. I determined when I grew up I would work until I could afford to travel overseas—first to give my ever-burdened mother a holiday and then to have my own adventure.

Another welcome distraction was being able to attend mass each week at the local Catholic church. In the small sandstone sanctuary I would lose myself in the ceremonies and the Latin liturgies. Sitting quietly beside my grandmother I would take in every detail, staring intently into the sorrowful eyes of Jesus, silently pleading for Him to rescue me. At the same time, a heady aroma filled the church and bells rang, transporting me into God's throne room.

On weekdays I would steal away to school where I became quite the celebrity. Despite standing out because I didn't have a school uniform and I often had welts on my legs from repeated whippings, I impressed the other children with my ability to analyse words and my unique repertoire of Latin hymns. In

1956, my primary school celebrated its first graduation of pupils and I was judged Dux of the school. But a year later, at the age of 13, I was finding it hard to juggle schoolwork with chores. Eventually it was all too hard. I was called into the principal's office.

"Unless your marks improve, you'll lose your bursary," she warned.

I remained silent.

"Have you any ambitions?" she prodded. "I thought you wanted to be a teacher. Have you changed your mind? Take this letter home to your parents."

Arriving home that day, I prayed mum wasn't in a bad mood. Instead I found her dozing in a chair, with our new sister wrapped in a bunny rug on her lap. She looked at me. I noticed how beautiful she was. Her hair glowed burnished auburn in the afternoon light and her hazel eyes were soft, ringed with dark lashes and welling with tears.

"Irene, I don't know how to tell you this," she was unusually gentle. "I may not be here next year. The doctors have found cancer in me; they told me I won't live past Easter."

"Oh mum . . . it can't be true," I cried. "What about the baby?"

She looked at me. "Would you leave school and look after the children for me?"

"Of course," I murmured, "but it's not going to happen. God won't let you die."

From that moment, I attended mass at every opportunity, desperately praying for a miracle.

In the months that followed, my mother's health deteriorated and I took on more responsibility at home, which didn't leave any time for a social life. My grandma Jessie stepped in, persuading my parents to let me go to a local dance once a week. It was there in the brightly lit dance hall in the Southern Suburbs of Sydney that the tall, gangly compere called for men to choose their partners for the "Pride of Erin" waltz. I was stunned when a young man approached me. His eyes were deep blue and sincere and he had a mass of wavy dark hair.

"May I have this dance?" he asked, with a deep, soft voice.

As I took his hand, my stomach fluttered and, for the first time in a long time, I felt beautiful.

Brian became my first steady boyfriend and was a great support through the tumultuous days that lay ahead.

◈　◈　◈

I was 16 when my mother died. My stepfather who was by her bedside at the hospice phoned to give me the news. "Your mother died this morning," he said.

Trembling, I hung up the receiver, looked over at my brothers and sisters and sat staring at the floor. It had been a sunny morning. Now grey clouds were rolling across the sky. Gusts of wind were shaking leaves off trees and spinning litter along the road. I shivered. "Please God, lift her above the storm. Let the angels carry her to you." Heavy rain began to drive across the verandah. Lightning zigzagged across the sky. It was as though nature was farewelling my mother and angels were howling in sympathy. The following morning, I put the children in front of the television, tied my clear plastic rain hat under my chin, put on a plastic raincoat, and headed to the local Catholic church. I took off my shoes and walked through all the puddles on the way. Pelting rain melded with my hot, salty tears as I finally felt free to cry for my dear mother and for myself.

Inside the church it was chill and quiet like a tomb. I dipped my fingers in the holy water, crossed myself and genuflected towards the altar. I knelt at the altar rail and prayed, "Why did you take her God? Why did you? We prayed. Why did you ignore us? Don't you care for us?"

There was nobody around, so I sat down quietly in one of the pews, put my head in my hands and cried.

I stopped quickly when I heard a noise at the back of the church. In came some men carrying a wooden box.

"God, please don't let that be my mother's coffin," I pleaded. "I don't think I could stand it here alone with her body."

When the men left, I walked up to the casket and read, "Cynthia Mary Richards 1925–1961." I stared at the name. Anger rose up within me as I looked up at the altar and then down at my mother's coffin.

"You're useless, God! I don't believe you're even there!" I shouted, wiping more tears from my eyes. Grabbing my raincoat, I pushed open the huge wooden doors and ran out into the drizzling rain, vowing never to go back to church again. The clouds were black and so was my soul. As far as I was concerned, I didn't need God and from then on I would make my own way in life.

3

SEARCHING

SYDNEY, AUSTRALIA, 1961-1982

WITH MY MOTHER GONE and no home help, I was forced to leave my final year of school unfinished.

Adding to my woes was an argumentative and abusive stepfather who had plans to take me on as his new wife. I was terrified of him, so I moved out of our family home and into a girls' hostel around the corner. Eventually my brothers and sisters were farmed out to relatives and then into foster care. I visited them occasionally, but by now much of my spare time was spent with my boyfriend, Brian, who was sweet and gentle and promised he would take care of me. I had fallen head over heels in love and looked forward to my new life as someone's sweetheart.

A few months into our relationship, Brian gave me a friendship ring and we began speaking of marriage. I couldn't believe he wanted to be with someone like me. I thought of myself as such a dull person with many problems. Brian ignored all of this and began taking me to stage shows and out to dinner. He phoned me every day—sometimes twice a day. "This must prove that he loves me," I wrote in my diary at the time. I, in turn, loved Brian for his manliness, his dependability, his protective attitude and his ready laugh.

"I wish we could get married now," I said to him one morning as we strolled the leafy avenues of Hyde Park, "but our parents will never give us permission." And then I had an idea. "If I get pregnant they will let us." Melting into each other's arms, we sealed the deal.

A few months later, after securing a job as a clerk at an insurance company in the city, I was on the bus going to work and I started feeling sick. As I stepped off the bus, I vomited violently in the gutter. I'd watched my mother endure seven pregnancies, so I knew what this meant. Three days later, Brian and I visited the doctor who confirmed the news—I was pregnant. Now Brian and I could finally be together. The news was met with mixed reactions. Brian's parents were shocked and my stepfather incensed. Despite his anger, he reluctantly signed the consent forms so I could marry. Brian and I were excited at the prospect of becoming parents and immediately began planning our wedding day.

On 23 March 1962, I awoke with a spring in my step. This was the start of my new life. After a frenetic morning of preparations we arrived at the Catholic church. I wore a three-quarter length white princess dress made of tulle. As the wedding march began I walked down the aisle grinning from ear to ear—all my dreams were about to come true. At the end of a wonderful day we drove to our small garden flat, sat on our only piece of furniture—a double bed—and talked for hours about all the highlights: much laughter, dancing and music.

I was 17 when I gave birth to my first child, Maree, who we thought looked Italian with her dark hair and exotic features. She looked a lot like Brian. Eighteen months later we had a son, Greg, who was quite different to his sister. He had blonde hair and chubby cheeks and entered the world with a deafening scream. Next came our pretty baby, Shelley, who astonished us all with a mass of thick golden brown hair. Four years after that, my fourth child, Heidi, was born and although she was an unexpected surprise, I was thrilled. Brian wanted to call her Pauline, but I loved the movie *Heidi* and so that's the name we chose. As happy as I was to have four healthy and beautiful children, and had planned to give them the childhood I never had, my days at home as a young mother with four small children were long and lonely. To make ends meet Brian worked two jobs and often wasn't home till late. With no sense of purpose and a past still haunting me, I slept a lot, watched TV and did little housework. Like my mother, I had become depressed.

Bored and desperate to find a distraction from the monotony of everyday life, I took on several new challenges. For a while I ran a family day care from my garage. Another time, I unleashed my creative side and began to teach copper art classes. On weekends everyone, including our dog, would go and watch Greg play soccer. I felt that I was a good mother, but became increasingly restless and dissatisfied with my life.

When all my children were at school, I convinced Brian I needed some mental stimulation, so I enrolled at a teacher training college. Literature and art opened up a whole new world for me and I met many fascinating people, including an older man whom I later worked with at an inner-city school. I can remember watching intently as all the children clambered over him in the classroom, stirring in me a longing to be loved the way a father would love his daughter. He responded to my infatuation by sending me poetry.

Over time, my obsession with this father-figure grew into a relationship with me convincing myself that I'd be happier with this man who was twenty years my senior. Call it depression or irrational behaviour or simply a longing to be loved, I did the unthinkable—I walked out on my family when my youngest was only 8 years old. But this, like other bad choices I had made in my young life, was doomed to fail. A few years into the relationship, the bubble burst and I ended up moving back with Brian and the kids. Not so much as Brian's wife, but more like a house guest.

In time, the disillusionment resurfaced. In my quest for peace, I began reading spiritual books on Buddhism. Becoming the essence of a non-being or reaching a state of Nirvana intrigued me. Eventually I planned a trek to the Himalayas. When Brian suggested he might accompany me, I refused. I was still trying to find myself. I left Australia with a suitcase full of expectations and an empty heart.

The mountains were breathtakingly beautiful and physically challenging. After several days, I left the party and took a trip to a Buddhist monastery, but in the end decided this wasn't for me.

At the end of my sojourn I returned to Sydney and Brian came to meet me at the airport. He was carrying a huge bouquet of flowers and had grown a moustache.

"I hardly recognise you," I said coldly. "Give me space, Brian—I am still trying to find myself." And that was it—the end of my sixteen-year marriage.

I remember looking in the mirror late one night and thinking how much I had aged. I was tired and haggard. Time was running out and even alcohol could do nothing to numb the senses or block the pain. I was 35 years old and my life had crumbled around me. I felt as though I had failed; I believed I had no future, only a shameful past. I counted my losses: my marriage to Brian, who was a good man, had fallen apart; my family home had been sold; and my disillusioned children were a mess.

My insatiable thirst for someone to love me was now taking me to nightclubs on a mission to find a soul mate. In dark, seedy bars, heaving with sweaty bodies, I had anxiously studied the room hoping to catch someone's eye. But nobody had taken any interest. I had become what I later would describe as a "geriatric disco queen" trawling the clubs looking for love.

Desperately lonely, I ended up moving into a small flat in a friend's backyard with a divorced man called Jeff whom I had met at an art cinema one night. This man intrigued me and life with him promised new possibilities. He was a filmmaker and author and was very intelligent. He was also oblivious to my mood swings, which were now bordering on suicidal. But even a new life with a man as interesting as Jeff, and all our joint business ventures, didn't ease my ever-increasing pain and feelings of rejection. My only therapy was to take long walks on the beach.

It was during one of these twilight walks, as a blustery wind churned up white horses across the sea, that I glanced up at a brightly lit surf club where a church service was taking place—the same church I had been invited to by a colleague of mine weeks earlier. I had shared my ongoing struggle with depression and she had suggested I join her one Sunday.

Pulling my hoodie tightly around my head, I took a closer look, but chose not to enter.

Weeks later, the small but growing church had moved to a converted warehouse near the surf club. I could no longer ignore the tugging at my heart, so I went along to a morning service. It was 28 November 1982. As I entered the building, young people ran past me laughing. A band was playing lively songs. Young men and women were clapping exuberantly; some were dancing. They looked so happy. Finding a seat at the back, I just watched and waited. When the music slowed, the young people closed their eyes and swayed. I looked to the floor. The youth band was singing "Jesus, Your Love Has Melted My Heart." As the music continued, I felt a surge of peace wash over me. Unbidden tears welled up from my soul and rolled down my cheeks. I lifted my arms and found myself lost in an intimate embrace with a mystery lover. Years of excruciating pain and inner turmoil were instantly lifted. All my searching had brought me to this moment and for the first time in my life I felt connected to my Creator.

Towards the end of the service the pastor, Phil Pringle, invited people to ask Jesus into their hearts. I thought, *I've made a mess of my life. I know You died for me Jesus. I've never before thought of asking You to take control of my life, but I do now.*

Right there in the hall, I gave my life to Jesus. That's when I heard God's still, small voice say to me, "Irene, everything is going to be alright from now on."

4

THE CALL

SYDNEY, AUSTRALIA, 1982-1990

IN THE WEEKS FOLLOWING my simple prayer of repentance, I immersed myself in the Bible, devouring scripture and holding on to God's promise that everything would be alright and that He'd stabilise my wayward children. This was the constant cry of my heart. My kids had suffered so much disruption to their lives and now I felt they deserved to experience the peace I had found. As I prayed and fasted and spoke out the word of God, God miraculously restored them. Within three years, my four children were all following Jesus. I was so grateful. It only seemed natural that I should ask God what I could do in return.

One of my first acts of obedience after becoming a Christian was to be water baptised. One warm Saturday afternoon, with church friends watching from the shore, I was fully immersed in a shallow-water lagoon. God promised me that my old character would die with Jesus Christ and that I would be raised up with Him.

Now filled with the Holy Spirit and spending hours reading my Bible, changes were noticeable to those around me. I was less agitated and had mellowed. For the first time in my life, I felt at peace. Jeff had even noticed the impact my new faith had on me, and asked if he could join me at church. It didn't take long before he, too, accepted Jesus and we began planning our wedding.

On 7 July 1983, Jeff and I made our vows at a Sunday morning church service. It was a simple ceremony attended by my children and a few friends. I can remember thinking on the day, *I am getting married again because I am terrified of being alone.* Nevertheless, Jeff and I began our new life together, taking on various business ventures: a tour bus, a cleaning business and a canteen at a technical college. We even wrote a children's book together. Our enterprises afforded us long summer breaks—an opportunity, as we saw it, to go on short-term mission trips around the world. We were privileged to visit the Philippines, Malaysia, India and Sri Lanka and saw God work powerfully though us—but I was still so restless.

In 1988, we took our first trip to Ethiopia to meet some of the thirty-five children we were sponsoring with World Vision. This was a turning point for us. As we locked eyes with skinny, listless children with bloated bellies and sad eyes, both Jeff and I felt the call to relocate to Africa permanently. Unsure of where to live, we began praying for our exact destination. We held onto Exodus 23:20, believing that God would send an angel ahead of us, to keep us on the path and to bring us to the place He had prepared for us.

❖   ❖   ❖

One night after dinner, Jeff placed a map of Africa down on our small kitchen table.

"I'd love to work in Ethiopia," I remarked, recounting what I knew from books I'd read. "It's a diverse civilisation with ancient art, music and literature—a very rich culture. And they are not as 'wild' as other Africans. The Ethiopians are descendants of the Queen of Sheba. What a heritage! What an exotic, romantic adventure it would be for us!" I rubbed Jeff's neck and smiled, picturing the two of us wandering through incense-misted churches, studying Byzantine glass windows, doing temple rubbings of ornate crosses.

"Be serious, honey," Jeff countered. "There's a lot of suffering people out there. Our aim should be to help them survive and build a future."

My eyes scanned neighbouring countries in the atlas as I pondered: Sudan . . . Kenya . . . Congo . . .

Jeff pointed to a small country next to Kenya and then proceeded to tell me about Uganda, once known as the "Pearl of Africa" until Idi Amin became president and began a campaign of terror. He ordered all the intellectuals to be killed, burnt mountains of books and destroyed towns. His army executed thousands of innocent people and shot many of the animals into extinction. Uganda has never recovered. Now AIDS was killing the new generation in the south. And in the north, rebels under the leadership of religious extremist Joseph Kony were kidnapping children and turning them into child soldiers and sex slaves. There was no schooling, because war had destroyed the infrastructure.

"I've heard that children spend their days sitting in the dust or hiding from bullets. There are thousands of destitute orphans there," said Jeff.

I was shocked. "How can such horrors be happening in this modern age? It's 1990! Why doesn't someone do something?"

"That's why we're going!" Jeff scolded.

"Well . . ." I hesitated. "It's a million miles away from our life here on Narrabeen Beach and our family, but if God is calling us, we must go."

Later that night in bed, I reflected on our conversation, even entertaining second thoughts. We lived in paradise and now we were about to move away to an unknown place—what on earth are we doing? A peace filled my bedroom and in that moment God reassured my heart. The following morning we began making plans.

Over the weeks that followed, Jeff and I approached several mission agencies for support. They were horrified at the prospect of two inexperienced Australians going to work in a war zone. Despite our backgrounds—Jeff was a skilled handyman and entrepreneur and I was a trained teacher—the response was always the same: "You have no experience and it's too dangerous."

We were discouraged, but unshakeable in our mission. Now it was just a matter of getting the timing right.

Weeks later, at a church conference, God spoke into my heart: "Irene, you've heard all this before and now it's time to go." I shared this revelation with Jeff, who simply smiled and told me the Lord had spoken to him about moving to Africa a week earlier.

Time to break the news to our family.

5

LETTING GO

SYDNEY, AUSTRALIA, 1991-1992

"OH MUM, AFRICA... really?" my daughter, Heidi, said when I shared my news. Church friends and family members were equally surprised and a little worried about our choice of location—a war zone! By the time Jeff and I had sold our two beach homes they understood that this wasn't a whim, it was a calling.

One balmy Saturday morning after advertising in the local paper, we held a yard sale—everything had to go. The proceeds were needed to fund our mission. On the day, our home was teeming with people looking for a bargain. I watched as strangers moved from room to room examining all my goods. Some puffed short breaths and polished the silvery cutlery that was heaped on a linen cloth; others examined the bindings on my precious books stacked neatly on my grandmother's carved dresser. My crystal bowls pinged as brightly coloured fingernails belonging to well-dressed women flicked their rims. I stood next to the window, opened the curtains to let in more light and smiled vaguely, answering a question: "Yes, they are all for sale. Everything must go." I sighed.

I wanted to keep only one item: Grandmother Jessie's rosary beads. Draping the pink glass beads across my fingers, I studied them, recalling her sturdy, weathered hands and imagining her bemused smile. What would she think of all this? I shook my head and quickly slipped them into my pocket, remembering her encouragement to live a "bigger" life. And that's exactly what I would be doing. Little solace, though, for a heart that was grieving. I felt torn. Letting go wasn't easy. I felt as if I was dying on my feet. I slumped down at the kitchen table and gently fingered the grooves in the oiled wood, etched by my grandson's metal car. For a moment, I could almost hear my grandchildren's chuckles as they munched their way through roast chicken on crusty bread rolls—Sunday lunch for the past six years.

"Are you really going to Africa? That's what the newspaper said." A woman interrupted my thoughts.

I nodded as I tipped my cutlery into a plastic bag and accepted her twenty-dollar note.

My daughter, Heidi, stared out the window. The sunlight turned her hair to spun gold. Her large blue eyes were moist. The greatest wrench was leaving my family.

"What about my family . . . ?" I had pleaded with God.

"Your youngest is 21. Leave them with Me," was His clear answer.

My 6-year-old grandson Jay sat on the edge of a chair, scuffing his feet on the carpet. He looked troubled.

"Excuse me, sport. This is my chair now. Wanna help me load it in my car?" Another stranger's question caused him to jump to his feet and glare, before moving to sit with his back against the wall.

Several hours later, almost everything had been sold or given away. The rooms were gloomy and empty, and so was my soul.

"Come on Jay," I grabbed my grandson's hand, "let's go for a walk."

A short distance away, we trudged over sand dunes and emerged onto Narrabeen Beach. A salty breeze tickled our nostrils and whipped through our hair as we feasted our eyes on the booming surf.

I gulped in the fresh air and took in the familiar surroundings—the beach had been a place of solace for me over the years. I had enjoyed many sunset strolls, family picnics and precious moments collecting shells with my grandchildren. Apart from time spent at home with family, this was what I would miss the most.

"Grandma, let's see if the sea eagle moved into the nest we dug." The small boy tugged my hand as we clambered over the dune fence and ran along the ridge. The silky soft sand had swallowed our hole, so we lay close together watching the cerise-coloured clouds scudding overhead. This was our special place and would be our last special time before I left. I sighed as I ruffled his hair: strong and brown. He loved bulldozers and dogs, and never showed fear. His father, like mine, had abandoned him before he was born, so I understood his stubborn determination to make his own way through life.

"Hey, Jayby baby, I'm going to miss you."

He shook my hand away, sat up, wrapped his arms tightly around his knees and scowled into the distance.

"The eagle's gone away . . . Now I've got no-one," he shouted.

He stood up suddenly and ran down the sand hill towards the water. The waves reared and crashed with thunderous roars—a stormy backdrop for the boy's grief.

❖ ❖ ❖

With our home sold, my children and I were mute with pain. We couldn't talk. No words could express our sadness at parting. I kept re-reading God's word: "Behold, I send an Angel before you to keep you in the way and to bring you into the place which I have prepared" (Ex. 23:20).

I could hear God urging, "Irene, you are my handiwork. I created you for My purpose, for good works which I have prepared in advance for you to do. This commission is set out before you as footsteps you will walk in" (see Eph. 2:10).

My face was set. No tears could turn me away from this God-ordained mission. A few weeks prior to leaving Australia we had our final family Christmas. On a home video captured by Jeff, I looked into the barrel of the camera, laughed and gave a farewell message to all my children. The family giggled at my silliness. I think the jokes and laughter about entering a war zone camouflaged our pain.

On Friday 10 January 1992, my four children, six grandchildren and friends gathered at Sydney Airport to wave us off. As the plane ascended, I rested my head back on the seat, looked out the window and allowed the tears to flow. In that moment, I heard God speak to me: "Irene, you are not just a heart. There is more happening in the heavenlies than your pain. This is not a senseless pain—as you truly pick up your cross and follow Me I will reward you with good things." Peacefully, I drifted off to sleep, still unsure of what we were getting into.

After a brief stopover and a few weeks training alongside some missionaries in Lira, Uganda, we were about to find out.

6

ON OUR WAY

KAMPALA, UGANDA, FEBRUARY 1992

IN THE 5 A.M. DARKNESS we arrived at the bus park in Kampala, Uganda. Stumbling over loose gravel, dodging between buses with their engines roaring, spewing out black smoke, Jeff hoisted me aboard a rattling tin bus as it lurched onto the main road.

"This is it," he said. "We'll go to the end of the line. I'm sure there will be no aid groups working there." Although we didn't know it then, our destination was Kitgum, a small community forty-five kilometres from the Sudan border.

The few passengers that were on the bus stared at us with open mouths then, one by one, lowered their heads and slept. We perched ourselves on a worn plastic bench and peered through a window that had no glass. A few minutes later a sharp nip on my ankle caused me to jump. The beady eye of a rooster underneath the seat warned me to keep my feet still.

I turned my attention to the scene outside. Scrawny men wearing ragged clothing ran wearily alongside the bus, pushing wooden carts heavy with bags of charcoal or huge piles of freshly harvested bananas. Their eyes were glazed over with exertion, veins throbbing as they gulped in air over swollen cracked lips.

Who had stolen their freedom and made them slaves to such a life? I wondered.

Beyond the bustle of the city, the bus chugged through lush countryside of banana and tea plantations dotted on rolling hills. Daylight had arrived. Looking up at the vibrant blue sky, my face was blasted by a strong breeze blowing through the open window. I rested my head on Jeff's shoulder and relaxed enough to doze. Several hours later, Jeff gently woke me as we crossed the Nile River over a narrow bridge at Karuma Falls. The awe-inspiring sight of the surging white water was soon replaced by apprehension, as we stared at the broken guardrail and the wreckage of an army bus that had plunged into the river.

Leaving the river behind, the vegetation became stunted and thorny. The road disintegrated into potholed dirt. As the temperature increased, my excitement diminished. Eyeing the dry scrubby bushes and towering elephant grass, I muttered, "God is this really the right place?"

Minutes later, soldiers boarded the bus. As we passed each village, they waved their guns. Gaunt villagers danced and cheered. I asked one soldier what was happening.

"This is one of the few buses to make it through rebel territory," he replied.

After ten long hours, the bus stopped beside a broken telegraph pole in a patch of dirt.

"Welcome to Kitgum!" the driver said, flashing us a toothy smile.

I clambered down the iron steps and stood in a small square lined with bamboo and tin shanties. In the glare of the afternoon sun, I squinted at a willy-willy (dust devil) spiralling up the road towards us, stirring up a corkscrew of litter, food scraps, rags and cow dung. The smell was putrid. I covered my mouth and nose.

A crowd of stick-thin villagers stared sternly, silently at the two white travellers, while a child screamed piteously and hid behind his mother's skirt.

Sometime later, we saw something moving across the ground. It was a woman—her body twisted with polio. She was crawling on all fours like a spider. I gasped. Jeff squeezed my hand and knelt down.

"Daughter of Abraham," he murmured softly.

The woman paused, shook a sandal off one of her hands and reached towards Jeff. As he shook her hand, the woman smiled. "*Kop ango?*" she returned his greeting.

Jeff asked, "Can I help you? Where are you going?"

She jerked her head towards a small shelter nearby, and on calloused knees continued her journey.

Many faces in the crowd softened. Several small boys were pushed forward by their friends and extended their hands. As we began to shake each hand, the crowd closed in around us and we were engulfed in a sea of ochre rags. The smell of sweaty, unwashed bodies assaulted me and reminded me that I was a long way from Sydney and Narrabeen Beach with its sunbathers and sea-washed bodies fragrant with coconut oil. There, sleek white gulls fluttered above turquoise surf. I looked into the African sky. Giant grey-winged vultures circled overhead and then swooped to land nearby, strutting 1.2-metres tall and foraging with long curved beaks in mounds of garbage.

Jeff was enjoying the crowd's attention. Children stroked his hairy arms and laughed. "Meow . . . meow" was their song. Looking at these children, my heart melted.

But something told me life in our new home wasn't going to be easy.

7

THE LAND OF HILLS AND VALLEYS

KITGUM, FEBRUARY-MAY 1992

USING A SERIES OF hand gestures we requested night-time lodgings for our first night in Kitgum. A youth escorted us to a nearby tin shed and pointed to a sign crudely painted in black: SCORPION LODGE. He pushed open a tin door and ushered us inside. Apart from a narrow shaft of light from the doorway falling across the dirt floor, the room was pitch-dark and windowless. He led me forward until I bumped into a wooden bed.

"Very soft," he said as he guided my hands onto the mattress, which seemed to be a rough hessian bag filled with lumpy rags.

"I hope there's no body in there," Jeff joked. "Let's leave our bags here, while we see the officials."

It was a short walk to the local government offices. They eyed us suspiciously.

"You want to do what?" one official demanded. For twenty years, the region had suffered war and strangers were distrusted.

Jeff patiently explained, "We need some land to build a primary school for destitute children. It will be free, and we will give them food and um . . ."

A young man leant forward with genuine interest, but another official snarled, "Destitute children! What do you mean destitute children? Who says Uganda has destitute children? Where are you from? What agency are you with? What is your real purpose here? Why did you leave your country? You need police clearance before you can visit here."

A large man in a rumpled suit leaned towards me. "Where's your family? What are you doing with them? You have children? Where are they?"

"My children," I faltered, "are far away in Australia." I gazed across his shoulder and looked through the window. Thin children trudged past, barefoot and aimless. "God blessed us by enabling us to raise them strong and healthy in Australia," I said. "Now we want to help yours."

The man guffawed, spraying spittle in my face. "I've never heard of anything like this in my life!"

Another official took over, "And how much will this project cost? What are you able to spend? And just how do you intend to finance it?"

Jeff explained. "First, we can use the money from the sale of our homes in Australia. Then we will get sponsors for your children."

The man's eyes narrowed. "Can you give me a figure . . . say $300,000?"

Jeff baulked. "We need to assess the needs of the community first."

The official persisted: "Let's say $300,000. A ten percent contribution would have to go to the local development authorities. Do you have that available?"

Jeff blinked. "Really!"

The pleasant young man interrupted, "These details can be concluded later." He opened his hands towards his colleagues, then looked at us and smiled. "Let's encourage and welcome this development to Kitgum. We've endured nothing but bad news these last twenty years."

The older man responded soothingly, "Well of course, it's early days. And there are many criteria you will have to meet. Rest assured, we are at your service as we work together to develop the district." Rising, he shook our hands and ushered us through the door.

Outside in the glare, my eyes scanned the dilapidated buildings and the dejected demeanour of the community. I sighed. Satan had been merciless to these people. Why should he make it easy for us to come in and rescue them? But I could not have foreseen the ruthlessness of his plans against us.

❖ ❖ ❖

A few days later, we returned by bus to Kampala, the capital, where we lived for the next three months. After settling in, I wrote a letter to my daughter, Heidi, updating her on our news. "We are staying in a clean house in Kampala that has electricity and running water—luxury! I have been bedridden for two days with a headache and a bad fever, but claimed God's promises."

I had no other news other than the frustration of registering our charity. Every day Jeff and I trudged around the city's streets, going from one government department to another, attempting to register our organisation, open bank accounts, finalise work permits, order water bores, and clear and register our car and caravan which were soon to arrive by sea.

One urgent requirement we had was to find a prominent Ugandan citizen to be our sponsor, without which we could not proceed. Appointments were made and cancelled, as many officials had little interest in two naive Australians with limited funds and no experience, intent on rescuing children.

Finally, we were introduced to Ben Okello Luwum—son of Saint Janani Luwum, who had been the Bishop of The Church of Uganda during Idi Amin's eight-year reign of terror.

Major General Idi Amin Dada, commander of the armed forces, had come into power in 1971, but this eccentric, egotistical and brutal dictator had some strange policies that included the expulsion of more than 50,000 Asians who were living and operating small businesses in Uganda. Estimates by Amnesty International and other organisations suggest that more than 300,000 Ugandans who disagreed with Amin's policies were massacred.

In 1977, with public executions increasing and university lecturers disappearing, Bishop Janani convened a meeting of church leaders. At the meeting, the elders agreed that someone should confront Amin and appeal to him to stop the atrocities. The Bishop himself volunteered.

Leaving their children at home, the Bishop and his wife, Mary, drove to the city hotel, which was Idi Amin's madhouse. Some floors were lavishly decorated, accommodating important guests but alternate floors housed prisoners kept in cages in inhumane conditions for his amusement.

Mary waited outside while her husband entered the hotel.

Several hours later, she was ordered to go home. The next day her husband's body was pictured in newspapers—he had been shot in the head and found in a mock car accident. Mary and her children fled for their lives into Kenya.

God promises He will avenge the death of His people (see 2 Thess. 1:6). Within eighteen months Idi Amin and his army had been driven out of Uganda.

Former Member of Parliament and certified accountant, the Hon. Ben Okello Luwum and his wife became honorary presidents of our Ugandan non-government organisation (NGO)—Childcare

International, which became known as Childcare Kitgum Servants (CKS).

❖ ❖ ❖

Now that we had our advocate, the next step was to fill in all the necessary documents and gather signatures from Kitgum officials. This meant long, bumpy 450-kilometre bus rides to and from the capital. Gasping in billowing dust, pressed shoulder to shoulder with distressed individuals and crying babies, and often crammed in-between bags of produce, we would only make one stop along the way for roasted cassava tubers and cordial. These trips were a feat of endurance which necessitated a full day of recovery afterwards.

After one such visit I was feeling extremely weak: malaria parasites had attacked my liver and tropical ulcers scarred my legs. I was resting in Scorpion Lodge when Jeff bustled in one afternoon.

"Some council clerks are outside. They want to show us four acres for our school. Do you think you can walk?"

I swung my swollen feet to the floor, slipped them into a pair of rubber thongs and began hobbling behind them.

One kilometre down a dirt road, we came to an area of scrubland dotted with mango trees. The town surveyor, Canaan Otim, emerged from the shade. He was a gentle giant with expansive gestures. Canaan slapped the council clerk's shoulder and challenged him.

"Just four acres? That is not even worth surveying. Give these good people ten acres. They are helping our children."

The clerk sucked hard on his cigarette, looked around and thought for a minute, then shook his head. "No, four acres is enough!"

I began to explain, "We could help more children if . . ."

Jeff frowned at me and muttered, "Go away and pray Irene."

I withdrew to some shade and read in my pocket Bible: "Consider now, for the LORD has chosen you to build a house for the sanctuary; be strong and do it . . . the leaders and all the people will be completely at your command" (1 Chron. 28:10–21).

A short time later, Jeff walked up to me, beaming. "The town council is giving us eighteen acres. Praise God!"

I rose and shook the surveyor's hand. "Tell me. Where is east?"

He pointed to the hills on my left.

My eyes swept the land and I sang, "As the sun rises from the east to the west, so will Jesus appear at His coming . . . And I will be here to see Him."

The clerks frowned and departed.

Jubilant, Jeff and I climbed a nearby hill, sat on a rock and watched the orange sun ball setting in the west. I opened my Bible and read: "For the land you go to possess is not like the land . . . from which you have come . . . [it] is a land of hills and valleys, which drinks water from the rain of heaven, a land for which the LORD your God cares" (Deut. 11:10–12).

Scattered huts and garden plots dotted a vast green plain stretching towards the mountains of Sudan in the north. At our feet, hundreds of splintered bullet cases studded the ground, mute testimony to the terror that had ruled this land for decades. Idi Amin's reign of terror had been followed by a return to power of Milton Obote, whose rule caused the deaths of half a million people. Seven years on, the Acholi of the north came face to face with evil yet again—in the form of the Lord's Resistance Army (LRA) led by religious extremist Joseph Kony, who claimed to be a spirit medium sent to overthrow the government and rule the country according to the Ten Commandments. His ideology was bizarre and his methods even more so. Anyone who didn't support his regime was terrorised. Under the cloak of darkness, unsuspecting villagers were targeted and brutalised in the most horrific way—not just with bombs and guns, but with machetes and hoes. Body parts would be cut off, innocent families murdered, homes burnt down, crops destroyed, women raped and children abducted then forced to join the ranks of this evil and growing militia.

This was to be the backdrop for our ministry.

"Jeff," I said, "let's make this our prayer mountain. We can dispatch angels, not bullets, to help these poor villagers."

Jeff sighed and looked around. "This country is so full of desperate need: the war has crippled the economy, the people are traumatised and abductions are rife—it's hard to know where to begin. But God encouraged me this morning," he said, reaching for my Bible. "It's 1 Chronicles 28:19: 'All this . . . the LORD made me understand in writing, by His hand upon me, all the works of these plans.' Now . . . where to begin? I think our first priority is to alleviate the physical suffering of as many orphans as we possibly can."

Sitting there in the pearly light, God gave us His plans: for a primary school to gather the masses and educate the illiterate children, water boreholes for washing bodies, a clinic dispensing free medicine and an agriculture-based feeding programme.

I was excited.

"The teachers will be Christians, so the school will be God-centred. Even the uniforms should be red to signify the blood covenant every child will have with Jesus. We will send the children home each afternoon to their guardians washed, fed, literate and singing thanks to God who rescued them."

Jeff beamed with pleasure, wrapped his arm around my shoulder and kissed me.

"Thank you for being such an amazing wife and helping me with this dream."

Hand in hand we strolled back to the lodge. Tomorrow we would travel back to the city to finalise preparations for settling in north Uganda.

I tried to sleep that night, but instead lay awake worrying. I rolled over to face my husband.

"Can we really set up camp on that land? . . . There's no electricity, no bathroom, no food. There's not even any water."

Jeff reassured me, "Don't you worry Irene. I'll take care of everything."

8

PARCELS AND PRAYERS

KAMPALA AND KITGUM, 1992

SEVERAL MONTHS INTO our new African adventure, we received good news: our container from Australia had finally docked at Mombasa, Kenya, before making the slow, bumpy journey by road to Kampala where we would meet up with it.

What a thrill it was to see our Land Cruiser roll out. A vehicle of our own meant no more ankle-pecking bus rides to and from the city. Next, our small caravan that was to be our home for the foreseeable future emerged. Despite its modest size, it had a small kitchen area, a table and a double bed. It was a mansion compared to Kitgum's crude mud huts with dung floors. Eagerly, I unlatched the aluminium door and climbed inside. Australian beach culture had arrived in landlocked Uganda. If I closed my eyes I could smell the sea spray and see the waves crashing along the sand.

I opened one of the kitchen drawers and carefully unwrapped my precious package of seashells: pearly turrets, purple pipis, cream cornucopias—treasures from the ocean. I picked out an iridescent ziggurat shell and held it up to the light. A translucent pink path spiralled to its peak, making me think of man's aspirations to reach God.

I wonder if this venture will bring us closer to Jesus, I thought, as I held the shell to my ear to listen to the sighing of the ocean. Inside, my soul ached. Jeff's face suddenly appeared at the door. Embarrassed, I quickly wrapped the shells and put them back in the drawer. He frowned.

"There you are. Look, there's no time for reminiscing now. We've got to get supplies. Are you coming with me?"

Our Land Cruiser edged its way into the sprawling city of Kampala—a kaleidoscope of shanties and open-air markets, flanked by mid-rise office buildings. Horns blasted as we slowly inched our way through relentless traffic jams. It was a chaotic scene as *boda bodas* (motorcycle and bicycle taxis), cars, bikes and people all converged into one. Along the road into town, every square inch of space was chock-full of someone selling something. From their makeshift bamboo and tin shacks, vendors displayed everything from bananas to bras. The place was abuzz with commerce and activity. Jeff parked the car next to the bustling open-air markets. I waited inside. Looking out of the window, I watched with interest as police patrolled the area carrying semi-automatic weapons. I was startled when a traffic controller approached and tapped at the window. He was short and stocky with bushy eyebrows. He looked angry.

"Where's the driver?" he scowled.

I pointed to the throng in the market—a noisy labyrinth teeming with brightly dressed vendors selling clothing, plastic utensils and second-hand shoes.

"You do know this is a very serious offence: driving with garage plates at the weekend? You will have to come with me to the court now. We will impound your vehicle. On Monday, you will be convicted and fined." He drew breath. "What do you think of that?"

My heart sank. We had visited government offices many times trying to get license plates and had been constantly disappointed. I popped my eyes, local style, and shrugged.

Frustrated by my witless impersonation, the traffic controller shouted, "Where is the driver?"

"He's somewhere in the market buying things for our orphan school in Kitgum," I replied.

"Ah, well," he said, his face softening, "on humanitarian grounds, I could let you go . . . But first, perhaps you have a gift for me?"

My mind was spinning. I realised I had broken the law and now perhaps I was going to pay for it. I shrugged at the man again and said, "I haven't got any money." He glared at me, so I quickly added, "Bananas! I've got bananas. Here you can have my bananas."

He bared his teeth and snarled, "I don't want bananas."

There followed a long period of silence . . . and then Jeff came into view, carrying jerry cans and saucepans.

The officer's face brightened. "You have committed a very serious offence. You should be convicted and fined." He paused. "However, on humanitarian grounds, I will let you go this time."

Jeff smiled broadly. "That's very considerate of you. Here's a tip for your trouble."

The man dismissed Jeff and went on his way.

Jeff sat beside me. "I've found a small shipping container to carry all the supplies we've just bought. Those boys over there will move it for $50," he said, pointing in the distance to a small blue tow truck. "You go and ride with them to direct them to the container terminal."

As I walked towards the boys, the "vehicle" came into view. I found it difficult to contain my shock. The vehicle was a truck cabin bolted to a battered 2.5-metre-long tray holding a small crane. I knew our container was six metres long. The sums didn't add up. Five young gung-ho Ugandans grinned and pointed to their logo: "ABNER BROS—ANYTHING. ANYWHERE. ANYTIME."

I gingerly climbed up into the cabin. The seat was a loose plank of wood; a bent and rusty metal canopy covered my head.

The driver waved to his mates who leapt from the back of the truck and began to push the vehicle downhill. I groaned and shut my eyes. With a shudder the engine spluttered into life and we lurched through the city. The driver held the wavering gear-stick in place while his feet shuffled between the clutch and brake pedals. I prayed and held the door tightly to prevent it flying open as we careered through the slums.

When we arrived at the container yard, it was immediately obvious our six-metre shipping container would not fit onto the truck's tray. We needed a miracle. The boys leapt into action, and in no time had winched a corner of the container up with chains so that half a metre of the container was supported by the truck's tray—the remaining five and a half metres had only air beneath it. Swaying from side to side, we travelled like this for ten kilometres. Each time the truck's rear wheels hit a pothole, we passengers in the cabin were lifted into the air. Eventually we arrived at the city container terminal where we could keep everything stored until we were ready to head to Kitgum.

The boys then convinced us they could handle the next assignment, which was to deliver fourteen heavy cast iron water bore pipes that were each six metres long. As the navigator, I watched as it took four stocky men to lift each pipe onto the tray, which again was much too small for the job. However, using steel chains, much prayer and African resourcefulness, we finally arrived at the storage depot at 5:05 p.m.

Closed!

We couldn't leave $5,000 worth of pipes unguarded and tied to an old truck overnight. But God moved the manager's heart and he allowed us to enter.

We had similar challenges buying and transporting other necessities: 500 sheets of roofing iron, 200 bags of cement, 80 sheets of plywood, metal drums of fuel, etc. As most building materials were unobtainable in northern Uganda, we needed to source supplies from central Uganda. We might have despaired if it wasn't for God encouraging our hearts and protecting us. On one occasion, our car was packed with a newly loaded full gas bottle. Our next purchase was a pile of 50 hoes, which the porter threw carelessly into the back. Unbeknown to us, this knocked the handle of the gas tap full on. As we were driving through an industrial area we thought the strong smell was factory smoke. When we realised the loud hissing was coming from somewhere in the back of our fully loaded vehicle, Jeff stopped, leapt out, wrenched open the door and turned off the gas just in time. Praise God that was not our exit day!

And the enemy went on his way thwarted, gnashing his teeth (see Ps. 37:12–13).

Our friendly surveyor, Canaan Otim, was not so fortunate. Just days after submitting our land survey to the Department of Lands in the city, he caught the 5 a.m. bus to Kitgum and was confronted by a thug waving a gun. After demanding money, the man asked Canaan where he was going. Then in a fit of rage, he shouted, "You people from the north should all be dead. You carry hand grenades in your bags!" And he shot him—ten times!

That night we visited him, lying with his shattered leg and arm in plaster. Hospital conditions were shocking: there was no food or painkillers. Patients brought their own mattresses into the wards and were escorted by carers who slept under the iron bed on a mat.

Several weeks after the shooting, an "army official" came to interview Canaan. However, the doctor became suspicious and immediately relocated the patient to a different floor—a fortunate move, as two hours later several men with guns came looking for their "friend" Canaan. They wanted to silence the complainant.

Facing seven more weeks immobilised in a hospital bed, with thugs gunning for him, Canaan was scared. We encouraged him to memorise Psalm 91, and he was amazed and delighted at the richness and practicality of the Bible. During our regular visits, and after his confrontation with death, Canaan gave control of his life to Jesus. He was hungry for God's word and wanted to discuss it continually. If God had sent us all the way to Uganda for this one soul, it was worth it, but our journey was far from over.

Now, if only we could get the clearances we needed.

$$\boxed{9}$$

KITGUM BOUND

KAMPALA AND KITGUM, 1992

SO MUCH RED TAPE.

Every decision seemed to take an eternity and gathering supplies was a long and laborious process. After weeks of trudging the streets, backed up by much prayer, we had completed all the necessary paperwork for registrations and permits, paid government taxes, and all supplies had been purchased and loaded. Jeff was to drive our packed Land Cruiser and tow our caravan, which was bursting at the seams with essentials for pioneer living. I was to follow in the truck carrying our container, which would also be towing a trailer loaded with building materials.

I felt apprehensive about the long journey ahead over pot-holed roads peppered with landmines and frequented by rebels. It would take a miracle of God for us to arrive safely. I ate and drank His word. "Be strong and courageous; do not be afraid nor dismayed . . . for there are more with us than with him. With him is an arm of flesh; but with us is the LORD our God, to help us and to fight our battles" (2 Chron. 32:7–8).

On the day of our departure, we drove to the storage yard to collect the container which was to be loaded onto a hired truck. Walking through the yard I tripped over the truck's gearbox which was lying on the ground and noticed the truck's back axle sitting on some bricks. This meant we weren't going anywhere soon. Perhaps because God knew the road was not safe that day.

In the meantime, young men who worked at the terminal yard clad in dirty, ripped trousers gritted their teeth, and with sweat beading their faces they heaved timber poles, chain mesh, boxes of Bibles, bags of cement and cast iron pipes onto our trailer. Under a blazing sun, Jeff joined them, lifting and pushing amid much laughter.

Several days later, the truck was reassembled with all the oily pipes bolted into place. I watched a huge crane as it navigated its way over hundreds of containers. It let down steel hooks which grabbed the four corners of our container. Spewing black smoke and roaring its engine, the crane heaved as it lifted the thirteen-ton weight and swung it like a matchbox above the truck. Watching from a safe distance, I breathed a sigh of relief as it gently lowered the container squarely onto the truck tray. We were ready to go.

Next morning at 4.30 a.m., Jeff drove away towing the packed caravan bound for Kitgum. At 7.30 a.m. my driver and mechanic wandered into the yard. After shunting back and forth, they finally hooked up the truck to the trailer. I clambered up into the cabin and took my seat. An iron bench behind the driver was littered with greasy jacks, spanners and pipes. The rusty metal roof was inches from my head. I rested my feet on the engine cover and was glad my sturdy shoes could absorb the heat.

As the driver edged into the morning traffic, the truck's engine began to protest at the weight. The brakes refused to hold, and when the driver changed to a lower gear, the gear-stick jumped. I had to hold it in place.

As the engine roared, I groaned, "Oh, no—$1,000 to hire this wreck! Only God can help us make it to Kitgum. Your strength is made perfect in our weakness, God. Don't leave us!"

Our twenty-one-metre-long rig edged through the Kampala streets, past concrete office blocks, whistling policemen, shouting newsboys, tin and mud shanties spilling down hillsides, naked children chasing chickens, and two-metre-wide barrows holding sweet potatoes.

Slowly we crawled along country roads, passing cool banana groves. Climbing uphill, people pushing wheelbarrows overtook us. As we rolled down the other side, the driver gripped the steering wheel to stop it shaking violently. The cabin filled with hot, grey exhaust fumes, and I began to feel faint.

Three hours out, we were driving through Luwero District, a township in the middle of Uganda that was still reeling from the effects of a bloodbath that had taken place between rebel groups in 1981. Knowing this made me very nervous. Suddenly, a policeman waved us to the side of the road. He examined the driver's papers and motioned for him to climb down. My heart sank as he escorted him down the road, around a bend and into the town. After waiting for ten minutes in the hot cabin, I climbed down and followed them, looking for a police station and muttering to myself, "I bind every demon hindering this journey, in Jesus' name." There on the verandah of an old yellow concrete building, my driver sat forlornly, flanked on either side by uniformed police constables.

"What's happening?" I asked.

They held up a tattered form showing the photo of a young man. I looked at my driver, his grey hair and his sorrowful eyes. Yes, time had definitely passed between his license issue and now.

"Expired license!" The constable barked.

"What does this mean?" I asked.

The officer in charge rose to his full height, his well-fed stomach almost bursting the buttons off his shirt; the driver shrank smaller onto the bench.

"It means he can't drive any more. It means we will take him to court and prosecute him and fine him. It means if he can't pay, we will put him in prison."

I feigned innocence. "When will all this happen?"

"Right now, lady, right now!"

I protested, "But we are on our way to Kitgum to build an orphan school."

Without comment, he turned his back on me.

I forced a quaver into my voice: "I can't drive the truck myself." Studying his broad back, I began to whimper.

There was an endless silence. Then he finally muttered, "Let the man go."

"Thank You, Jesus," I sighed.

With the sun beating down fiercely, we resumed our journey. As the day wore on the driver was in great pain from his shoulder and elbow as he wrestled to hold the gear-stick in place while our monster hurtled down every hillside. He was especially cautious on the steep descent to the bridge crossing the River Nile. Playful baboons frolicked beside us as we successfully climbed the northern hill. Now we were in a different region, climatically and spiritually. My eyes scanned the scrubby brown bush for khaki-clad ambushers.

Abandoned farmhouses, their walls drilled with bullet holes, were silent witnesses to past terror. Mercifully, the sun was sinking and we only had thirty minutes of cool twilight before we plunged into deep darkness. We drove on, the truck's headlights only lighting road hazards seconds before we were in them. Although Jeff was in Lira—a small town about a hundred kilometres away—it was obvious we would not reach there that night. At the next village we climbed down in pitch-blackness. I was led to a small round mud hut and given a fried egg on bread and a basin of water for washing. A tiny candle revealed my bed was freshly made. This was African hospitality at its best—ready to greet strangers at any time. Clean and satisfied, I sat outside looking at the brilliance of the stars and delighted by darting fireflies.

Next morning at 9.30 a.m. we found Jeff anxiously waiting for us in Lira. He had spent a sleepless night wondering where we were and was angry at having paid $1,000 to hire a 1962 truck without working gears, brakes or a licensed driver. But then again, he had his own story of troubles. He told me the back of our over-packed caravan had sagged, detaching the front end from the chassis. The entire load had shifted to the back, flinging the front into the air. He had spent hours repacking and redistributing the weight. Then, as he was driving along the caravan door had flung open, allowing red dust to blow in and cover all of our precious belongings. After sharing our woes with each other we set off again.

For the next, most dangerous part of the road, we left in convoy at 10.30 a.m., but were soon stopped by a police roadblock. As the officer began to note down the many faults in the truck, it seemed we would be delayed indefinitely. Under my breath, I prayed. The official changed his attitude suddenly, and grudgingly waved us on.

Nearing our destination we passed children half-hidden in tall grass and billowing shrubs, their eyes wide at seeing our rigs. Some screamed in terror to see a mobile home complete with windows like rolling eyes, moving along the road. Thirty kilometres out of Kitgum, we were waved down by a stalled utility truck. The tray was full of fish, curling their tails underneath a burning sun. The driver begged us to tow him to town. We agreed, and used some rope to drag his utility behind our trailer. The rope broke several times, especially climbing hills.

That afternoon, we finally arrived. I was excited to see the mud houses and mango trees of Kitgum. God had sent His angel before us to keep us on track and to bring us to the place He had prepared for us (see Exod. 23:20).

Gaunt villagers gathered on the roadside staring open-mouthed at our strange procession—more like a travelling circus —as it entered town: a white mud-covered Land Cruiser towing a dusty mobile home, followed by an ancient truck roaring through its gears, loaded with a red container and towing a trailer filled with timber poles, chain mesh and boxes, pulling by rope an old utility filled with reeking fish! At the sparse open-air marketplace we untied our smelly burden. The owner put down a mat and shovelled out his fish for display. He was instantly surrounded by excited women and children all bidding for this rare but sun-spoilt treat that had made such a grand entrance.

Dusty children waved, jumped up and down and flashed wide smiles as we drove through town, down a narrow track onto our land and parked under a giant tamarind tree. Because of recent rains, it was green and lovely. As curious children gathered around our caravan, I looked for something to dispel their fear of two strange *mzungu* (white people) who had set up camp near to their huts. Opening one of the drawers inside the caravan, I pulled out a bag of mixed sweets, stood in the doorway and began sucking wildly in front of the children.

"Mmm," I said licking my lips. "They are delicious—want one?"

They all looked at me blankly and took a step back. I passed one to Jeff who relished his sweet treat. Slowly the children inched forward and accepted a sweet—these were to be my new friends.

Taking some deckchairs from the caravan, we shared a flask of tea and biscuits with my driver.

"Well done, mate," Jeff smiled and handed him a tube of Goanna salve for his aching joints.

Huge rain clouds rolled across the horizon from east to west. I touched Jeff's hand and whispered, "We will have ringside seats when Jesus comes back."

He looked into my eyes. "You are amazing Irene. I thank God for you." He yawned. "Hey, I need a rest. Let's clear our bed."

He dismissed the driver. "See you in the morning, mate. We'll unload then."

Our successful day was celebrated with a blissful sleep within the safety of our caravan. Outside the night was filled with the sounds of Africa: chirruping insects, strange noises and howling dogs disturbed by witch doctors' drums. But we slept nestled in each other's arms, satisfied that both of us were exactly where we were meant to be.

It wouldn't be long before reality sunk in.

10

FRUSTRATIONS

KITGUM, 1992

WE WOKE THE NEXT MORNING to the shouts of excited villagers and clambered out of our caravan carrying a basin, towel and paper. After filling up our bowl from a local borehole, we went in search of some long grass for private bathing. Back home, a long warm shower was a welcome start to the day; here my steamy grass bath didn't invite lingering.

After breakfast our driver appeared grumbling, "There's no crane in town to lift the container down." As Jeff groaned, an official hurried towards us.

"You can't unload anything until you have the necessary permits," he said. "You will have to come back to my office."

With a shrug, Jeff walked into town. I stood there helpless, surrounded by chattering villagers bemused by the spectacle. I turned to face Celestino, our newly appointed worker who I'd met in Kampala and who would now be working with us at the project site.

He smiled. "Please, Mama, let me help you. I know how to unload the truck."

He asked the driver to get him some rope and then, giving orders in the local Acholi language, he directed the crowd, which by now had grown in number, to retreat and stand in a line. He then unwound a long rope in front of them and told them to lift it up and hold it, making a fence using human posts.

Jeff returned and chose seven strong men to help. The container doors were opened and after three hours of labour under the hot sun, Jeff and the workers had emptied it.

Next, Celestino attached the steel rope of our winch to the container's back corners, then wrapped it around the tamarind tree and called for the driver to slowly edge the truck forwards, away from the tree. The container slid towards the end of the tray, balanced for some seconds, then crashed to the ground in a cloud of dust. We all cheered.

We watched in awe as the men, covered in dust and sweat, began repacking the grounded container with the iron sheets, cement, food, furniture and tools. The villagers who were standing watching proceedings under the fierce sun were pointing and laughing at our modern chairs and cupboards. Hours later, everything valuable was locked in the container, apart from some hessian packing sacks that were still lying around. The labourers grabbed them eagerly.

"Good beds, Mama," they said beaming. We were one short, but Celestino happily carried away a cardboard carton as his new bed.

It was easy to love these appreciative, tireless workers. Labour was always abundant and we were happy to contribute to the local economy, so the next morning we invited them to work for us. They happily worked alongside Jeff, who had acquired a range of handyman skills over the years, back in Australia. Together they unloaded the trailer, fenced the site, dug pit latrines, cleared acres and planted maize—all in our first week in Kitgum.

❖ ❖ ❖

As each day presented a new crisis, my love and admiration for my husband of nearly ten years deepened. One evening I leaned back in his arms and looked up into his eyes.

"This is where the rubber hits the road," I murmured. "How do you do it, honey? Dealing with dust storms, insect swarms, tropical ulcers, malaria, constant beggars and intolerable heat—all the challenges of Africa. Sorts the men from the boys. What a man I married!"

He seemed to dismiss my praise. "I know it's tough, but it was God's plan for us to come to Kitgum," he said matter-of-factly. "We need to draw on His strength every day. What a privilege to be His ambassador. When I see the locals hacking the rock-hard soil, I fear starvation for them, but then I remember His promises: "The blameless spend their days under the LORD's care . . . in times of disaster they will not wither; in days of famine they will enjoy plenty" (Ps. 37:18–19 NIV).

Jeff knew God's promises as part of his life. I wasn't quite so gracious. My constant muttering was, "In my weakness, God, Your strength is made perfect." I was struggling to keep up my lifetime habits of order and perfection, while caring for my husband without water or electricity. It seemed an impossible task for this white woman. Unable to dig pit latrines or handle the heavier jobs, I looked after all the domestic chores. But it was tough.

Small routine jobs that had been so easy in Australia were such a challenge. During our first week in Kitgum, I queued for water at the local water borehole and carried a heavy twenty-litre jerry can 200 metres to our compound, where I attempted to scrub Jeff's clothing by hand. Washing our bed sheets and towels in cold water was frustrating—everything was soiled and dusty brown. Eventually, some local girls took pity on us and took over our laundry. They even ironed Jeff's shirts with a charcoal-filled iron box, so he began to look smart again. But I felt he was disappointed in me.

My attempts to cook our limited rations of beans and maize over a wood fire were equally frustrating. My legs stung as my polyester skirts melted against my skin. I scoured the local markets for familiar vegetables, but only found yams and aniseed. Frequently my eyes filled with tears as Jeff rose from our candle-lit foldaway table positioned beneath a starry sky and poured his soupy beans on the grass. How we longed for roast chicken. Remembering baked dinners made our mouths water. Over the following weeks, as his weight decreased, I became ashamed and concerned that I wasn't the wife I should be, so I started making him "chocolate pudding" out of sweetened millet porridge. This seemed to sustain him.

Eventually, an African girl called Freda came to our rescue and cooked us meals of dried fish in peanut sauce. A wave of sadness engulfed me as I noticed Jeff respond to her competent service.

One morning, I watched as Jeff installed our solar panels.

"We'll soon have music," he said as he placed our cassette player on an outdoor shelf.

"We need it connected inside our caravan," I objected.

He frowned and continued working.

"Freda needs music," he shrugged.

"What about me?" I complained. "I am your wife—don't I come first?"

I'm losing him . . . I thought. Seeing how zealous Jeff seemed to be about everything, while I was grappling with my own inadequacies, created insecurities I found hard to shake off. Indeed, my rising jealousies and escalating self-doubt amid the hardships seemed to be driving away the man I had been married to for nearly a decade. I became aware of the small signs: the care and concern for others and the feeling that he was distancing himself from me. I couldn't help but feel that my ruddy Irish skin breaking down in the heat, compounded by blotchy bouts of crying, added to my diminishing appeal.

Despite the ups and downs of married life, we had always enjoyed missionary trips together: visiting exotic cultures, dispensing love and prayer alongside practical help, then flying away, feeling satisfied and eager to plan our next adventure. I moaned when I realised that this time there was no return ticket and no home waiting in Australia. This was a life sentence we had willingly walked into. "But God," I wailed, "You must have anaesthetised us back in Australia to cause us to sell our homes and burn all our bridges."

I couldn't hear if He answered.

I tried to re-focus my energies. One morning, I took a trip to the markets to buy clothing for all the local children. As I distributed T-shirts and men's white business shirts and shorts, the children babbled excitedly. Covering their nakedness in oversized outfits gave me a sense of satisfaction and for a time took my mind off my struggling marriage.

In the evenings, as the red sun ball dipped below the horizon, painting the sky burnt orange, I climbed the nearby hill and thought of Jesus' trials at Golgotha. Watching the villagers winding their way home to their round mud huts carrying water and firewood, with their children listlessly in tow, I began to feel God's heartbeat for the community—His grieving heart for their hard labour to survive, locked up in their prisons of ignorance, superstition and sickness.

As I observed these beautiful people, I sang in heaven's language songs of deliverance for His created people, for every feeble villager, every crushed child. God would use us to lift them from earth's dunghills and seat them at His banqueting table. I closed my eyes and caught a vision of their tear-stained faces, their arms outstretched towards heaven. I saw children, smiling—thousands of them, dressed in white satin and lace, seated at a magnificent feast, served delicious foods by beautiful angels.

Energised by this picture, I stood up, brushed myself off and resolved to start work immediately.

11

FREE TO SING

KITGUM, MAY 1992

AS RAINS COOLED the days in May, I started to run informal lessons for the children in the area. Each day, after a small breakfast of porridge and tea, I packed a bag of books, tambourines, alphabet charts, puppets and a camping stool. Protected under the shade of my umbrella, I strolled through shoulder-high grass towards town, often being startled by gaudy grasshoppers that randomly jumped across my path. And then two by two, ragged children would emerge to follow me as I sang "Come along with me to my Father's house . . ." I often felt like the pied piper with my little procession tagging along behind me.

By the time I had reached the large mango tree, the group had swelled to about a hundred children. Some were tiny 4-year-olds with babies tied to their backs. Others were unschooled village children and gangly, curious teenagers. Sitting on my camping stool, I would wiggle a puppet and sing, "If You're Happy That Jesus Loves You, Clap Your Hands." As the children mastered each song, they were eager to learn more.

I could not use the usual tools of a kindergarten teacher: play dough—because the children were so hungry they would eat it; cardboard cartons for building blocks—because they would be taken for bedding; dressing up clothing—because it would be commandeered to cover their nakedness. Writing names in the dust, counting pebbles, alphabet charts and Bible stories were my tools of the trade.

To overcome the language barrier, I became a one-woman circus, acting out gospel dramas with exaggerated facial expressions and much jumping, kneeling and dancing. Sometimes I'd ask one of the English-speaking locals to translate for me.

At first, the children sat silently, looking puzzled, but eventually they began to smile. In time, they got so excited and exuberant that they mimicked my repertoire, and this drew a large crowd of women who stood at the back and watched the spectacle. Untouched by technology, the children were delightful, innocent and eager to learn.

Most of these children had never been to school before. Unlike our western culture that has been familiar with the written word for centuries, the Acholi of northern Uganda have relied on oral tradition—stories and songs—to transfer their knowledge. Their perceptions and instincts are much keener than those of city dwellers. My techniques seemed to work well despite our cultural differences. Perhaps the only hindrance to learning was the profound trauma many of them had experienced living through years of civil war. Apart from our noisy midday sessions, there was an uneasy silence in the community. Everyone was alert for sounds of battle: alarms, gunshots, bombs. They walked silently, smiled shyly, their natural rhythm and song stifled within them.

One silent evening I was walking around the compound praying, when the breeze brought a refrain to my ears: "Now we're happy Jesus loves us, clap our hands."

A thick quiet swallowed the words. I strained my ears. Did I imagine it?

"Now we're happy Jesus loves us, and we've really got to show it . . ." The voices of the children bounced from village to village gathering strength, until it boomed like a heavenly choir.

Every evening thereafter, the singing continued until the sun went down. God had put the song back into the hearts of the children. Even today, those children, who are now adults, can recite the words to the songs I taught them all those years earlier under the trees.

During one school session under the shade of a large mango tree, I showed a picture of Jesus healing a sick child and said to the children, "Jesus is real and alive. He wants every one of you to be healthy. Who is sick among you?"

They were quick to respond. "James is sick in his house," they offered.

I stood up and replied, "Well let's go and pray for him."

We filed through the grass until we came to a typical Acholi hut—round mud brick with a thatched roof. Although it was very dark inside, I could make out the body of a thin boy lying on a mat on the dirty floor. He lifted his head, rolled his eyes, and then closed them again. I took in a breath, then whispered, "Dear Father, please let them see You heal this boy so they won't go to witch doctors anymore."

Aloud I prayed, "Thank You, Jesus, that You carried James's sickness in Your own body on the cross 2,000 years ago. By Your wounds, James has been healed. Please release Your healing power through his body now." I waited a few moments. The children jostled around me, peering anxiously into the darkness to see if the prayer had worked. The boy lay motionless on the floor, so we left quietly.

Back under the tree, the children again bowed their heads and prayed for James. Death was a common visitor here, so my faith levels were low. Moments later there was a commotion at the back of the crowd as children made a space for James to sit down. He was smiling and nodding to his friends. "Jesus healed me!" he declared.

It was the first of many miracles. As the children came to know the person of the Holy Spirit, they saw his power healing their friends of tuberculosis, malaria, dysentery, conjunctivitis and ringworm. As I witnessed their faith levels rise, I taught them to pray for each other. "Hands up if you're sick," I'd say. "Now, those children who are sitting next to them, lay hands on them and say these words: 'Sickness go, in Jesus' name! Leave their body. Leave their soul. Leave their spirit. Jesus, by Your wounds they've been healed; Holy Spirit, thank You for releasing Your healing!'"

Many children who had previously sat ashen-faced, unable to walk or eat, with the spirit of death embracing them, were soon able to run, eat and laugh after we had prayed.

After weeks of teaching, I discovered that the English language was not essential to the children's understanding of the spirit world—perhaps in part this was due to the Acholi culture being deeply spiritual. Long before missionaries arrived, the Acholi had consulted spirit mediums or traditional healers to reverse the curse of sickness. They believed in a class of spirit called "Jok" that they viewed as the source of the sickness. They attempted to counter the spirit through sacrifices and rituals.

As I taught them about Jesus, the children began seeing miracles and were keen to get all their friends healed. One afternoon, the children guided me to a hut. Inside, a boy called Kenneth was lying on a small mat and shivering with fever. One leg was swollen and smelt gangrenous. His eyes were tightly shut. While he was trying to seek oblivion through sleep, he was waving away a swarm of flies that were tormenting him. His suffering made me mad at the devil. I commanded the devil to leave and then prayed.

As I washed and dressed the boy's leg, I noticed the scars of razor slashes on his neck and upper arms, a sign of a witch doctor's intervention to ward off evil spirits, which is common practice in northern Uganda. Witch doctors are viewed as prophets who are able to discern why a person is facing disaster and reverse curses. But the tradition has become exploitative and many witch doctors have become charlatans, overcharging for their services. Celestino had once told me that when a child has a fever they are often taken to a witch doctor for treatment.

I showed Kenneth's mother the story of Jesus driving out a demon (see Luke 11) in a picture Bible and explained that although witch doctors may appear to have healing powers, when demons leave a person they roam about looking for a new home and then often return to the individual, bringing more illnesses. As I continued to explain Bible truths, neighbours gathered around me astonished that anyone should come so far to show care for them. An elder brought up a chair and insisted I sit down as he addressed the crowd. A teenage boy interpreted.

"We have been called the most backward tribe in Uganda. Now these two *mzungu* have come to camp amongst us. They get water from our borehole. They treat our sick people. They are planning a free school for our children. Let us do all we can to help them."

One middle-aged woman, wearing an oversized man's check shirt and a long colourful skirt, shuffled forward and presented me with a grass broom. A bare-chested small child deposited a heavy pumpkin on my lap. Kenneth's mother presented me with a chicken—but this bundle of flapping black feathers was very different to the sanitised trays of chicken breast I was used to buying from Australian supermarkets. Oh how we longed for roast chicken! But when I asked her if she could possibly kill it and bring it to my fireplace she exclaimed, "Oh no, only a witch doctor carries dead chickens. My daughters would never get a husband!" As the crowd chuckled, I wondered if these people would ever leave their dependence on witch doctors and if I would ever satisfy my craving for a roast chicken dinner.

┌─────┐
│ 12 │
└─────┘

EVIL PLANS

KITGUM, 1992

THAT NIGHT I had a dream . . .

The sky was filled with invisible generals reporting to the ruling spirits of sickness and despair.

"These whites come in His authority—I shudder to mention His name. And He's backing their prayers. Babies are getting healed and she's blasting all our traditions: the slashing with razor blades; the pulling out of infants' teeth; the submerging of newborns in boiling water. She's going into huts to pray for sick children. Six crossed over into His kingdom yesterday. She wrestled one man away from us just before he breathed his last. He missed hell's fires by one hour."

A roar of indignation went through the sky.

"And the man—he never tires. He's building fences and digging alongside our people. He gives them big meals and bonuses. He's making them laugh and, worst of all, he's giving them back the dignity we've spent years stripping away."

"Enough!" the ruling spirits bellowed. "These two whites are not immortal like us, they are only humans. We'll show them just how frail they are!"

"Excuse me, sirs," a spirit slyly interrupted. "There are not just two of them. They have many praying for their safety back in their home country. And He's actually listening to them. A number of our traps—the exploding gas bottle, the falling tree branch, the bus ambushes, the attack of malaria parasites and the swarms of flies have all been nullified. Our troops are in turmoil. Some of our witch doctors are considering relocating to another district. We will lose all the control we have taken years to establish."

The rulers began writing.

"We'll deal with your complaints one by one . . . But first, let's put these two front-liners out of action before they bring in reinforcements. Send observers to find out their weaknesses . . . In what situations are their souls vulnerable? Too fatigued to communicate with their God? Sickness? . . . Frustration? . . . Bombard them! Now go."

I woke to the sound of howling dogs as spirits moved through the district.

Jeff stirred. "Are you okay?" he murmured.

I snuggled into his back and was reassured.

In the following weeks, a series of attacks reduced us to tears of frustration. The tropical ulcers on my legs flared up with blood poisoning. I was forced to join the long lines of chronically ill women and children at the local hospital, whose sad eyes sympathised with my immobility. Our kerosene stove exploded twice, with flames shooting three metres high. Violent winds, preceding the rainy season, rattled our corrugated iron shelter while I was bathing, then tore it apart flinging sheets of iron across the fields.

One morning, 200 thin men queued at our gate begging for work in response to a false rumour that we were recruiting. My eyes took in their gaunt cheekbones and their bloodshot eyes.

"Please sir," they begged Jeff. "Please. Anything. We will dig pit latrines. Put up barbed-wire fencing. Anything!"

Jeff shook his head. "I'm sorry. We already employ too many. We have no more money."

He turned away abruptly and I hurried to catch up with him.

"You did the right thing, honey. We can't be responsible for all the adults too," I said, touching his arm, but he shook me off.

Our moods swung wildly as our bodies were persistently disturbed by bouts of malaria and dysentery.

One evening, as I was about to hobble up my prayer hill and beseech God about the situations, I discovered the army had taken up position 200 metres away and were blasting the hillside with bullets for target practice.

Were we discouraged? Were we dismayed? Devastated is probably an apt description!

But we read Judges 6 and, like Gideon, we prayed: "Lord, if You are with us, why has all this happened to us? Where are all Your miracles? Lord, have You abandoned us?" As we read more, we understood God was letting us experience the frailty of our human bodies so we wouldn't claim glory for ourselves and say our own strength had saved us (see Judg. 7:2).

Then God's Holy Spirit came on Jeff and he marched around the land praying loudly in tongues, giving the demons their eviction notice. Using the words of Nehemiah he claimed victory: "The God of heaven will give us success. We His servants will start rebuilding, but as for you [mocking and accusing spirits], you have no share," no rights, nor claim, nor any place here (Neh. 2:20 NIV).

Hobbling after him, I added my favourite: "Because the Lord delights in us, He will give us dominion in this land. We do not fear the former inhabitants. Their protection has left them, and the Lord is with us" (paraphrased from Num. 14:8–9).

13

MOSES BRICKS

KITGUM, 1992

WE HAD BIG PLANS—too big to tackle alone—so Jeff employed eighteen village men to work alongside him on the land we had been given. They laboured industriously and tirelessly, clearing fields, planting crops, digging latrines. We could see their self-esteem improving each day as we affirmed their value by giving them morning porridge, a big lunch, wages plus bonuses, hoes, seeds and Bibles. One time, we bought them all colourful gumboots from the markets. A necessity—or so I thought! We were all highly amused when one of the boots got stuck on the foot of our builder and needed to be yanked off with great force. These were our first African friends and we were keen to bring them closer to the love and goodness of God.

"I am already Christian like you," one announced one afternoon after lunch.

"Lovely," I smiled. "What about your family? How many children do you have?"

"Fifteen . . . I think," he replied.

"Oh, your poor wife!"

"I have three wives," he disclosed.

Wow! I thought to myself. *This is a challenge.*

Like witchcraft, polygamy is also common in northern Uganda. In a country where women outnumber men, one of the "advantages" polygamy offers is the opportunity to inherit property. Moreover, according to the Acholi culture, a real man's worth is determined by the number of wives and children he has. I once heard a second wife referred to as a "side-dish." While this might appear sexist in a western culture, I was reluctant to challenge deeply entrenched beliefs. I also learnt that women are married to the clan, not so much the individual husband. In African culture, the lines between immediate and extended families are blurred. Your cousin is referred to as your brother and your uncle as your father. It was complicated, so I asked God to deal with this.

I turned to his friend and asked, "What about you?"

"I only have one wife," he answered quietly.

"It must be hard to have only one wife in a polygamous society," I smiled.

He shrugged. "I used to be rich. I had 400 cows and sold all their milk. But the Karimajong raiders took them all in 1988. Now I am too poor. I can only afford one wife."

Another worker mocked him: "But he is a bad man. He does the wrong thing. His brother died last year and he is ignoring the widow. He will not take her as his wife!"

"But if he is a Christian—?" I quizzed.

I was interrupted.

"No," they argued. "That doesn't change our laws. It is an African tradition. You must take your brother's family as your own. He cannot avoid his responsibility. This is how our clans have survived for so long."

"And how did your brother die?" I asked.

"That sickness . . . 'slim' . . . I mean AIDS," he murmured.

The group went silent.

My knowledge of AIDS was limited, although I had come to understand that polygamy, promiscuity and forced rapes had increased the risk of AIDS and that this disease was depleting the Acholi population.

The pain in their eyes warned us against asking more. Instead we emphasised moving forward to a good future for their children.

❖ ❖ ❖

"We need to start building the permanent school building," Jeff announced one morning in June 1992.

He began by directing the men to make bricks. It was hard work under a fierce sun and reminded me of the Hebrew slaves toiling for Pharaoh—except our workers were paid. Their method was traditional. Bare-footed men would stomp in knee-high mud that had been doused with water until they felt they had achieved the right pliability. This gluggy mixture would be shovelled into moulds and carried metres away where they would be carefully laid out to dry in the sun. Later they were stacked in kilns made from mud and baked for twenty-four hours.

With tremendous effort the men made 18,000 hand-moulded bricks. While we waited for them to bake, we began clearing bush stumps from the future school site.

But our plans for our first school building had to be put on hold as severe weather battered the region. We were quite unprepared for the violent storms of a landlocked country like Uganda. Australia's coastal showers came gently, but here wild winds from Sudan carried in the rainclouds. It was unnerving to bathe in our corrugated iron shelter with sudden winds pounding it like an invisible hammer previewing heavy rain.

One night storm clouds blew in from the heated landmass of Kenya. Lightning flashed and torrential rain sent floods of water across the land. Like sodden dominoes, the bricks we had made toppled to be reclaimed by a sea of mud.

Next morning, Jeff and I surveyed the damage and cried when we saw the devastation. The workers shrugged, while Celestino explained, "We were just following your directions boss. It is the rainy season here from March to October. We'll start again in the dry months—November to March. Meanwhile, we'll continue planting maize and beans to store for feeding the orphans during the dry months." As there is no back-up employment in Kitgum, all energies are geared to planting, harvesting and storing supplies for the dry months when the landscape is reduced to dust and thornbushes.

In the months that followed, Jeff and I often awoke to the thudding sound of digging hoes, heralding a watery sunrise. As villagers prepared their rain-soaked earth, I enjoyed waking early to dig alongside these Africans as they instinctively responded to the rhythm of the earth's seasons: splitting the rich soil, depositing seeds, tending to the green sprouts as they appeared, and anticipating the harvest. It reminded me of the stories in the Bible of sowing and reaping, seed time and harvest.

Throughout the wet season I often walked with the children as they foraged for edible leaves. The grass was lush and sweet-smelling, alive with buzzing insects and yellow butterflies fluttering, while scarlet-breasted birds perched precariously on maize stems, which bowed and swayed beneath their weight. The children offered me berries from lantana bushes. The seed was large, but the taste lingered like blackcurrants.

With every climatic scene change I had a front-row seat to a meteorological extravaganza. In the afternoon the scorching heat would be broken by torrential rainstorms. Pillars of white cloud would shuffle across a vibrant blue sky, slowly blanketing it lead-grey and then spill sheets of rain onto the thirsty ground. Villagers would run for cover, taking a welcome rest from their toil as they watched the raindrops turn the ground into rivulets, producing muddy floodwaters that cut gullies across the earth. Ducks and children revelled in the downpour, sloshing underneath overflowing gutters and swishing along drains. After thirty minutes or so the clouds would roll away and sunlight would glisten on a washed world. Too late in the day to re-establish its dominance, the sun would bow out in a fiery display of red-gold rays across the horizon. There is no twilight on the equator, so black night switches off another day and another grand performance.

In order to survive in a land with such erratic weather patterns, the community learns to adapt—a discipline we, too, would discover in the weeks ahead.

14

BREAKING THE CURSE

KITGUM, 1992

IT'S OFTEN SAID that to be a good teacher, one has to become a great learner. Although I was the white teacher with the western training and the alphabet charts, I had become a student of Acholi traditions and culture. As I spent time with the locals, I discovered a social system where every individual is essential to the community and knows their place and to whom they belong. I also learnt that surviving in a land where bartering is the main currency necessitated altering my thinking patterns.

Co-operation and interdependence are essential traits for the community's survival. Competition and independent thinking threaten the community's cohesion and so are not tolerated. Enforcing boundaries of personal territory, individual possessions and privacy is considered rude and unsociable. Disputes involving divorce, land or property are settled in lengthy public negotiations chaired by clan elders whose experience and age are highly valued. Unconditional tolerance flows within the clan. Every issue involving land, arranged marriages, development or education is examined at village meetings where every person's opinion is welcomed and considered.

If an outsider is to fit in, they must respect and honour decisions made by community elders. So when it was suggested by elders that I begin more classes for the children in the slum areas of town, I naturally obliged.

The young people who lived in and around Kitgum Town, which was about two kilometres from our project site, were unschooled and spent their days sneaking into video halls that were screening violent movies. I would often head to the courtroom building with Pastor Faustino, the minister of the local church we now attended. Once there we would set up a video-player, generator and TV screen and play *The Jesus Film*. A crowd of about fifty people would arrive and sit hypnotised, mouths wide open as they watched moving scenes unfold on the small screen. When the movie was over, Pastor Faustino would stand up and give a passionate Gospel message followed by a call for salvation. Hands would be raised and futures sealed.

On other days of the week, with Jeff away in Kampala renovating a house we'd bought there as a base, I'd set up my informal class under the trees. Usually it wasn't long before a large crowd gathered. The older children were mesmerised by adventure stories from the Bible, which they were encouraged to act out. In time, 300 children gathered each afternoon to learn to read and count and to sing and dance before God. Released from their sadness and bad memories of warfare, they embraced the truth that they had a Father in heaven who loved them and who would make them healthy and happy. During my lessons, I would note the condition of the children. Bloated bellies and red hair was a sign of *kwashiorkor*, a form of malnutrition brought on by a lack of protein in the diet. Eventually, I employed our cook, Freda, to prepare meals for the children.

One afternoon, Freda had prepared enough beans and *posho* for forty children. *Posho* is a staple for Ugandans—a dough made from maize (cornmeal) and water, which is often rolled into a ball and is dipped into a bowl of soupy beans. It is similar to polenta. I explained to those who had gathered, "We have enough food for only forty children. Please help me pick out the needy ones."

With much laughter, they pointed to their skinny friends. But their smiles soon faded when I dismissed them without food, whilst trying to placate them with the words, "Thank God you are very strong." They left sullenly.

Meanwhile, the forty thinnest ones sat quietly in groups of four as I ladled the beans and *posho* into communal bowls. They thanked God, then ate hungrily, silently. When they had finished, I recorded their names and family conditions. Ages were guesswork as no birth records were kept. I began taking photos of them for potential sponsors and arranging home visits.

One of the boys, named Mozambique—a 13-year-old orphan who lived with his aunt—returned very distressed. He had been abused by the "strong" children who were hiding along the roadside. Later, when I found them lying in wait in the long grass, I rebuked them and threatened them with exclusion from my "school" and from receiving books. They were unhappy—not at the loss of benefits, but for upsetting me and for the apparent separation from their white "mama."

Every morning at 11 a.m. the children would bring me their needy friends for feeding. James, who had been miraculously healed, introduced two of his friends to me. The first was a younger boy of about 9 years old called Denis Olanya, who wore his shirt over his head like a shawl. When we placed him in the wash line prior to feeding, he baulked at having to remove his covering. But I insisted, so he tentatively took off his shirt revealing weeping fly-blown sores all over his scalp. The smell was overpowering. With gritted teeth, I soaped him all over, rinsed him and applied tea tree ointment to his head, then topped him off with a cap. This little boy no longer stooped over like the hunchback of Notre Dame. He walked proudly, upright—his cap proclaiming, "ZOO KEEPER Taronga Park." (This once sickly child grew to become one of our youth pastors, a radio presenter and vocational school teacher, and has recently graduated in business management.)

The other friend was a shy, gangly youth called Labele, a name which means "the witch doctor gave him to me." His brow was creased in confusion above eyes that were puzzled and bloodshot. "He doesn't hear or talk," James explained. "He hasn't since he was born."

My heart melted and I felt sad as I offered food to this boy who had been trapped in his silent world for fourteen years. He ate ravenously, his eyes darting around the circle of children. Then he paced around the edge of the crowd as they gathered for school. I watched his eyes widen as the children sang and danced, shaking bells and clapping wood sticks. He leant forward to see the pictures as I displayed them: elephants, giraffes, flowers—animals and flora never seen in Kitgum.

Then he was gone!

I didn't see him leave. I felt sad but continued teaching. Each child prayed for a sick friend, including Denis's scarred scalp. Sunlight dappled their faces. The mango tree's leaves rustled bright green overhead. I looked up into its foliage. There was Labele's face peering down, like some shy forest creature, hidden but watching.

From then on, at every school session he was there above me, staring at the children's faces, looking at their silent moving mouths as I held up pictures and written words. A new language was learnt through his eyes only. He caught a glimpse of a new and beautiful world like heaven, where people smiled, animals frolicked and flowers bloomed instead of bomb smoke.

❖ ❖ ❖

Even though Jeff wasn't around much I found little time to fret, as the need was so great. In the end, I employed six local women to help me with the huge task of washing all the children in our crudely constructed brick bathing shelter. Taking care of the expense of soap and scarcity of water by installing two water boreholes on our site, I soon saw an astounding improvement in the children. With clean hair and skin, cut nails, dressed sores and full bellies, these children were becoming articulate and dignified—the way God intended.

Early one morning, there was a rattling at my caravan door. Labele's mother was standing there. She smiled at me with bloodshot eyes and presented me with a clay pot full of sweet potatoes and crinkly lemons. Acholi words rolled from her tongue as young James interpreted.

"She wants to know if you will help her build a new hut. The one she lives in is collapsing. Her husband was killed by rebels and she has no-one else to help her."

"I can't give money away," I hesitated, "but I could find work for her . . . Yes . . . if she comes tomorrow I will pay her to help wash children. Also, I can buy sweet potatoes from her every week, if she has enough for her own children."

The mother, Leonara, was frowning as James translated. Labele stood nearby, locked in his silent world.

"Does she agree?" I asked.

Again the musical language tripped off her tongue.

"She says she is not feeling well."

I noted the dark cloud over her face and her ragged red dress hanging limply over her bony frame.

"You tell her, she must not look to Irene." And then I turned to face her: "God created you and has been waiting all these years for you to talk to Him. Unless you follow Jesus Christ, the devil will keep robbing you. Even if I give you money, you will only lose it unless He protects you."

She considered this dispassionately, staring at the ground and shaking her head.

I shrugged and continued, "Leonara, if you don't belong to Jesus, the devil controls your life and he's a cruel master. Already he has robbed you: two husbands killed, two babies dead and Labele who's deaf and dumb."

She lifted her eyes towards Labele and prattled urgently in Acholi. James interpreted: "She asks if she joins you, will you destroy her ancestral shrine?" He went on to explain, "You see, she had a baby born feet first. Of course, it died. They buried it one way, then she buried it another. She wants to know if you will destroy that place."

I reassured her that I wouldn't disturb the child's grave and that she could begin working with us the following week.

That night, Jeff and I were awakened by bloodcurdling screams. We lay alert in the darkness, listening intently. Incessant drumming began, interspersed with raucous laughter. The Holy Spirit was telling me it was Labele's family. Then I heard His still, quiet voice: "Do not allow Leonara to pray over any of your children . . . Do not eat any food she brings you."

In the morning Celestino confirmed our fears. "Don't associate with Labele's mother—her food may be poisoned," he told us, then went on to explain that the Acholi have a tradition whereby when a child is born with a deformity they believe it is a gift from the spirits. When it dies, they bury it with special words. After two years they exhume the body, and place the skull in a pot with eyes looking towards the house. They believe the spirit of the person who died will protect the family. Every year the witch doctor performs a ceremony where he kills a chicken or goat, sprinkles its blood around and adds its head to the pot as a gift for the spirit. Also, the child's father or brother has his head shaved in a special way, leaving tufts of long hair. He then lies on animal skin and is carried around with dancing and singing whilst the women prepare a broth in a certain way to be eaten "in communion" with the spirits.

I thanked him for forewarning me about the food.

"Did they disturb you last night?" he asked. "The ceremonies will last all week."

I shrugged. "I can wear earplugs . . . but African shrines are certainly different to the usual candles and floral offerings!"

I was losing sleep because of the witch doctors' nightly drumming and hysterical chanting. Rather than appease spirits, their raucous incantations were only strengthening the spirit of death.

Many mornings began with the sound of wailing as people mourned the death of family members from malnutrition or malaria. Our Land Cruiser was often commandeered as the local "hearse," returning shroud-wrapped bodies for burial in their villages. On these sad occasions, my heart ached for the clean beaches of Australia—civilisation, running water and electricity.

It wouldn't be long.

15

OUR FIRST TRIP HOME

SYDNEY, SEPTEMBER 1992

OUR FIRST EIGHT MONTHS in Kitgum had been frustrating in many ways, yet at the same time so fulfilling.

In September 1992 we returned to Australia to see our family. My three daughters, my son and six grandchildren met me at Mascot Airport. They gasped at my reduced weight and my sun-bleached hair. They laughed to see my swollen, infected feet in a pair of thongs.

"Mum, you've really gone African. Are you alright?" my son joked. "I mean, do you have to go into quarantine, or something?"

We kissed and hugged, not knowing that I would break out in contagious hepatitis within a fortnight. (Everyone was very brave when they had to have their injections.) It was so refreshing to be back in Australia. Although I now called Kitgum "home," I enjoyed everything Australia had to offer and the time I was able to spend with family. While I shared myself around, staying at each of my children's houses, Jeff stayed with his parents, reassuring them that he was okay. Over the next two months, we enjoyed a variety of delicious foods prepared by friends and family, we relished the luxury of hot running water, reading at night by electric light, English conversations and humour. I never quite understood the Acholi humour and didn't know what the Africans were laughing at half the time. I had missed Aussie banter.

Over several weeks, we divided our time between family gatherings and speaking engagements to promote child sponsorship. Faithful supporters—mostly friends from church and family—would gather at my daughter Shelley's house, hungry to hear my African stories and receive an update on our newly established project. In only seven months we had dug several pit latrines, fenced off the compound and built a bamboo and thatched shelter for school and morning assembly. Although many of our contributors received our newsletters, face-to-face contact was much more effective. Those who turned up to our meetings gave us an encouraging response and assured us of their continuing support for our vision of building extra classrooms in order to meet the growing demand. Up to this point, we had been relying on the money from the sale of our homes, but we knew this wouldn't last long. It was time to be more deliberate with our fundraising efforts.

As we neared the end of our holiday, I tried to make every moment count as I stored up precious memories watching ferries skim across Sydney Harbour, the kindness and loving embrace of friends and seeing my grandchildren. I loved watching Sarah and Luke jumping waves at the beach, digging mouse caves in the sand dunes with Jay. How I laughed to see his little brother Caleb's peculiar locomotion as he bounced on his bottom across the floor at top speed. How my eyes feasted on granddaughters Holly and Melody as they studied animals at the zoo. My daughters Maree, Shelley and Heidi arranged shopping excursions to the mall, where the range of produce was confusing to me after only having small tomatoes and pumpkin leaves to choose from.

All too soon, it was time to leave and I was very emotional. Tears welled in our eyes as our minds tumbled with words we should be saying and things we hadn't had time to do. Maybe next time . . .

As the plane rose, my heart felt as if it was breaking. The carefully woven fabric of our family was being ripped apart once again. Hot tears spilled down my cheeks. Flying across Australia's heart, the pilot drew our attention to Ayer's Rock. Even from that height, the rock was a huge monolith, pulsating with strange light. I began to sob. Jeff reached across and pulled down the window shade. I recalled how Jesus had to "set His face" towards His cruel destination in Jerusalem. I heard His voice, "Unless a grain of wheat falls to the ground and dies, it remains only a single seed. But if it dies, it produces many seeds . . . Whoever serves Me must follow Me; and where I am, My servant also will be" (John 12:24–26 NIV). Shutting off my emotions was the only way I could survive the separation from my family.

So that's what I did.

16

CHILD SPONSORSHIP BEGINS

KITGUM, 1992

TWENTY-FOUR HOURS AFTER leaving Australia we landed at Entebbe Airport. Stepping off the plane, we came face to face with the familiar seventies-style arrivals hall displaying the sign "Welcome to Entebbe International Airport." How strange it felt to be back on African soil.

An hour later, we were in downtown Kampala, squelching through muddy alleys lined with bamboo markets, looking for a kerosene stove, buckets, tinned stew and toothpaste, as we dodged the barrels of guns slung over the shoulders of soldiers. We stepped aside as men thumped past, unseeing—their backs bowed beneath the cruel weights of grain or cement. A man carrying cartons on his head tripped. Bottles of oil spilt across the ground, rolling in the mud. Bystanders laughed and scrambled to retrieve the bottles from wheels of passing trucks. Once supplies were sourced, it was time to get down to the business of securing our tenure in Kitgum.

With hopeful hearts, we climbed the stairs of a government building to collect our charity certificate. Months earlier we had submitted a sheaf of documents. Without permission, we could not build anything, nor even stay in the country.

The receptionist yawned. "There's no-one around. They wouldn't have processed it yet. The man who has to sign it is overseas."

We recognised a strong spiritual hindrance operating. Time for spiritual warfare.

The next day, I remained in our room at a lodge in Kampala and fasted to loose the "chains of injustice" so that our application would be released (see Isaiah 58:6–9 NIV). I prayed and spoke God's Word.

At 4:30 that afternoon Jeff appeared, triumphantly, waving the precious certificate that stated that Childcare International was recognised by the Ugandan government as an organisation permitted to build schools, clinics, feeding centres and churches to meet the needs of orphaned and destitute children. We could legally continue with the work.

With renewed energy, we loaded our car with supplies: 60 blankets, 230 banana tree seedlings, timber, mechanical parts and jerry cans of fuel. Jeff negotiated the 450 kilometres of pot-holed road up to Kitgum. After six weeks away, we wondered what we would find there. Had we tested God too much, leaving thousands of dollars' worth of building materials and electrical equipment unguarded in a desperately poor area of African scrub, while we had been busy drumming up support in Australia? I muttered a familiar prayer: "Thank You God that because I enjoy Your advice and do not despise Your correction, I know that my property is safe. I shall check all my belongings and find nothing missing" (see Job 5:24).

Celestino rushed out to greet us, smiling broadly and shaking our hands energetically. Behind him, our compound resembled an English country garden, with rows of fat cabbages, lines of carrots and huge red tomatoes growing unashamedly out of the red earth. All was peaceful and in order. About eighty laughing children surrounded us, while Celestino waited patiently to show us his other achievements: two new water boreholes, bags of harvested beans and corn and our potholed entrance repaired. We shared the news about our new permit with Celestino and chatted excitedly about our plans for expansion. As we talked, Australia seemed a million miles away. We were home; it felt right to be back in Uganda. We were well rested and ready for the task ahead of us.

That evening I prepared dinner by the light of a kerosene lamp: soup from our fresh vegetables. We ate contentedly, watching the full moon rising like a searchlight. Jeff and I discussed what response we might expect from our Australian friends with whom we had shared this promise: "If you spend yourself on behalf of the hungry and satisfy the needs of the oppressed, then your light will rise in the darkness, and your night will become like the noonday. The LORD will guide you always; He will satisfy your needs in a sun-scorched land and will strengthen your frame . . . you will be called Repairer of Broken Walls, Restorer of Streets with Dwellings" (Isaiah 58:10–12 NIV). Our stories highlighting the plight of vulnerable children in Kitgum had motivated many of our friends to take up sponsorship, which we believed to be one of the most effective ways of helping the community.

Several days later, accompanied by Pastor Faustino Okello, I trekked the area equipped with sunscreen, an umbrella, camera and notebook to look for suitable children to sponsor. Strolling through the towering grass, we visited families who lived in mud huts, and spoke to ancient grandmothers and guardians about the condition of their children. At the beginning of the year, when we had parked our caravan in the middle of a community of villagers who had been displaced by the war, we noted that the community had nothing: no seeds, hoes or possessions. Most existed on a diet consisting solely of cassava, which wasn't enough to sustain them. Their rust-coloured hair and bloated limbs were a constant reminder of bodies crying out for nutrition. The need was enormous. During one of these patrols we were followed by two young brothers who had shaved heads. As Pastor Faustino translated, they told us their names: Denis Okot (meaning "rejected") and Willie Opoka (meaning "broken family"). Deserted by both parents, they were in the care of an older brother who worked as a poorly paid tailor in town—which meant the boys were often left unsupervised. These boys spent their days roaming the scrub catching tiny birds or field mice to roast.

With sponsorship money, I planned to improve the children's diet by providing them with beans and millet. A care-worker would supervise daily bathing to deter lice and scabies. Most importantly, they would attend our school and be given clean clothes, pens and books. We were determined to release the community from the prison of illiteracy that was confining them to a life of ignorance and fearful superstition. I noted the logistics of meeting all the children's needs: adequate clothing, blankets, and clinics for medical treatment. They would need classrooms and a permanent school. In addition, poultry, hoes and seeds would need to be given to their guardians to ensure the whole family's quality of life improved.

This kind of development was sure to stretch our limited finances. Nevertheless we were quietly confident God would supply the money we needed in order to pay our labourers, teachers and cooks and for the construction costs of drilling water boreholes and building classrooms, purchasing medicines for our community clinic and, finally, the cost of tools, seeds and fruit trees for the farms. There was a lot to consider. Although we were receiving tax exemptions from the Ugandan government for vehicles and materials bought, it wasn't enough. As I pondered this and prayed, we received good news: a Christian organisation in the USA had agreed to send us a very generous donation each month. We praised God for His continued provision.

Another emerging prayer point was the antiquated communications system. Keeping in touch with my family was frustrating. Letters took several months to arrive at either end and the radio phone at the Kitgum post office was expensive: $23 for three crackly minutes.

In May 1992 my middle daughter, Shelley, had written and told me she was pregnant—news I longed for. But by the time the letter reached me, she had miscarried. Several months later, she received my reply congratulating her and acknowledging that her tummy would no doubt be growing. Hmm . . .

Over the years, I missed several key events due to the lack of communication. In more recent years I have been very thankful for Facebook.

17

RED TAPE

KITGUM, 1992

IN A COMMUNITY DECIMATED by war, bricks were scarce. The bricks our workers had laboriously moulded had turned into slush in the torrential rain, which meant we needed to find more. Eventually, Jeff located a stack of hand-built baked bricks next to a swampy river. He paid $1,000 and hired a tractor and trailer to carry them from the riverside to our project site. Under the scorching sun, we followed the trailer full of our labourers, weaving past huts and across sorghum fields. Recently flooded, the ground was a quagmire. The tractor sank. So we went into town to hire a truck to help. It also sank to its axles. The scene became farcical as ever-helpful villagers and children sank up to their knees trying to push the vehicles this way and that. Wheels spun, speckling everyone with mud. After what seemed like hours, Jeff pulled the lorry free, to the sound of great cheering. He supervised the stacking of bricks on the lorry and was loading 1,000 bricks into our car when the truck driver revved his truck across a potato field and became hopelessly stuck again.

Despite the sweltering heat, there were no frayed tempers, only side-splitting laughter from the locals—especially when a local drunk reeled out of the trees and entertained everyone in an impeccable British accent.

"BBC is my name. I am a British-trained general reporting for duty," he said. "Look lively, chaps. This tractor can't sleep here tonight. All hands on deck. Move along smartly." As he spoke, he swung a stick like a baton, causing the children to shriek with excitement and leap out of his way.

Three days later, most of the bricks were still down by the riverside. Some were stacked on the truck, still stuck in the muddy potato field. Others had been offloaded and were sinking into mud. We had to pay $100 compensation for damaged crops. A week later the ground was dry enough to move tractor- and lorry-loads of bricks and sand to the site of our first school, ready for Jeff and his builders to begin construction.

While Jeff sweated under the African sun, I prayed for the release of essential documents: five-year work permits, school registration and land title. It seemed as though our work was subject to endless approvals. Nevertheless, we claimed God's promise: "Do not be afraid. Stand firm and you will see the deliverance the LORD will bring you today . . . the LORD will fight for you; you need only to be still" (Exod. 14:13–14 NIV).

One afternoon, officials told us the Prime Minister wanted to visit our site in Kitgum and asked if they could borrow our Land Cruiser for his transport.

"No objection . . . Will you release our plans?"

"Er . . . Come and see us tomorrow."

The very next day I climbed the stairs of the old building in Kampala. Years of grime and peeling paint stippled the walls. I was optimistic. The clerk was irritated.

"You can see for yourself, madam. Your plans are in the cupboard. And the cupboard is locked. The boss has gone on safari. We don't know when he's coming back."

I persisted: "Where are the keys? The Prime Minister is visiting us and he'll want to see our plans."

With great reluctance they released a girl to direct me. We drove four kilometres away to a hut in the village. Stepping over mounds of sorghum drying in the sun, she disappeared inside the hut, emerging moments later clutching the keys.

As I tried to reverse the car along the narrow track, the front wheels went over a hump. The back wheels were spinning in sand and the engine grunted to a stop. I turned the ignition key repeatedly without effect. The car would not restart. I got out of the car and began to walk back towards town under the glare of an unforgiving sun. Villagers peddled past, none of them able to drive. A tractor approached. I waved it down.

"You can drive can't you? Can you get my car going?"

The tractor driver gallantly leapt down and ran to my car. I hurried behind. As I settled into the passenger seat, he was muttering, "'Can you drive?' she says. 'Can you drive?'" He turned the ignition key while pressing the accelerator flat to the floor. The car engine roared to life.

"Thank you," I said, touching his arm.

He shrugged me off and, laughing wildly, accelerated at full speed towards the small hut. Squawking chickens scattered.

"Stop!" I screamed. He ignored me. So I pulled the handbrake on hard. We lurched to a halt.

The smell of alcohol hit me. This guy was rotten drunk; alcoholism is a real problem in northern Uganda. The pattern of daily life interrupted by war means men who once held traditional farming roles have now found themselves devoid of land, animals and purpose. With no education and training and nothing to do, they numb themselves with the local brew. This man clearly had a job, but was still drunk.

"I'll drive. You get out!" I ordered.

"No," he persisted. "I can drive," he slurred.

I leant across him, opened the door and pushed him out. He staggered off towards the road. After drawing deep breaths, I carefully reversed back along the track, but the car got stuck on the hump again. Tears of frustration welled in my eyes until I saw in the rear-view mirror a gang of youths walking past.

"Oh please, can you help," I cried.

They studied the situation for a moment, then began rocking and pushing the car body up and over the ridge.

The tractor driver's face appeared at my window. "Give me beer money," he growled.

The next moment, open palms were waving in my face. I dropped a handful of coins into one. "Thanks so much, boys. Buy some sodas."

Back in the city building, I found the clerks anxiously consulting one another in whispers and scurrying from one office to another. Finally a junior clerk came to me with his apologies. "I'm sorry. The key opened the boss's door but not his cupboard. There is no way we can get your plans for you."

I took a deep breath. God hadn't saved me from a drunken driver to bear this nonsense.

"Can I see the man in charge?" I asked.

Following him along the dusty hallway, I muttered under my breath, "In Jesus' name I bind every obstructing force."

I was ushered into the office of the assistant to the boss, where I sat down opposite a slight man with a furrowed brow, who kept turning his pen over and over between nicotine-stained fingers. He placed his pen behind one ear and turned his palms upwards and shrugged.

"We have done all we can do."

I sighed. "Well . . . the Prime Minister will be very unhappy to see that the plans haven't been approved."

A silence hung thickly between us.

Suddenly the junior clerk burst through the door carrying all the architectural drawings for our school buildings. He unrolled them across the desk and together they examined them. The clerk noted, "They are not signed yet. We can't release them."

"I know . . . I know," the assistant's voice quivered. He looked at me—his eyes pleading that I understand. "Please come back tomorrow. If my boss has not arrived back, I'll sign them myself." He spoke softly. "I am for development . . ."

Several days later, Jeff and I were busy finalising preparations for the Prime Minister's visit to Kitgum. We erected a tarpaulin shade house. Chicken and sweet potatoes were cooking. The best crockery was arranged. Excited, well-scrubbed children were gathered at the gate, eager to sing and present their drawings of Kitgum life to our honoured guest. They cheered us as we drove past to collect him from Kampala.

Our first stop in the city was the first government office to collect our building plans. The boss's assistant sighed loudly as we walked in.

"Bring me the stamp," he ordered his clerk. He slowly opened his stamp pad, applied the ink, and stamped the plans page by page with a heavy hand, then lifted his pen, sighed again, hesitated for a moment and then, with shaky hands, signed his name page by page. His eyes stared vacantly past us. When he'd finished, he rolled the plans, secured them with a rubber band and pushed them across the desk. We shook hands, offered him a $10 gift and exited. Once on the stairs, we triumphantly whispered "Alleluia! We've got our plans!"

Next stop, the Prime Minister's office.

A stern official reached for Jeff's car keys. "Just leave your car here. We want it on standby. But we cannot use you as driver. Protocol, you understand."

Jeff protested, "That car is our only vehicle. No-one drives it except me."

Another official intervened: "How is everything with you? I am sorry we have been too busy to inform you, but unfortunately the Prime Minister's schedule does not allow time to visit your project. However, we are confident of your co-operation in allowing us to use your car as you have promised." A line of men glared at us, awaiting Jeff's response.

"Sorry. No visit. No car. Goodbye!"

Our staff had gathered expectantly in Kitgum. Despite being disappointed about the Prime Minister not showing up, they were jubilant to see the building plans approved.

"Now at last we can begin building," said Celestino. "But for now, let's feast on chicken and sodas."

18

OUR FIRST CHRISTMAS

KITGUM, DECEMBER 1992

ANYONE WHO HAS EVER worked in Africa will tell you that development is not a destination, it's a journey, and a slow one at that. After ten months of haggling with officials and sourcing supplies we had made some progress at the project site, but not as quickly as we would have liked. Perhaps it was all a little too slow for my husband, who now spent much of his time in the city, regularly making the 900-kilometre-round journey to unravel government legalities, eat steak and chips and care for some of Kampala's street children.

My only company while Jeff was away was my dog, Caleb—a stray who had wandered around the village in search of food. I took him in as a puppy and he became my constant companion. Caleb was black like a panther and loped through the grass as if he was. At first he was fierce, especially if I scolded him, but as I took him for a daily walk on a chain his wild streak was subdued. He ate mainly beans, like me, except when I rewarded him with dried whitebait. Whenever he scored a bone—a rare prize in Kitgum—he'd promptly hide it by burying it. There were many nights when Caleb would leave my side briefly, returning with the foul-smelling object. Like an English gentleman savouring his after-dinner pipe, Caleb chewed and slurped and licked. He relished his bone. I put up with the smell in exchange for his protection. I enjoyed having him by my side as I sat on my deck-chair under a canopy of stars, praying and looking over the dark valley for flashing torch lights. This was a sign of rebels silently raiding huts to abduct children. I had learnt that fire flares meant villagers, but torch beams signalled evil.

Evil came in many forms.

One dark night as I was putting away dishes in my cara-van annex, Caleb was barking at my feet. The light of my torch showed a thin black snake coiled against the wall. Another eve-ning, as I was cleaning my teeth in the moonlight, Caleb alerted me to a two-metre-long cobra slithering by. A week later I was about to step down from my caravan, when Caleb barked fu-riously. Once again, he had alerted me. A giant black scorpion with its stinging tail curved upwards like a sickle was waiting on the step. I dispatched it with a hoe handle kept nearby for such occasions.

On 27 November 1992, the night we were ambushed, Caleb didn't bark—he whimpered.

At around 2 a.m. while Jeff and I were fast asleep, five shad-owy figures brandishing AK-47s had crept through the tall sor-ghum, cut an opening in our wire fence and thrown a large rock at our caravan. We thought they might kill us.

We dispatched these thugs, not with a hoe or an axe, but with a weapon much more powerful—the name of Jesus.

❖　❖　❖

Christmas was around the corner and my garden was a field of stubble. The land was cracked and rigid from the scorching sun. By the middle of the day my shadow was reduced to a tiny circle around my feet the shape of my large round sunhat. At this time of year the earth is always brick-red and brick-hard. Most plants die. Only thornbushes and large black scorpions survive.

Villagers often take advantage of the dry season to repair their grass roofs or make mud bricks, but most of the time they stay indoors, conserving energy for the hard digging and planting work that will begin with the first rains. There is a sense of waiting. Waiting and watching and trusting nature—trusting in God's preordained rhythms. My stomach, on the other hand, was not accustomed to waiting and I began to crave fresh vegetables and fruit. So on Christmas Eve I braved the local market, which looked rather empty compared with the bustling, treasure-filled Christmas markets back in Australia. Although there was an undercurrent of excitement among the crowds, the produce was always the same, as were the sellers. Old women wizened by the sun would sit alongside teenage girls, selling small piles of leaves, tiny pyramids of tomatoes or mounds of maize flour. Locals would meander between vendors, wistfully studying the rows of blackened smoke-dried fish. At $2 a piece it was too expensive to buy, but the pungent smell was free for all to enjoy.

As I struggled along with my heavy load of sweet potatoes, the sellers smiled *"Cam karama maber"* (eat well at Christmas). Now that was debatable. I was contemplating a few withered lemons when I felt a persistent tapping on my elbow. I turned around to face a man eyeball to eyeball, who appeared to be demon-possessed: his eyes were bloodshot, his face and head smeared with ash. Dressed in filthy rags pinned together with wire and paper clips, he tapped at my bag and then curled his hand like a claw at my face. I stepped backwards, but he put his face close to mine and snarled. I saw the razor blade glinting between his teeth. He swung his head from side to side, carving a lethal arc through the air. This man was full of devils, threatening me.

A sense of indignation rose within me. Overcoming any fear, I put my bag down and beckoned to him to come to a nearby wall. I focused fully on his eyes and said, "In the name of JESUS CHRIST, go away!"

He reeled aside as if I'd hit him. Then, without a backward glance, he scrambled back through the market.

I returned to my bag. "How much for five lemons?" I asked.

The seller was wide-eyed and speechless.

"*Lubanga ber*" (our God is good), I explained.

She smiled broadly and threw in some lemons for free.

That afternoon I set up paint pots and paper so the children could make angels, stars and sheep for a poster. There under the mango tree, with each child using a well-chewed twig as paintbrush, they created a beautiful poster of the infant Jesus in the stable, under a sky full of angels and stars.

As we began to clean up, one of the children painted a bracelet of lime green around their black wrist. Another painted a red headband across their brow. Then I saw a child with the name JESUS across their forehead. Then another. The idea spread like wildfire. Every child was painting their friend's face with patterns around the name JESUS. These African children were delightful as they adorned themselves with colour. Soon my compound was filled with 120 children jumping around with excitement, their thin black arms patterned with colour and the name of JESUS. They spilled out onto the road and then, with laughing and singing, began a spontaneous Christmas procession into town.

At midnight on Christmas Eve, Jeff and I were woken by a cacophony: tins rattling, drums pounding, unearthly screams. As I stepped out of the caravan, the black night sky was filled with eerie smoke as firesticks were being flung into the air.

Celestino came to reassure me. "It's to scare the devils away from baby Jesus."

Nearby, children were whooping and running through the scrub, holding smoking sticks up high and drawing a trail of sparks.

As we drifted back into an uneasy sleep, we were disturbed by terrible screams from across the river. Someone was in pain—or possessed. The screams were deadened by loud rapid drumbeats. A witch doctor's ceremony was in progress, probably exorcising some superstitious woman by slashing her with a razor across her cheeks or shaving her head. She would survive and wear her scars proudly. Only the fluttering in her eyes would show something was amiss.

On Christmas morning the sun struggled to shine through the smoke haze. After a quick bowl of maize porridge and mug of tea, I enlisted the help of some small boys to fix the poster to our fence. While villagers paused to admire this splash of colour in a parched landscape, trouble broke out between the boys. An older boy had noticed head lice on Luke, one of my helpers, and was tormenting him. Luke bowed his head against the nativity poster and cried. He could not bear the shame. I thought of his dirty bedding: a hessian rag on the earth floor. Then I recalled the shame of Jesus, our King, lying in an animal's feed trough 2,000 years ago.

"Don't cry, Luke," I tried to comfort him. "Come and I'll give you some of Jeff's shampoo." This downcast little boy followed me to the caravan. There I found medicated lotion. Luke's face lit up. He grabbed it and ran to the water borehole where he lathered his head.

His friends watched quietly. I asked them if they had head lice.

His friend Denis answered, "Of course. It troubles me very much."

As I held out the bottle, they all leapt to their feet and eagerly put their heads under the spout of the water borehole and began to work up a good lather. As the sun rose higher on this Christmas morning, I shared the happiness of these ragged orphans having clean itch-free heads.

Freda started cooking Christmas dinner: beans!

At midday, Jeff sat down with twenty village men in a circle. The women sat separately on the grass. Two hundred children ran unsupervised around the perimeter. We waited for the beans to soften . . . and waited . . . and waited.

The children were hungry and tempers were fraying, so I called them to join me under a tree where for three hours I told them stories and taught them every song I knew. The women looked dejected. They lacked the stamina and ideas to help me and, as usual, were lost in their own thoughts. Not to be defeated, I proved that God's strength is made perfect in our weakness (see 2 Cor. 12:9). The children and I enjoyed three hours of singing and dancing before our King. The Holy Spirit inspired me and lifted me above my tiredness. I introduced memory verses and God showed us the music in His words. As the children rapped out the words: In God I trust / I'm not afraid / what can man / do to me? (from Ps. 56:11), they stamped in time with the rhythm and punched the air with their hands. Fine dust sparkled gold in the sunlight, rising in clouds around their thin legs.

God gave me a vision of their grandfathers preparing for warfare, dressed in leopard skins, stamping in the dust and chanting war cries to terrify the enemy. The children embraced my suggestion that they, too, were warriors, fighting a battle against the devils that had invaded their land and robbed them of parents and food. I told them their dancing and chanting of God's Word would terrorise the enemy so much he would flee the district.

They sat in rapt attention as I told the Nativity story by holding up Christmas cards. As I opened a musical card, the children gasped with surprise to hear it play "We Wish You a Merry Christmas." Two hundred faces beamed with pleasure. They seemed as captivated as children crowding around decorated shop windows in a big city.

Finally Christmas dinner was ready. Five children sat around each bowl, as was their usual habit. The bowls were licked clean too quickly, so I began to serve seconds. But this proved disastrous: the children broke ranks and rioted. Two hundred ravenous children began shouting and jostling, shovelling food into their mouths. It was a reminder of their past; these children had known intense hunger. Two of the mothers came waving sticks and order was restored. In that moment of being able to satisfy their hunger, I thanked God that He had brought Jeff and me to Kitgum to help these people who had suffered so much. I prayed that He would protect and support us so we could stay.

At 7 p.m. the sun, a giant cerise-coloured ball framed by a dove-grey sky, began to drop to the horizon. The remainder of the children sat around on mats, reluctant to return to their huts. I considered their thin bodies and their big sad eyes. This Christmas these children had received no brightly wrapped presents and no treats, but they knew the goodness of Jesus. An indescribable peace blanketed us. I was exhausted, but so content.

"Hey, come and see your Christmas present," shouted Jeff later that night.

How happy I was to see the gas cylinder rigged up to my caravan stove. No more rising at 5 a.m. to fan stubborn charcoal into flame, which often proved hazardous. My eyes would sting with the smoke; my arms and hands would go black from the charcoal as I sleepily smeared ash slurry over the saucepans to stop them burning black. Over time, my hands became infected and I discovered the lime in the ash was scarring my hands. No more polyester skirts melting against my legs. What luxury! Turn a knob and instant heat for cooking porridge. It was ingenious.

I also found a way to get hot bathing water for Jeff. Leaving a jerry can of water in the hot sun all day made almost boiling water. My challenge was keeping it safe from passing "borrowers." Conversely, for cool drinking water the local clay pots made excellent refrigerators. The only downside was the slow seepage, which created large puddles and invited a company of very ugly, noisy frogs who croaked happily all night. Now *that* was a welcome sound.

19

TRAINING GROUND

KITGUM, JANUARY-APRIL 1993

IT HAD BEEN SEVERAL WEEKS since my birthday on 30 December, and I was anxious to hear from my family. I had missed our traditional family Christmas lunch and could only imagine how much fun they must have had, sharing a variety of foods, passing around presents and finishing the day off with delicious Christmas cake—my favourite! When my birthday passed without a word from my youngest, Heidi, I began to get worried. Then, one morning the snail mail postal service delivered an envelope from Australia—the birthday card I had been expecting. I heaved a sigh of relief, sat on my foldaway chair in the shade and hastily ripped open the envelope. Like a hungry animal, I devoured every word. My heart was aching for my family. I committed each one of my children and grandchildren to God, asking Him to protect them. Then I felt the Lord speak to me and say, "No more weeping, no regrets, for your work will be rewarded."

I pondered the work God had already done through our hands amongst the locals in this dusty outback town. Approximately 360 children were now gathering each day under the trees in varying parts of town as I taught them a Bible story and a memory verse. Then, at lunchtime I would head to the markets to buy dried fish, millet flour, green leaves and bananas, and carry it back to the school by 2 p.m. in time to feed all the children their first meal of the day. Tummies full, I would begin teaching again. I delighted in this precious time with the children and cherished the moments when they grasped an understanding of Jesus.

Although my days were busy teaching around town, my nights, while Jeff was away in Kampala, were often lonely and at times nerve-racking. Sometimes I'd have a whinge to God about being on my own and then I would feel guilty. Over time, God taught me to "get over myself" and to praise Him for the positives: no stress, no junky TV shows, no striving to be perfect. He showed me that all I had to do was look at the starry sky, breathe in the clean air and be content in the knowledge that I was outworking His plan for the north of Uganda. Occasionally, I would regress and find myself moaning about the food, the bouts of malaria and the fear of being murdered in my caravan while I slept. It kept me awake at night—but then I learnt to sleep like a baby in the loving arms of the Father. Still . . . danger was always lurking.

One night as I was heading to the outside pit latrine, I heard a *zing, bang*! About twelve bullets whistled past me. I decided I didn't need the toilet that badly and went back to the caravan and listened. My dog started whimpering outside the door, so I let him in and turned off the light. Sitting in the pitch-dark, my heart was thumping, but I knew that God was with me. Caleb jumped on the bed and started chewing my shoes. Then he climbed all over me, which, oddly enough, was more disturbing than the stray bullets. I was about to put him out when I heard *zing, bang*! More bullets flew past. I sat still. Eventually it went quiet and I put Caleb outside to sleep. I lay on my bed, took a deep breath, said a prayer and fell into a deep sleep. The Lord Jesus sustained me. As each day passed, I began to realise how much spiritual warfare I was dealing with. I was being trained for battle.

Days later, I was deployed.

Our local policeman, Richard, had previously been diagnosed with HIV/AIDS. At this point he was wrestling with the spirit of death, and it looked as though he would die, so I asked God what was going on and He told me that the battle would be hard, but he would win.

Rolling up my sleeves, I marched into Richard's home and asked all the unsaved mourners to move away. "This is war," I told them. Together with two other Christians, I took authority and commanded every demon to leave Richard's body. What a battle! Through most of the night his body was racked with terror and pain. He was convulsing on the bed, but Richard didn't want to give up and we were not about to give up praying. About 1 a.m. the smell of death wafted through the room. I went outside and sang victory songs to God. The next day we read Psalm 23 to Richard, who by this time was unconscious. Unperturbed by this, we continued to pray.

Days later this young man sat up in bed, and over the following weeks was miraculously healed. I wrote a letter to Heidi to share the news of Richard's healing. I closed the letter by writing, "It's all a bit more exciting for a granny than bowling, isn't it!"

But my enthusiasm was short lived, as the enemy decided to turn up the heat.

20

THE SOUND OF SILENCE

KITGUM, MAY 1993

"LUNCH READY?" asked Jeff, who had just arrived back from Kampala to work on the project site. He and Celestino sat down under the caravan annex. He mopped his forehead. "It's hot out there, but we've made good progress. Two classrooms are set out."

Freda was ladling out their beans, while I offered a bowl of chopped tomatoes.

A boy stopped his bicycle and handed Jeff an envelope from the chief. Jeff read the letter, then flung it across the table.

"Blazing idiots!"

I looked at the letter:

To the Directors of Childcare Kitgum Servants,

We are informing you that as you haven't complied with local expectations, your activities with African children are illegal, especially in relation to compensation for the mango trees you now enjoy. ALL feeding, washing, medication and schooling activities must cease forthwith. Locals stand ready to enforce this ban.

> You are forbidden contact with any African child. Any
> child found entering your premises will be detained for
> his/her own protection.

This was yet another blow.

That afternoon, fifty children gathered at the gate for lunch. I swallowed back tears as I told them I had been ordered not to touch or feed them. They just stood staring at the ground, hiding the hunger and confusion they felt inside. People of a war zone soon learn that revealing emotions can mark them as condemned.

I carried some bandages along the road to tend to my special friend James. Afflicted with sickle cell anaemia, his body had little strength to heal a tropical ulcer. He said nothing as I explained that I couldn't return for a while. Only his eyes conveyed his gratitude for the soothing ointment and bandages. In the darkness of his hut, I allowed the bitter tears welling up within me to spill down my face.

Every morning and afternoon, destitute children had gathered in the shade of trees around Kitgum Town to sing and dance and hear stories. Villagers passing by would smile and nod their head to the singing. Suddenly the children were dispersed. There was only the sound of insects buzzing in the heat. The songs of the children had been silenced.

My prayers were angry and urgent. I quoted scripture: "Who is this uncircumcised Philistine that he should defy the armies of the living God?" (1 Sam. 17:26). And then I prayed, "Father God, You have always been my only Father. Because I am afflicted in this, my service for You threatened with closure, I call out to You. I stand strong in Your word and I'm reminded that You promise to protect the widows and the fatherless." Then I quoted the whole of Psalm 2.

Two weeks later, as I walked into town to plead with elders to lift the ban, I passed my former pupils, now sitting mute and dirty, with their ribs sticking out. But the elders were unmoved by my pleas.

One Friday afternoon a mother ran crying to me, begging me to drive her five sick children to hospital. They were too sick to walk. Before I reached town, my car was road-blocked by thugs who wrenched open the doors and ordered the children to return home. In the rear view mirror, I watched them hobbling down the narrow track. My heart broke.

❖ ❖ ❖

Despite the forced closure of CKS, we pressed on with the work of building the school. However, one morning angry voices broke the early calm.

"Don't you threaten me, woman!"

I looked across the school yard and gasped to see a woman advancing towards Jeff, screeching in Acholi. I ran forward till Celestino restrained me.

"She refuses to move, and her hut is blocking the building of the school," he explained.

The woman had been ordered by the government to move and had been handsomely compensated, but still refused to budge. Several of our builders ran to the distressed woman and disarmed her. She turned and fled along the road wailing loudly.

Jeff muttered to one worker then walked over to our container, returning with a can of fuel which he began splashing over the hut's grass roof. With the lick of a lighted match the roof burst into flames. As it collapsed inwards, Jeff called for hoes and, following his lead, the builders demolished the mud-brick walls.

I stood speechless, not believing my eyes. Dirty with ash and sweat, Jeff went to have a wash in our bathing shelter. When he emerged I said, "We are under a lot of pressure Jeff. I'm going to start a forty-day fast."

Jeff stared ahead past the scrub to the valley.

"I said I'm going to start a forty-day fast," I repeated.

Jeff murmured, "You want a medal?" He looked at me critically. "Well, you do what you need to do. I've had enough. I'm going to Kampala to chase up our work permits. Okay by you?" he added sarcastically.

I stared at him for a moment. His eyes were cold. I felt as though a knife were being thrust into my heart. My old friend, rejection, was back—although stoically I would never admit it. I quickly dismissed my hurt and responded as cheerily as I could.

"No, that's fine with me. I can get on with my fast without having to cook. You go. And rest as well—come back recharged."

I punched his shoulder playfully, but he stood still and coolly said, "I'll take Celestino for company."

"But that will leave all the work for me," I objected.

"One less to cook for!" Jeff's mind was set.

❖ ❖ ❖

Shortly before Jeff left for Kampala we noticed our dog, Caleb, was staggering around. A local vet had diagnosed tick fever and gave him two injections. "If that doesn't work, it must be poison," he told us. "Villagers get angry when dogs steal their eggs."

We spent an anxious weekend. Caleb sat on the caravan floor close to me, eyes and ears alert for every sound, every smell. It was when he needed to move, dragging himself across the ground with his front paws, that he moaned. And each time he did, he looked up at us with his sad eyes, appealing for help. On Sunday morning, he'd wedged himself under the caravan, shivering. He struggled to lift his head and lick our hands. We pulled him out and placed him next to the warmth of the charcoal stove, where he rallied and ate two eggs. He was now panting in the heat, so I sponged him down and we carried him inside away from the hot winds.

That afternoon, Jeff and I sat praying. Caleb rested his head on Jeff's leg. We knew it was over. The vet came and gave him an injection to put him to sleep. He was very peaceful, but sometimes he trembled and he'd look up at us. We prayed urgently, wrestling with the spirit of death for our Caleb.

"God, please don't let him suffer," I prayed. I opened my eyes to see Caleb's head slip off Jeff's knee. His laboured breath had stopped.

Jeff's eyes filled with tears. "He's gone . . . This blasted place kills everything you love." He stood up and left the caravan, slamming the door after him. He was on his way to Kampala.

I gazed at Caleb. He looked like he was sleeping. Caleb never slept when we were around. He was always romping and gnawing and playing. Now his toys: an old cow horn and a giant snail shell lay next to him. Engulfed in sadness, I just stared at Caleb's lifeless body and allowed the tears to flow freely. I thanked God I'd spent this last hour with my special companion. His work was finished. He'd saved me from snakes and scorpions; he'd given me his company and unconditional love in a place where I had no-one other than Jeff—and now he, too, was slipping away from me.

I knew what I needed to do.

21

BREAKING STRONGHOLDS

KITGUM, MAY-JUNE 1993

BEFORE BEGINNING the marathon fast, I wrote in my journal:

> *I am prompted to fast for the total defeat of the demonic forces ruling the Kitgum community. God hates unjust measures. Yet when I balance out our year of harsh living conditions against very meagre results, it is clear that stronger spiritual weapons are needed. Throughout history ordinary people have fasted to get extraordinary results. Like Ezra, I fast to see evil cancelled. Like Daniel, I need supernatural knowledge and wisdom. Like Jehoshaphat, I want victory over any attacks. Like Moses, I will have a personal encounter with God. Like Hannah, I will birth what God has conceived in my soul. Like Jesus, I will minister in the full power of God's Holy Spirit.*

I was reassured by Matthew 6:18: "Your Father who sees in secret will reward you openly." So, having waved goodbye to Jeff, I began.

Day 1: My mind was in turmoil with questions like, "Why was it going so wrong? Being hit by malaria and dysentery so often renders me useless—God, should we really be here?" But the sun eventually set and the first day was over.

Day 2: I was dizzy with hunger and sadness and slept.

Day 3: I enjoyed the close presence of God's Holy Spirit.

Day 4: A troublesome growth on my eye disappeared overnight.

Day 5: I walked to the chief's house and asked him how he could ignore his own African orphans with swollen stomachs waiting outside my gate.

Day 6: The chief was badgered by my sympathisers and scribbled a note withdrawing his previous accusation against us. But as it was unofficial, it had no clout.

Day 9: A sick man was miraculously healed as I prayed for him.

Day 18: I talked to government officials who agreed that all hindrances to our project development should be removed in the forthcoming development co-ordination meeting.

Day 23: I anticipated a showdown meeting with the chief. The meeting went on for five hours. The chief called Childcare illegal and challenged our application. He said that we had broken their laws by entering rural areas without obtaining security clearance in writing. Some members leapt to their feet shouting that ignorance of the law was no excuse, that our passports should be confiscated! I left thinking about all the times Moses had gone to see Pharaoh.

Day 24: Seventy development committee members threatened to report the chief's behaviour to the President of Uganda.

Day 27: The chief called me to his house and told me that I could get our go-ahead letter from his secretary. I asked him what it said. "I don't know. Whatever you want it to say. I'm busy. You dictate it," was his reply. His secretary's typewriter was broken, so I asked for some headed paper and said I would write it at home and bring it back for him to sign. I carried the precious paper home and wrote, "This serves to advise that Childcare Kitgum Servants has community permission to operate freely in northern Uganda without any hindrance."

Day 28: Our gates opened wide to receive 200 children for feeding, singing and stories. Classes under the trees around town also recommenced.

Day 30: I was jubilant that I had only ten more days to go. One villager asked me, "Are you okay Aunty?

Your volume seems to be shrinking!"

Day 31: A motorbike roared into the compound. I was
ordered to ride in to the District Intelligence
Office, where I was grilled. What were we doing
to Ugandan army personnel? Were we starting a
cult? Were we from Cuba? Were we supporting
the Lord's Resistance Army? Why didn't we
respect the Acholi traditions? What was our
real reason for coming to this war zone in north
Uganda? Where was my husband? Maybe I was
delirious from hunger, but my mind was con-
centrating on angels. Angels ministered to Jesus
(Mark 1:13); an angel appeared to Paul (Acts
27:23–24); Father God was sending His advocate, the Holy Spirit (John 14:26). Eventually,
the army personnel shook their heads and released me. Escorted by my angelic bodyguards,
I wandered back home down the dirt track,
recalling the rewards of fasting (Deut. 32:9–14).

Day 37: I only had three days to last before sinking my
teeth into bean soup. Locals warned me to begin
eating solids very slowly, as many die after a
famine when their system can't adjust to eating
again.

Day 40: The final day eventually arrived!

Fasting is supposed to strengthen your spiritual nature above
your flesh, but every day I was dreaming about the feast I would
enjoy when the forty days were completed. I prepared for myself

a treat of kebabs—chunks of local cow skewered on bamboo and roasted over coals. For the side dish I stewed cassava tubers and dried green leaves with sesame seed paste. The feast was delicious, especially for a starving person. I couldn't quite swallow the meat, instead chewing it over and over, like an Eskimo wearing down their teeth on seal skin. But it felt good to exercise my jaws. I finished with millet porridge, three bananas and some biscuits. My stomach gurgled with pleasure and I went to bed to dream of breakfast.

Life can be cruel! I'll spare you the details, but leaning over a pit latrine is no way for a lady to spend her night. For several days I shuddered at the mention of food and crept around, too weak to work. Then one day I found just what I needed at the back of my caravan cupboard: two tiny tins of baby food. Now that was delicious!

As I recovered I was elated. I had broken the back of the enemy and truly installed Jesus as supreme Lord over the work of Childcare Kitgum Servants.

Time to get on with it.

22

PRESSING ON

IN SPITE OF ROADBLOCKS and soldiers positioned everywhere, I was now free to move around other regions that had been decimated by war. Peter, a retired teacher, and I explored the rocky terrain of Lamola in the Gulu district. Beneath the blazing sun, sweat trickled down my back, flies stuck to my face and my ears were filled with the buzzing of insects. As we passed through each village, groups of thin, unkempt children peered cautiously from the doorways of their huts. Some had never seen a white person before.

One boy shimmied up a tree in fright, leaving his small brother clawing at the trunk and screaming pitifully *"Konya! Konya!"* (Help! Help!). I approached him with open arms to reassure him I was a kind lady, but this only increased his terror and he scrambled up behind his brother hiding in the leaves above. With wide eyes he shrieked, *"Satan, Satan. In aye won jok."*

Peter laughed. "He's calling you a devil. He says your father was a ghost."

As we moved on to the next *samba* (garden plot), I was feeling like an alien, especially as my ear could not discern individual words in a jumble of language. As Peter recorded children's details, I sat on any nearby rock noting the unbelievable poverty of this community. Their housing was mud slapped over sticks, now exposed by heavy rains. Termite tunnels ascended the walls, reaching a grass and bamboo roof structure which had been eaten away. Stepping inside one of these huts was like entering a time warp. The room was totally dark. The floor was set hard with smeared cow dung that had been swept clean with a grass broom. Against one wall there was a clay stove and in the centre of the room, a smoking circle holding one blackened clay pot. Hanging from the roof by string was an assortment of old metal dishes and pots. Also suspended upside down were dried bundles of seeds on maize or millet stems—precious seed for next season's planting. A straw tray holding some wilted greens near a seeping clay water pot completed the kitchen and pantry. A rolled-up grass mat marked the sleeping area. This was all the peasant farmer owned—a simple biodegradable lifestyle.

As they attempted to climb above the poverty level by selling excess crops, they were constantly thwarted by dowries, medical costs and school fees. How could one manage when a kilogram of sugar costs a whole day's wages, a packet of tea costs two days' pay, a tube of toothpaste costs three days' pay, a second-hand shirt will set a farmer back three days' pay and a term of primary school a month's pay? Discouragement and apathy are constant companions in this part of Africa. The only hope for these people was for them to give God control of their lives, so they would then experience His hope in their spirit and His blessings.

As we continued our journey, we noted that children living in the worst conditions were dependent on parents who had been disabled by war injuries—those who could only crawl and who were unable to plant food or even get water to wash themselves. It was such a miserable existence. We met men who had survived the scourge of war, but who now sought oblivion in the local brew.

This, however, only exacerbated their frustration and rage, which they vented on their traumatised children.

After much walking, we recorded the names and situations of eighty illiterate children over the age of 12, who we had found sitting staring into the dust, while local schools were filled with keen children, fortunate enough to have families who could pay school fees and uniform costs. It was a wonderful experience to walk the eighty children to the marketplace where tailors, who were sitting at ancient treadle machines, measured them to be fitted for new school uniforms. They could not keep still they were so excited.

Next, we paid for their enrollment at several local schools until our school block was built. They enjoyed school routine and discipline and then every afternoon rushed to my informal "under the mango trees" school, eager to show off their knowledge and sing the loudest.

With the older children's education arranged, I was still overwhelmed with all the younger and traumatised children needing attention. It was difficult to find local women willing to help me with the washing and feeding of the children because war's tragedies had smothered their natural joy and energy.

I was experiencing physical exhaustion myself, as I conducted three classes in different parts of town as well as checking on my other "schools" run by villagers who I had recruited and trained. As I looked at the assembled children who sat at my feet under the tree, my heart was troubled. Some sat in rapt attention and remembered every word of my Bible stories, while others sat staring at the ground. They were the ones lost in grief. With no water boreholes in the area, most were dirty with neglect, their heads caked with dust and sores, their hands swollen and lumpy with scabies. Babies were tied to the back of toddlers—their faces moist fly-traps. Others sat in the dirt searching each other's hair for lice—such terrible conditions for God's precious children.

I looked down at my own feet. My skin was dusty and cracking. I brushed the flies away from insect bites that had turned into tropical ulcers on my legs. Suffering repeated bouts of malaria and weakened by an insufficient diet, I had to admit this was a tough place. As I heard my voice droning, I tried to boost myself with more energy. Sometimes the children and I needed to sing louder and praise God with more determination in order to drown the heavy drumming of the witch doctors. By the end of the lesson, God's Spirit would inevitably fill us and the sky would ring with the proclamation, "We're going to shout it here in Kitgum, Jesus is Lord!"

❖   ❖   ❖

It had been several weeks since Jeff and Celestino had left for Kampala.

"There is a lot of paperwork to sort out and renovation work to complete," Jeff explained before he left.

And while I knew this to be true, his absence bothered me. He was away for much of the year, setting up a project to help street children in Kampala. He planned to convert our house in Kampala into a refuge.

Every now and then, I'd walk to the post office and call him on the radio phone. Villagers who sat on nearby bench seats averted their eyes, but I could tell they were listening to every word.

"I miss you darling . . . Yes, I am fine. Freda and Peter are looking after me. When do you think you will be coming home?"

I often thought of Moses, struggling in the wilderness alone. He remembered the comforts of civilisation, yet dealt with disappointments, frustrations and often lost patience with the murmurings of the people. Yet it was there in the wilderness that Moses spoke with God. I, too, was being given my instructions in the wilderness. The enforced isolation caused me to listen more keenly, often with tears, to the quiet voice of the Holy Spirit. Sometimes it felt as though the communication was hampered by static on the line. During these times I realised that the more I died to self and my own desires the clearer God's guidance would be. At times I would cry out in frustration, "God, how vast is the distance between the villagers' understanding and mine."

Then God would gently remind me, "How vast is the distance between your understanding and Mine." And then He would say, "Trust Me, Irene."

23

A SPECIAL VISITOR

KITGUM, CHRISTMAS 1993

I SAT IN 43°C HEAT in my small makeshift tin office, which looked more like a garden shed, shuffling through paperwork, preparing wages and picture folders for potential sponsors. Although my correction fluid was like concrete and my typewriter stiff with grit, I was in good spirits as I listened to a soothing cassette recording showcasing birdsongs of Australia. The chiming of the bellbirds took me back to my most recent visit to Australia in October of 1993: picnics by the harbour, strolls through the zoo hand in hand with my grandchildren; time spent at cosmopolitan Bondi—a vast expanse of white sandy beach, dotted with bright sun umbrellas shading the thousands of people who occupied every square inch of sand. I had noted with interest the melting pot of people from all walks of life: Japanese tourists on the boardwalk taking video footage; young mothers pushing designer prams; balding elderly men buffed and tanned, clad in speedos doing push-ups on the grass; and Italians sitting at pavement cafes, feasting on pasta and red wine. Nearer to my line of sight were my own grandchildren building sandcastles and digging for treasure. These were all precious memories of time spent with family. For me, these were valuable snapshots of another life back in Australia that I would file in my mind's cache to be recalled when life in Africa became challenging or mundane.

As usual, this annual sojourn had flown by and I had all too soon found myself bidding tearful farewells to family and friends at Sydney Airport. This time round it had been slightly easier, as Jeff and I were accompanied by my 23-year-old daughter, Heidi. At 7.00 a.m., we checked our baggage in at the counter and watched the scales rise: eighty kilograms overweight! But how could we leave behind all the books, videos, cassettes and printers given to us by faithful supporters. Over my shoulder I carried a bag full of precious toy cars and marbles—a gift to the children in Africa from my grandson, Jay. When we explained our mission to the check-in staff we received favour yet again, as the airline waived the fee.

After a perfect twenty-two-hour flight, Heidi was excited to touch down on African soil. Her eyes shone as she glided across the tarmac. Within moments, we were clearing customs and hugging our manager, Celestino. But where was Jeff? He was supposed to be getting the car, but had been gone for half an hour. As we waited for the luggage, he finally arrived with the car and he was looking angry. A beefy-looking policeman with a frown on his face jumped out of the passenger seat. Jeff was arguing with him. The officer became even more aggressive when he saw our luggage and began waving Jeff's license around and threatening to take Jeff down to the police station.

Welcome home! I thought to myself and then sighed. All I could do was sing my favourite warfare song: "He is the King of Kings."

The policeman looked startled. "Are you Christians?" he asked.

Jeff responded by telling him that Jesus was our Lord and Saviour.

"What about them?" the burly officer pointed at us. "Yes, He is their Lord also," Jeff responded, nodding toward us. At this point the officer's voice softened and he began to stutter, "If . . . if you're Christians, I'd better let you go." And with that, he slunk away.

We leapt into the car, elated. This was divine favour. In future, we decided to speak His name immediately—it was much more effective than normal conversation.

Besides, war zones were not normal places, as Heidi was about to discover.

Africa was a complete culture shock for my sheltered daughter. Although she had travelled to Asia, she was not prepared for the conditions she would face in the north of Uganda: the oppressive heat, the isolation and the grinding poverty—a world away from her life on the Northern Beaches of Sydney. For a few months she worked alongside the locals putting Band-Aids on the children, peeling potatoes and helping me with the paperwork.

Once Heidi was settled, I decided to travel to Kampala to assist Jeff with a pre-Christmas lunch he was hosting for seventy street children who had been rounded up from their makeshift homes around garbage containers in the city bus park. Arms around each other, full of mock bravado, these boys were shifty-eyed and suspicious of our motives at first. But when gathered in a local church hall decorated with balloons and filled with the aroma of good food, they mellowed and were receptive to the presence of God.

I stayed at our Kampala house, which had recently been painted and fitted with a few mattresses, but not much else, as Jeff was busy turning the home into a permanent refuge for street children. Already he had employed several staff: Paul—a dynamic house-father; Sam—a tall, gentle teacher; Teddy—an older lady skilled in turning beans, goat and cabbage into delicious meals; and Anna—a university graduate, ambitious enough to ensure our Kampala refuge became a showplace that donors would be keen to support.

After two full days, it was time for me to reluctantly say goodbye to Jeff and travel back to Kitgum by bus.

"When will you be coming back to Kitgum?" I asked Jeff. "I'm finding it hard by myself."

He looked around the house, looked at Anna and said, "It's going to take a lot of renovation to get the house up to scratch. I don't know how long it will take."

Although Jeff's response bothered me, I had learnt as a child to accept things as they were and not question too much. However, I did leave wondering about Anna. I began the bus journey by opening my Christmas card and letter from Jeff, which began with "My Darling Irene . . ." In his letter, he told me he loved me and missed me and couldn't wait to be back with me. All my fears were allayed—especially when I read, "To the beautiful wife God has given me." With a sigh of contentment, I closed the card. The bus, held together by wire, was jammed to capacity, with more than a hundred people filling every possible space. As the day's heat increased, dust and sweat blended with the smell of dried fish, bags of grain and engine fumes—a stinky concoction. It was a sense-assaulting experience to be hemmed in by hot bodies, with poultry underfoot pecking at my ankles, lurching from side to side each time the engine roared.

Smoke began to fill the bus—the radiator was empty. A passing cyclist was commandeered to get water from the nearest swamp. While those of us with seats held onto our space, the other passengers alighted and sat listlessly on the road in the heat. As quickly as the driver filled the radiator, water gushed onto the road. Crumpled newspaper and maize flour glue were pressed into the leaks. Under an unrelenting African sun and several jerry can trips later, the bus began to limp along, having to stop repeatedly as black smoke filled the interior and more water had to be collected by passing cyclists. With the sun setting fast, I was contemplating the long walk down the dark laneway to home, when suddenly the bus slipped off the road into a watery ditch. Under the glow of the moonlight, we had to climb down and watch the men, who were up to their knees in mud, attempt to push the bus out of the ditch. We looked around nervously. This was rebel-held territory and the sounds coming from our bus were like that of a wounded animal, inviting attack. I joined everyone in collecting rocks and tree branches. They pushed again. But the wheels stubbornly dug deeper into the watery quagmire. By midnight the passengers had lit a fire, and one by one lay on the rocky ground to sleep. Overhead was a glorious canopy of stars, but my bones ached from the cold ground, so I got back on the bus and spent the next few hours snoozing on a bench. At first light I joined the other passengers around the fire. They began to grumble and complain, "Why is God punishing us like this?"

So I told them, "There were two criminals hanging on crosses on either side of Jesus. The first criminal kept complaining to Jesus, 'Why don't you save me?' Jesus ignored him. But the other man recognised Jesus as his Lord and Jesus told him that that very day he would be welcomed into the kingdom of God. Your day will change if you recognise Jesus Christ is Lord."

They all looked at me sullenly and growled, "Why are you trying to take us away from the religion of our ancestors?" I knew what they meant, as there were pockets of the community who still held on to the belief that their dead ancestors had special powers. In pre-colonial times, an ancestral shrine was found in almost every homestead. At the *abila* or *kac*, which are shrines made from wood or stone, sacrifices and prayers were offered to their ancestors on various occasions. Moreover, they asked them for blessings and thanked them for success in a hunt or battle, the birth of children, a good harvest and other good fortune. When disease or other calamity struck the community, people would typically turn to their ancestors for assistance. This explained, in part, their unwillingness to seek Jesus for answers.

The bus remained bogged down all morning. By midday we were joined by local villagers who arrived to stare and murmur, "Sorry . . . sorry." They disappeared, then a short time later returned with hoes and axes. With their muscles straining underneath mud-caked skin, one man swung his axe, while other men dug around the wheels with their hoes. The driver fired the engine and the bus ploughed forward amidst much cheering. Silently, but with broad smiles, the villagers retreated into the scrub—village heroes, swallowed up by the brittle yellow landscape they inhabit. Thirty-two hours after I had begun my journey, I arrived back in Kitgum to join my 200 children and my daughter, Heidi—just in time to celebrate Christmas together.

❖ ❖ ❖

On Christmas day 1993, Heidi and I visited Kitgum prison, which is within walking distance of the project site. Most of the cases are capital offences: rape, defilement, murder, assault or domestic violence that can only be tried in the High Court. I had been visiting the prison since arriving in 1992. Although I didn't quite understand the spiritual dynamics there, the prisoners seemed to be addicted to the Holy Spirit's presence and the healing love of God that accompanied my visits each Sunday. Stepping into the prison hall was an assault on the senses, as the prisoners were kept in the halls with no access to toilets.

The smell was overwhelming, but as I led praise and worship, preached and prayed, all the things of this world became shadows in the light of Jesus. There were weekly salvations and baptisms in the Holy Spirit, and soon thirty-five prisoners were clamouring for water baptism. As Heidi played her guitar under God's anointing, the prisoners thought she was an angel from heaven. She gave her testimony and I gave an altar call. That's when one of the prisoners said to me, "Mama, we are all already saved." But in my spirit I knew there was someone else.

"The Holy Spirit tells me there is someone who has not given his heart to Jesus," I said, pointing to a young man leaning against a wall. The inmates all laughed.

"Yes, he is the new inmate," they answered.

The young man shook his head as if to tell me he wasn't ready, so I told him it was fine and that he could think about it during the week. Then I added, under the Holy Spirit's prompting, "Be very careful, there are many murderers in this prison."

Immediately, he clambered to the front, fell down on his knees and accepted Jesus as Lord. After the prayer, I asked him what he had been charged with.

"Murder," he replied.

Heidi and I walked home in the scorching heat and sat down to Christmas dinner consisting of beans and *posho* with a hundred orphans. Then I started the generator and played *The Jungle Book* to a gathering of 500 or more. They shrieked with laughter to see marching elephants and dancing monkeys. We finished by singing along to a cassette playing worship songs like "Come Let Us Adore Him," "Oh, I Love Jesus" and the "Lord's Prayer."

Several weeks later as Heidi prepared to fly back to Australia, I asked her to fill in a questionnaire about her time in Kitgum— something that might entice tourists to visit. But it seemed as though she wanted to keep Kitgum simple and undiscovered.

This is what she wrote:

Accommodation: *Tin shed—hotter than a furnace*

Food: *Chew 'n' spew then rush to the loo*

Climate: *50°C—hot like a hairdryer blowing on your face all day*

Nightlife: *Listen for robbers, witch doctors' drums and count the stars—29,672, 29,673 . . .*

Concierge: *Mum, who keeps saying, "Don't worry, it's a genuine African experience."*

Local McDonald's: *In your dreams*

Communications: *Watch satellites pass over at night, Morse code*

Tourist attractions: *Mum and stray dogs*

Medical facilities: *Paracetamol and Band-Aids from Dr. Mum*

Suggestions for improvement: *Turn down the heat, employ a chef, train a guard dog, catch the next plane out*

Attractions: *Hundreds of big-eyed, huggable children who desperately need Mum and Jesus*

Heidi never returned to Africa, but had a greater appreciation for the work Jeff and I were doing.

24

BETRAYAL

KITGUM, MARCH 1994

THERE WERE A NUMBER of children who really captured my heart. In 1994 it was 10-year-old Francis Olanya—a little boy who had the face of an angel and a voice to match. One evening, Peter, who was at this time dormitory house-father, brought him to me as I cooked supper in the caravan annex. Francis' face was downcast.

Peter explained the reason why: "Last night Francis came running to my place terribly upset. You know the witch doctor who has been drumming all week? That's his mother. She beat him last night because he refused to help make brew for her customers. Then she told him to do her drumming, which he also refused. So she got her boyfriend to beat him again. Francis told them he's now saved and won't do any more work for the devil. Can we fit him in here with the other boys?"

"Sure, sit down there Francis," I said, motioning the other children to make space for him. "We have a special treat—I have cooked bean burgers. You will love them . . . I hope."

The children watched as I prattled and bustled and scooped mounds of bean mush and tomatoes into bowls.

"Didn't quite stick together. I'm sorry."

Sitting along two benches, a little hesitant to eat the dish set before them, the children exchanged glances. Eyes squeezed shut, the children uttered a long prayer of thanks for the food, then opened their eyes and looked into their bowls, perhaps expecting that a miracle might have transformed this soggy mixture into something more palatable. I shrugged and began purposefully swallowing the nutrients before me.

"This is good," said Peter. He stopped eating for a moment and handed over a grubby envelope addressed to me in Jeff's handwriting. "This was given to me on the bus."

I felt a knot in my stomach. I took a deep breath, knowing what this meant. For years Jeff and I had faced issues in our marriage, but in the back of my mind I had always hoped moving to Uganda would bring us closer as a couple. Instead, the challenges just magnified the problems.

With the children settled and a full moon rising golden before me, I opened the envelope gingerly and leant towards the kerosene lantern. The letter confirmed that as far as Jeff was concerned, our marriage was over and that there would be no possibility of reconciliation.

Hot tears welled in my eyes.

From the corner of my eye, I could see Peter was watching me.

"Some sad news?" he asked.

I couldn't speak. I sat and stared at the letter. Although Jeff had told me before he'd left for Kampala that he'd had enough, I still found it hard to believe. I buried my face in my arms and sobbed. I felt betrayed.

"He can't leave me," I said. "We were in this together. How can he leave me here alone?"

Peter took my hand and responded softly, "You are not alone, Irene. I am here with you. I will never leave you. I will always look after you."

He put his arm around my shoulder, but I shrugged him off. I needed to be alone. I ran into my little caravan, shut the door behind me and threw myself onto our bed and wept.

Betrayed.

Abandoned.

Images flashed through my mind. The letter my grandmother had received from my father refusing to have any involvement with his child. My elusive mother whose attention I constantly craved; me as a 4-year-old sitting on a seat in a deserted school yard, night closing in, my eyes searching the tree canopy overhead and seeing gargoyles watching me as I waited for one of my stepfathers to come and get me. I don't remember how I got home that night, but I do recall the terror invading the darkness. Today was just another brick in the wall of my aching heart.

That night, I fell into a fitful sleep full of vivid dreams. Jeff and I were playing with orangutans in a Borneo jungle, then paddling canoes in Malaysia in order to reach the hill tribes. We were walking the Via Dolorosa in Jerusalem, Mount Legaspi, an active volcano in the Philippines, and then our final destination, travelling to northern Uganda to rescue war-ravaged children. Surely our adventures were not going to end this way.

The following morning, I decided to call Jeff on the radio phone at the post office. I took my place on a bench alongside the queue of despairing relatives, desperate to tell their city family of the plight of their children. Finally it was my turn. I connected with Jeff, took a deep breath and began.

"I got your letter. Over."

Through much static he answered, "Don't bother trying to get me to change my mind, Irene. I told you that! Over . . . What are you calling me for? Over."

"Jeff, we are a team. We will always be a team. We've done so much together. Over."

". . . Are you there Jeff? . . ."

The postmaster switched off the machine. "Aunty, we have lost the connection," he said.

"Please try again," I begged.

The tall, lanky postmaster motioned to the ever-growing queue. "Maybe you try later this afternoon Aunty. Many people have problems."

"I'm sorry . . . of course . . ." Tears welled up in my eyes as I stumbled back into the harsh sunlight. Inside I felt hollow.

Peter was waiting for me. "When is Jeff coming back?" he asked.

"I don't think he is, Peter. I don't know what to do."

The following week was a blur. Fearing they had lost their boss—Jeff—our workers were troubled. Villagers were reporting rebel group activity, just five kilometres away.

I felt no fear—only sadness. Each night, I shut my caravan door and fell exhausted onto my bed. For months, a dark cloud engulfed me. I had no energy and no appetite. There was no-one to talk to. My family was thousands of kilometres away and I had no way of communicating with them.

I had never felt so alone.

25

STRUCK DOWN
BUT NOT DESTROYED

KITGUM, 1994

RIGHT FOOT, LEFT FOOT, right foot, left foot . . . The bags of tomatoes and onions weighed heavily on my arms as I trudged the two kilometres back to the Childcare site. I set my mind on my chores ahead: cooking lunch for the 2 p.m. class, singing, Bible stories and writing lessons in the dust for 150 children. I walked to another "classroom" under the tree on the edge of town, stopping to pray for patients in one ward of the government hospital.

My responsibilities seemed overwhelming. There were 200 children in our care who were consuming large amounts of food. I needed to send an SOS out to the villages to purchase 2,000 kilogrammes of beans, as our harvest was only 500 kilogrammes. We needed more money to purchase food.

I gathered the children and told them we needed to pray. Then I decided to try and talk to Jeff again.

The postmaster connected me quickly.

"Jeff, are you there?" . . . static and beeping.

Then, I could hear him speaking. He was mid-sentence, ". . . told you, you can't persuade me to change my mind, so don't try.

Irene, we are not building anything together anymore. I will only come there when you leave. Over."

"Leave?" I responded immediately. "Where Jeff? Where do I go? Over."

"That's your decision, Irene, but I suggest you go back to your family in Australia. I can put Celestino in charge of everything in Kitgum and I will run the school from Kampala. This is the best option if you love the children."

I was choked up, but managed to respond, "The children will suffer because our donors will not support you. Please come back so we can talk. I also need the car to carry the maize and beans. Over."

He paused, and then said coolly, "You will have to learn to manage without the car. We agreed—you would keep the caravan and I would take the car. Besides, I have found a buyer. Over."

I raised my voice. "Jeff, how can you leave me here without a car and with rebels all around?"

With one last burst of static, the call was terminated.

I shuffled past the sympathetic eyes of the post office staff and emerged once again into the glaring sunlight. I gritted my teeth. I had shed many tears over Jeff's decision to leave me. Now I was angry.

"I'll have to get a bicycle," I decided. So I did.

A week later, I collected my ladies' bike from the market. I was almost 50 years old and I had never ridden a bike in my life, but I wasn't going to let that stop me.

The first challenge was to figure out what to wear. Women in northern Uganda are not respected if they wear trousers, so my first attempt saw me careering down a track with my long skirt billowing over my shoulders. Not a good look for a lady! I wheeled my bike back to my caravan and dressed again. This time I compromised by wearing a skirt over trousers and then set out to collect my supplies from town.

As I attempted to hold the handlebars steady, the rutted track I was riding along turned into a gully, and then into a ditch, eventually throwing me off into a potato field. Fortunately it was a soft landing. I wiped myself down and wheeled the bike the rest of the way. Ladies in the market pointed to my muddied trouser knees and chattered in Luo.

One of the women explained to me, "They want to know why you have been praying in the mud."

❖ ❖ ❖

I spent a lot of time praying after Jeff left. With the project in my hands, now more than ever I needed direction from the Holy Spirit and divine protection for the long trips I would need to make to Kampala.

As there were no banks in Kitgum, my only option was to make the ten-hour trip by bus to Kampala to do my banking. Every two months I'd hop on a bus, crowded with produce and people, for the perilous journey to replenish funds.

These trips followed a familiar pattern. A convoy of old metal buses would leave Kitgum Bus Park accompanied by trucks overflowing with gun-wielding soldiers. Then we'd make our 450-kilometre journey over bumpy, potholed roads in the scorching heat, often scanning the vegetation for khaki-clad rebels or sunlight glinting off bayonets.

Knowing an ambush was likely, I always began these journeys with a prayer based on Isaiah 35:8. "Thank You Lord that we travel on the highway of holiness where no evil thing can come—where only the redeemed of the Lord travel. In the name of the Lord Jesus Christ, I cancel every plan assigned against us involving any baby, bird, animal, pedestrian, bicycle, motorbike, vehicle, mechanical breakdown or rebel. We shall return safely to Kitgum with singing and rejoicing in our hearts."

Once safely in Kampala, I would stop at the city post office to collect faxes and mail from my family in Australia, then go on to the bank to withdraw 16,000,000 Ugandan shillings in cash (which at the time was equal to about $8,000)—enough money to last us two months. As there was no change in Kitgum, the money was given to me in small notes which filled a beach bag. I would carry this back to the guesthouse, before travelling back to Kitgum the next day.

For the next fourteen years, I carried the money in a big beach bag this way, eventually increasing the necessary funds to 240,000,000 shillings ($120,000) for two months, until there was a reliable bank in Kitgum. The bank tellers were intrigued and concerned by a lone white woman making a large bank transaction.

"Where is your security?" they'd ask, looking around for accompanying security guards.

"Outside," I would answer casually, tucking wads of notes into my beach bag, completely confident that God's angels were assigned to me.

On one occasion, as I exited the bank and crossed the road to walk to a taxi stand, three men, who seemed to appear from nowhere, hemmed me in by walking beside, behind and in front of me. The gangly one with dreadlocks and beady eyes kept turning his head and staring into my eyes. Perhaps it was witchcraft, but his eyes seemed to flare like yellow lightning. I gripped my bag tighter. All of a sudden, he walked swiftly ahead, then turned round abruptly and strode towards me. On reaching me, he clawed at my neck, but then continued walking. I felt for my gold cross. It was still there. Then the man who was beside me strode ahead, swivelled round and lunged at me. I stepped off the footpath to escape. A truck barrelling towards me blasted its horn. I jumped back onto the footpath as it roared past. The men fled. With my heart thumping, I took a taxi back to the guesthouse.

Transporting the money back to Kitgum was no less challenging. For several years, the buses stopped running because so many of them were ambushed and set alight.

On many occasions, the only way back to Kitgum was to sit atop bags of produce on the back of a truck with other villagers. It had the advantage of good visibility and almost automatic ejection if ambushed. The journey was never ideal—we were frequently delayed, arriving in Kitgum Town at around midnight, and were always covered in red dust.

With my bag full of money firmly clutched under my arm, I'd walk the two kilometres down the dirt track, often backwards, my eyes searching the pitch-blackness of the bush on either side. Rebels could have been in any village along the way. I'd sing, "Thy word is a lamp unto my feet and a light unto my path" until I reached the project site. Once safely inside our compound, I'd unlock my caravan door, have a quick basin wash in ice-cold water and fall into bed, satisfied that the money was there for the children's food and medicine and for the workers' wages and building materials.

Years later, in 2008, an automatic teller machine (ATM) was finally installed in Kitgum, so most of our Ugandan staff were able to collect their wages with their own microchipped cards. I praised God for keeping me safe throughout the season of commuting through a war zone.

Sometimes, the only thing I feared was fear itself.

Like Job, what I feared the most was about to come upon me.

26

ANOTHER FIERY DART

KITGUM AND SYDNEY, 1994-1995

A LETTER ARRIVED in the post. It was from Shelley, my eldest daughter.

"Dear Mum," she wrote, "we are sorry to hear about you and Jeff. We know you haven't been happy for a long time, so maybe this is for the best. Our prayers are with you as you continue to help the children."

I folded the letter and placed it under my pillow, strengthened in the knowledge that my children supported my ministry, even if I faced the future alone.

From time to time, I felt overwhelmed and discouraged by the task ahead of me. Occasionally, I had fleeting thoughts about leaving Africa, but these were short-lived, as I would look out of my caravan door and catch sight of the children running around the compound. Despite my loneliness and my heartache, I could never desert them.

At least I had our faithful manager, Celestino, to keep me company. He would be returning from Kampala any day now.

But his arrival was not as I expected. In his bag were documents for me to sign and return to Jeff in the city. The pain was crushing, as it reinforced the fact that my marriage was indeed over. Celestino gave me no answers when I asked him about Jeff and quizzed him about Anna, the university graduate working in the Kampala house. I had suspected for some time that she and Jeff were close. Jeff and I had been separated for twelve months which, according to Australian law, meant we could divorce. Reluctantly, I signed the papers. Then I bought Jeff's share of the house we had purchased for street children in Kampala.

"Don't fret Aunty. I will be back soon to help you with the work here," Celestino reassured me. "You have started a good thing, and together with God we will finish it well." Leaving me with this promise, he departed for the city.

While Celestino was away, I prayerfully considered how I should let our donors know about Jeff's resignation. In the October/November 1994 newsletter to our supporters, I wrote:

> Jeff and I suffered a direct hit. He has resigned from all involvement in Childcare International and is returning to Australia . . . I have been running Kitgum school/farm/feeding centre alone since February 1993. I will continue to be obedient to God's calling, privileged to serve my Lord by serving His children.
>
> The good news is that Childcare International is going from strength to strength, under the direction of our Lord Jesus Christ. I am taking over Jeff's half share of the Kampala house, which was been beautifully renovated to accommodate up to twenty-five street children, so let's pray for furnishings, for godly staff and victory.

In the newsletter I assured donors that work was continuing: we had built four new workshops for vocational students, gathered ten more orphans, employed three church pastors, and built four new classrooms to roof height.

Several days later, Peter handed me a large brown envelope.

"What's this?" I asked.

He smiled gently, then replied, "I told you that you can trust me. I am watching out for you."

Inside was a sheaf of handwritten letters. As I pulled them out, I recognised Jeff's handwriting. It was correspondence between Jeff and Celestino planning their takeover.

"Madam is not prepared to run, as we had planned earlier . . ." Celestino had written. "We are like two generals in a war zone— you in Kampala and me in Kitgum."

I was aghast to discover that Jeff and Celestino had such devious plans. My mind was in turmoil. With Celestino absent, I supressed my fears and took time to think. Celestino was a good project manager. Our fledgling staff admired him and followed his instructions. So I decided that reconciliation was the best way forward.

When Celestino returned from Kampala, I sat down with him and we talked.

"Celestino, I know you are not comfortable with working for a female boss. (Having worked in Africa for three years, I understood the community's attitudes towards women in leadership, so his reaction was not altogether unexpected.) However, Australian donors will never support Jeff and the woman he is planning to marry. I am the only answer for the project going forward. I admire your work ethic and all the staff respect you. Couldn't we work together for the good of the community and the children?"

He stared at the ground.

"I fear that donors might think we are scattered and unable to continue," I added. I took a deep breath and kept talking. "I would like to take you to Australia and introduce you as our project manager. Do you think we can show a united front to win back their confidence?"

Grudgingly, he agreed.

It was an unusual and somewhat sad trip back to Australia. While board members hosted Celestino, I spent alternate weeks with my children going over events leading up to my separation from Jeff. On the outside I tried to appear indifferent; on the inside I was deeply hurt. But after a month with my family I felt strengthened and ready to continue with the work in Kitgum. Donors and board members were appeased by my explanations of the breakdown and impressed by Celestino's quiet demeanour and apparent earnestness. As we boarded the flight back to Uganda, I was confident that we had settled any doubts in supporters' minds and was ready to face the challenges. Every day more children were arriving at the Childcare centre desperate for clean water, medicine, clothing, schooling, breakfast and lunch, but most importantly the teachings of Jesus Christ—a hope beyond their war-torn lives.

To assist me with the mammoth task ahead I employed David Livingstone, a local Acholi, who had himself been a victim of war and who had a heart for the plight of vulnerable children. With his skills—which included carpentry, driving, mechanics, building and his mastery of several languages—he would become a driving force in our project.

❖ ❖ ❖

As our new school opened in February of 1995, Celestino opened the gates and a procession of stick-thin people streamed through. After prayer and singing, our 300 registered orphans went off to their classes. Then the work of interviewing 200 others began. Some of the children were accompanied by their aged grandmothers, but most had turned up on their own. They told Celestino how their parents had been killed in the latest bomb blast and how they had walked for days to reach the security of a town like Kitgum. Their clothes were rags. Without any money for food or school fees, these children faced a hopeless future.

As Celestino recorded names and details, the 200 watched expectantly, silent except for some hacking coughs in the crowd. The grandmothers pushed forward the little ones they loved and pleaded their cases with furrowed brows and extended palms.

I especially remember one bony grandmother, whose face was deeply wrinkled, her eyes red-hot like coals. As she studied my fair hair and white skin her face softened. For many, I was the first white person they had ever seen. Although we were about the same age, her life of subsistence farming had taken its toll: her knees were swollen and painful. As she sat down on the ground she grimaced in pain. Her four grandchildren gathered around her like chickens. I thought of my own seven grandchildren so far away in a country that, in comparison, was so blessed. She pushed her four grandchildren forward and began to relate the story of her daughter's death. I could tell her heart was aching.

Celestino waited patiently for her to finish, then responded gently, "Please . . . we can only take three."

The woman shrugged, let out a little sigh, and then said, "I will take the smallest one back with me." Tears rolled down her dusty cheeks.

"He's only little, I think we can squeeze him in," I intervened.

Everyone laughed and the small boy, looking up at his grandmother, began to smile when he understood what we were saying.

I looked over at Celestino and smiled.

He didn't smile back.

27

THERE IS NO
CONDEMNATION

KITGUM, 1995

CELESTINO AND OTHERS gathered at our first staff
meeting since the start of term. I was eager to share with our
nineteen Christian staff members news from our recent trip to
Australia, but before I had a chance to speak, Celestino took
the floor and hurled a raft of accusations against me, including
a rumour that I had taken one of the new staff members as my
husband.

I was speechless.

I later learnt that Celestino and a pastor of a local church
had ignited a destructive rumour that had spread like wildfire
throughout the town. Their plan was to have me removed and
take over the project.

The meeting left me in no doubt about their intentions.

"Aunty is not being honest with you," he shouted and pointed at me. He went on with his barrage of abuse, including a
complaint about me not paying our staff fairly.

The staff looked on quietly. I was astounded.

"We want Jeff back. We don't want a woman to lead us!" A
worker crossed the floor, his eyes blazing. He demanded three

months' pay and hit me in the face with a heavy book.

I shrieked.

The children, who were watching from outside, began crying. One of my teachers ran over to me and stood in front of me to offer protection.

Trembling and humiliated, I said to the workers, "I am closing the project till Monday and am going to fast for three days. I advise you all to do the same. You are all dismissed. On Monday I expect you here at 8.30 a.m. to reapply for your jobs and begin work."

Tearfully, I locked myself in my caravan until Pastor Faustino called me out.

"Aunty, come out here. You must take your rightful position as our leader. You are like Moses. You will lead us out of slavery," he said. "Please read Joshua 1. God is with you, as He was with Moses and Joshua. Are you employed by Celestino or did you employ Celestino?"

I didn't respond.

After the staff meeting, Celestino had left immediately by truck for Kampala, where he dispatched a fax to all the board members:

"It is as I feared and shared with you. Madam has closed the school, dismissed the workers and has moved into a hotel."

On his return to Kitgum, he triumphantly slid their answer under my caravan door.

"Dear Irene, we grew to love and trust Celestino when he stayed with us here. We are most alarmed by his report of your erratic behaviour and feel we must withhold any further funding until his allegations have been thoroughly investigated."

I was deeply saddened by their lack of trust in me, but not surprised by their response, given the archaic communication system and their ignorance of local traditions. So I sent Peter to the city to fax my reply: "This is all untrue. And I pray you will see this. Please release a further $10,000 (proceeds from the sale of my house) from my bank account so I can continue caring for the children. Celestino will be dismissed, as will his henchmen. Any further correspondence from him is without authority." After careful checking of the facts, I was fully exonerated.

A week and a half later our errant workers stood at the gate threatening anyone who entered. Ten members of staff braved the picket—one of whom was our school secretary, who is still working with us nearly twenty years on. When the troublemakers came to me, I stood my ground and announced, "Sorry, you have all dismissed yourselves—there will be no pay. Now go, as I have work to do."

Later that morning I took my place at the blackboard to teach the children, some of whom had travelled long distances to be at school that morning.

Over the weeks that followed I was kept busy covering for the dismissed workers, interviewing and appointing locals for vacant positions, and praying more earnestly than ever for the work. The days were exhausting and the nights were tense. Rebels continued to prowl the district and the army carried out their bombing in the dark. Knowing that I now had enemies amongst disgruntled ex-workers, I recited Psalm 91 a little louder each night. But I continually asked God why I no longer had a loving husband to support me or anyone to protect me.

I was desperate for answers.

One day, I crossed a local sports field on my way back from town and noticed a crusade was taking place. I went to take a closer look.

From the stage, the speaker called out, "That *mzungu* up the back."

I looked up.

"Yes, you."

I kept walking until a few people in the crowd stopped me and said, "He means you, lady."

I walked to the front of the stage where the preacher prayed and prophesied over me: "Men have condemned you. But God is with you. He will never leave you. Your righteousness will be established by the words of your mouth and the fruit of your hands. Does that mean anything to you?"

All I could say was, "Thank You, Jesus! I am ready to carry on with Your work."

28

KAMPALA'S STREET CHILDREN

KAMPALA, 1995

IT HAD BEEN A TOUGH YEAR. Demand was growing, resources were diminishing and the coup staged by my staff had been devastating. I felt the need to take a break from the pressures at the Kitgum Childcare site and check on the progress of our Kampala street children's home. This was my first trip to the city since Jeff had returned to Australia.

After a fairly typical bus journey, I arrived tired and a bit dishevelled, but ready for a city tour with our house-father Paul.

As we walked through the large overcrowded bus park, we scanned the scruffy boys weaving their way through the vehicles. "Uncle Paul, Uncle Paul," they called, as he distributed bread, which they devoured hungrily.

Some of the boys were slumped against the garbage dump. Most were high, pressing petrol-soaked rags against their nostrils and breathing the fumes deep into their lungs.

One of the boys, whose name was Abdul, told me a story I would never forget. His dying mother's words to him were, "Keep walking until you reach the west. You'll find your daddy there, where the sun goes down." He had cradled her head and squeezed her bony hand until it was stone cold, with tears rolling down his dusty face. He was only 8 years old and now he was totally alone. With a backwards glance to the refugee-camp huts, his home for the past six months, he set off along the hot dusty road towards Kampala in the west.

Exhausted from his trek, he arrived in the city and found a spot on the pavement. As he looked up he saw a sea of angry faces—passers-by who ignored his pleas for help. Hands pushed him aside roughly. Then he saw a mosque—its dome shining in the setting sun. A loudspeaker began wailing prayers across the city. He ran to the gate but was refused entry, so he sat on the curb expectantly searching every face that entered, until he fell into a fitful sleep. At 5.00 a.m. the call to morning prayer wailed in the new day. The young boy lifted his head from the pavement to see a good pair of leather shoes and a long white *kanzu* (a full-length tunic). The face of a gaunt young man stared down at him. Although he recognised the eyes, the mouth was slightly twisted as he spoke. "You're a lying dog just like your mother. If you shame me like this again, I'll kill you. Go and find your real father," he said, throwing a coin at the boy and then walking away.

As the coin bounced on the footpath, another young boy who had been watching the exchange sprang on it. "Ha, it's mine!" he declared and ran away. Abdul chased him to where a group of boys were washing under a broken water pipe.

"What's your name?" they demanded. "You'll work with us . . . agreed?"

"Yes," Abdul responded.

Scrounging food from the rubbish bins by day, sleeping curled up with the others like a litter of puppies each night, Abdul began his new life as a street kid.

By the time I met Abdul, he was slouched in the mud, oblivious to the poverty and despair around him. He wasn't alone—several young people sat beside him. As I watched their eyes rolling, their limbs twitching, I leant down to touch a youth. He leapt to his feet, shaking a rock in my face. "You . . . you white witch. Don't touch me."

Paul quickly restrained him, pushed me clear and shook his head. "They are not well today," he muttered. "We will come back another day."

"Wait," he said, then grabbed the hand of Abdul. "You're a good boy and you're too young to be here. Do you want to see Aunty Irene's house? There are many friends there for you. You'll eat good food and go to school."

Without a word, the small boy climbed onto the luggage rack of Paul's bicycle. I boarded a *matatu* (a colourful African bus) for the short ride back to our street children's home—a single-storey concrete house located in Rubaga, a suburb of Kampala.

The following week I heard that a street boy leader called Mayombee had visited our house. Looking sharp in new jeans and shirt, and wearing a diving watch, he began telling the boys of the riches waiting for them back on the streets. Sensing he was up to no good Paul evicted him, however for several days the young man sat outside the back wall whispering the promises of easy money and freedom on the streets.

Lured by the possibilities, Abdul, dressed in his Sunday best, walked into Kampala town. His old friends greeted him warmly and they shared roast maize with him at the back of the city markets. As the chilly night air descended, dampening his hair and shirt, they offered him a "welcome home" treat: a rag soaked in jet fuel.

As he breathed the fumes, his head rocked, his eyes rolled and the cold night air was replaced with a warm euphoria. Soon he was curled up by his friends. Around midnight he was awakened by a boot kicking his back. He found himself alone, deserted by his friends and facing three youths, who beat him severely. They ripped off his shoes, his shirt and trousers. Naked and bloodied, he crawled to an open drain and washed the blood from his face. He tied a rag around his waist and cowered under some cardboard. As the grey dawn light uncovered the depressing scene, Abdul's friends sought him out and offered him tablets. He gulped them down to ease his throbbing head. When Paul found him, he was irrational and yelling, "Get away from me. You don't love me. You always favour the other boys. I'm going to go there and kill them all."

That evening in the home, other rescued street boys prayed fervently for their "prodigal brother." Several days later, Paul found him again. This time Abdul was broken. His eyes filled with tears as he whispered, "Take me home, Uncle Paul."

Mayombee continued his secret visits, whispering enticing promises through the wall, until he had lured three of our children back to the gang. By the time Paul found them, jet fuel had disturbed their minds and made them violent.

Back at the home the children prayed even more fervently. Paul awoke from a deep sleep one night to hear a voice outside his window. "Give me a drink of water, please." He found it was Mayombee crouching in the dirt, his body beaten, his clothes torn. "Let me stay here," he begged. Another soul saved.

Over the years many street children have been rescued and have grown up there. Many have gone on to become teachers and college graduates. Although I had a heart for our boys in the city, my primary calling was to northern Uganda.

And as it turned out, the children of Kitgum needed me more than ever.

Age of innocence
– me at two.

Mum six weeks before her death.

Early days with Brian.

Marrying my sweetheart.

Me as a young Mum.

My beleaguered caravan.

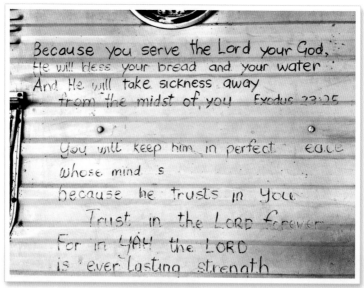

Because you serve the Lord your God,
He will bless your bread and your water
And He will take sickness away
from the midst of you   Exodus 23:25

You will keep him in perfect   peace
whose mind s
because he trusts in You
Trust in the LORD forever
For in YAH the LORD
is everlasting strength

My caravan covered in God's Word.

Early days – lots of curious visitors.

Writing – one of my great pleasures.

Lining up to be washed.

Finding water
– who would have thought!

My new African friends
and my faithful dog, Caleb.

In the
beginning
– teaching
under the
trees.

Praying for abducted relatives.

Night commuters....

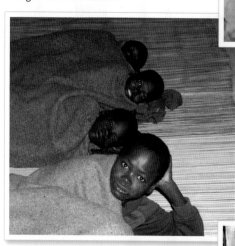

An irresistible need.

Vulnerable children –
ideal targets for the LRA.

IDP camps – a depressing reality.

Many of our students came
from IDP camps.

A typical dusty
Kitgum road.

Village life – meeting the locals.

Saying goodbye to family never got any easier...

.... But seeing them every year gave me strength to continue.

Just a few of my fifteen grandchildren.

Introducing my African friends to my favourite beaches.

Our bedford truck
transported tonnes of supplies.

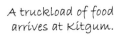

John Paul and me with our new
Landcruiser – a much-needed gift.

A truckload of food
arrives at Kitgum.

Kampala to Kitgum
– always a challenge.

Playground
– all the way from Hong Kong.

Always the teacher.

Look what God can do with obedience.

One of our school assemblies.

Inquisitive and eager to learn.

Finding sponsors for all
of these precious children.

Photo courtesy of Jon Love

Former student, Patrick,
teaches in an IGF classroom.

Enjoying the new equipment.

A future and a hope...

Graduation Day.

Learning to sew
and earn an income.

Feeding the children
– a mammoth task!

The Gospel story through the eyes of our resident artist, Everest.

Many hands make light work.

Former child soldiers
learning a trade.

.... and our faithful staff.

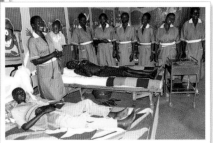

Gloryland Junction AIDS Hospice....

Photo courtesy of Jon Love

Cooking – backbreaking work.

"Good morning, Kitgum!"

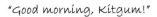

Dormitories for resident orphans.

"Come to Mama."

Mama Irene.

Always room for more.

Filming the Daystar documentary.

Momentarily distracted....
poor baby!

Prisca – "She smiles
at her future" (Proverbs 31)

Dr. Vincent – achieving
God given potential.

Rose – running her own
successful business.

Everest – the maestro at work.

What an honour!
Receiving my
Order of Australia.

Final interview with Daystar.

Meeting the President of Uganda.

Mama Irene's Kitgum memorial service – 10,000 say their goodbyes.

With Paul and Alice Zagorski.

Praying for the work of IGF
with some of the African team.

Founding chairman of IGF USA,
Drayton Nabers.

The wheels keep turning – our IGF leaders.

KITGUM, UGANDA

BEFORE....

AFTER....

29

WIDOWS AND ORPHANS

KITGUM, 1995-1998

BY MID-1995 close to 1,000 children from our district had been abducted by rebels. Some were to be trained to fight against the Ugandan army; those who were too young to handle guns were sold to the Sudanese as slaves in exchange for guns. Hearing this stirred in me a righteous anger. These children needed me to demonstrate the lordship of Jesus Christ in a practical way. As reports of rebel attacks increased, the Spirit of God moved in an even greater way throughout the communities. Villagers were keen to hear about Jesus Christ as the loving anchor for their souls in troubled times. Town officials began borrowing videos from Pastor Faustino to help bring calm and order to the community.

In the evenings, under the dim light of a flickering paraffin lamp, I would sit at my small laminate table huddled over my Bible, sipping hot sweet tea and praying for safety and protection for our community. I drew the curtains tightly so as not to let any chink of light show across the dark fields and attract attention. Somewhere out there in the chilling African night bands of rebels, under the influence of spirit mediums, were prowling—men and boys who had undergone brutal training in

Sudan. These militants were ruthless in their quest to take or destroy anything they could in order to survive. Along the way, they left a patchwork of destruction: the charred remains of huts, rotting animal corpses, ravaged soil where sorghum and maize once stood proudly, and desperate mothers who sat in the dirt mourning the abduction of their children. Northern Uganda was in crisis; the spirit and the life of the Acholi race had all but been extinguished.

Fear of the rebels sparked the beginnings of a massive migration from villages into Internally Displaced Person (IDP) camps established by the Ugandan government to provide protection against the rebels and to deter rebel activity. In time, more than 1.5 million people would leave their huts and their land and relocate to one of the twenty-three IDP camps peppered throughout northern Uganda. The conditions were far from ideal: small mud and thatch huts or tents butting up against each other on a parcel of land too small to cultivate. Cramped living conditions and apathy were characteristics of these compounds. Inhabitants were hungry and malnourished, and the lack of clean water and adequate sanitation resulted in many health problems such as malaria, cholera and dysentery. It was humiliating to be reliant upon external aid and the resulting idleness brought a wide range of negative effects on the whole community.

In comparison, we had a sanctuary filled with light and provision as we cared for 1,200 children each day with much hope, love and singing.

In time, word about the work of Childcare spread to the IDP camps and many children who needed supplementary feeding above their ration of one mug of beans and two mugs of flour per week turned up every afternoon and queued outside my caravan. With gaunt faces, skin stretched over cheekbones and ribs and knees swollen above twig-like legs, they'd quietly line up for a biscuit and a cup of milk to last them through the night until we could give them porridge and lunch the following day.

In the mornings the children would stand quietly in line waiting for their mug of sweet porridge. At lunchtime, they would cram beans and *posho* into their hungry mouths. After they had eaten, the children would pray a blessing for the donors around the world whose support had bought them food, blankets and clothing. This was such a touching scene, yet my heart would be torn at having to turn away 500 extra children who arrived each morning desperate for food, care and schooling. Without any shelter, I couldn't let them sit all day in the hot sun, so I'd have to send them away.

Displaced adults also came begging for help, sharing stories of unimaginable horror. Our office clerk's father and brother who were living in an IDP camp decided to risk going back to their *samba*, rather than starve. Rebels caught them digging, tied them up, and then axed them to death. Another father and son, also starving, biked to their compound. As they loaded a bag of sorghum onto their bike, rebels dropped from the trees. The father fled, but when he returned he found they had gouged his son's eyes out as a deterrent.

Some took extreme measures in order to protect their family. I remember one time a disabled father turned up and begged me to take his children, rather than subject them to this fate. With tears streaming down his face, he told me he couldn't physically defend the children against the rebels. I accepted the children, but wept over the scene that followed. Hand in hand, his two children stood at the gate watching silently—their large eyes welling up as their father rolled his wheelchair with difficulty up the long, dirt road. They looked puzzled and scared—no doubt, wondering if they would ever see him again. He turned his head once. I could see from a distance his palms wiping the tears that were streaming down his weathered, dusty face at the pain of leaving his precious children behind. I could not erase this image from my mind. A few hours later, I was walking to the market when I overtook the father who was still making his way painfully and slowly up the road. My heart went out to him. I suggested that he return to our project site and stay with us until his children were settled. He gratefully accepted and took on the role of an office clerk, also helping to dispense medicines when the need arose.

One sweltering afternoon a thin woman from a neighbouring IDP camp knelt at my gate. Her hair was matted and her cheeks were gaunt. She looked like a scarecrow with her shabby black dress, beneath a threadbare coat. In her Acholi dialect she began to tell me her problems. As I listened, not understanding her words, my eyes filled with tears. The compassion of God towards her led me to wrap my arms around her. I embraced this beautiful creation of God, now reduced to a filthy rag doll. She slumped into my arms. As I held her tightly, tears flowed between us, transcending any language barriers. She pressed a dirty scrap of paper into my hands which translated said, "My name is Grace Aleng. My husband was abducted by rebels last year. I don't know if he's dead or alive. My husband and I and our four children were living in the village of Palabek. In July, the rebels took my 12-year-old son. We ran into town. Now we live in the camp. We are starving and I have no clothes or blankets for my children. I don't know what to do."

I felt compelled to offer Grace employment at Childcare. Her job was to dispense medicines to the queues of children who needed daily medication for malaria, wounds, chest infections and parasites. The day I visited Grace's tent in the camp, she proudly showed me her struggling vegetable patch of tiny tomatoes and some sticks of sorghum. As I watched her 2-year-old daughter,

Nanny, toddling toward a cesspool of filthy, disease-ridden water, once again I felt led to help her and offered her a hut on the project site, which she eagerly accepted. Every morning, I awoke to the sound of Grace singing hymns as she prepared breakfast for our forty resident orphans. Grace became a beloved house-mother. Dressed in fresh clothes and eating regular meals, Grace took her rightful place as a daughter of the King of Kings. There were many others like Grace—weather-beaten, forsaken women in rags—who were transformed into His beloved women of dignity, dressed in regal traditional *gomesi* (a floor-length, brightly coloured dress), playing tambourines and rejoicing in the dance.

One morning a 4-year-old orphaned boy from one of the surrounding IDP camps, who was almost unable to stand up on his stick-thin legs, wandered into our school. We fed him some porridge and opened up yet another group: a nursery for the malnourished. Pretty soon, despondent grandmothers were sending starving little ones to our school.

❖   ❖   ❖

By the end of 1997, our eighteen classrooms were overflowing with more than ninety children in each. Every one of them was receiving schooling, breakfast porridge, lunchtime beans and *posho*, medical care, washing and soap, practical agricultural experience, animal husbandry and basic vocational training. Moreover, Childcare had built a sewing room, a clinic, several offices and a newly donated kitchen. On site we had sunk two freshwater boreholes, erected a children's bathing centre and latrines, and built staff quarters and animal sheds. Every child was given a school uniform and blankets.

Day after day, the CKS children witnessed that the practical love of Jesus Christ is more powerful and life-changing than the incantations, sacrifices and herbs of the local witch doctors. I never ceased to be amazed at the ongoing miracle of being able to provide such practical care for thousands.

Outside our flimsy wire fence, chaos and war reigned. Inside the Childcare sanctuary, we lived in a different kingdom where, by the grace of God, we continued to make progress.

30

THIS IS THE DAY
THE LORD HAS MADE

KITGUM, 1997-1999

EVERY MORNING I would open eyes full of faith in my spirit, but in the natural I was slightly surprised to still be here on this earth. During the night rebels continued to ravage the district. Surely this middle-aged white woman alone in her caravan was an easy target? As each day passed, I breathed a prayer of thanks to God that He had protected me through the night. As the first sunbeams of light rolled over the hill, across the field into my caravan, I'd turn up Vivaldi on my cassette player and kick the door open to let in the rays of light, then call, "puss, puss," to the stray cat that lived in the tree, and give it some milk in a small saucer.

"Lord, show me Your glory today," I would say while pouring coffee from my thermos. Then I would stand at the doorway, cup in hand, watching the dawn sky morph from silver-grey to metallic gold.

Around my caravan, our resident children would chop wood and stir up clouds of fine golden dust as they swept the compound. Others would sing at the tops of their voices as they stirred the large pot of porridge. It was a happy scene.

Most mornings Simon Peter, one of the children, would stand at my doorstep smiling shyly and saying, *"Ichoo maber? (You rested well?)"*

"Iyo. In koho? (Yes. What about you?)" I'd reply.

"Do you want porridge Aunty?" he would ask me.

"Just half a cup," I'd say, watching him skip towards the fire.

Under my breath, I would utter a quiet "thank You" to Jesus for healing him. Months earlier his aged mother had brought him to us. He was emaciated, unable to digest food and one side of his chest was swollen. His leg swung uselessly, the skin peeling off in strips. His mother explained that her boy had walked on snake poison smeared on the pathway to their hut by a jealous neighbor. Doctors could do no more; they'd sent Simon Peter home to die. I knew God would heal the boy, as he lived under the praises and prayer that resounded around the CKS school site. God had certainly lifted this ailing child from the dust and set his feet on a rock.

As he ladled out fifty mugs of porridge, I searched out some of the other recent arrivals and smiled to see some of their obvious healings. Stephen, aged 12, used to crawl in the dirt, but was so improved that he was now able to walk using crutches. Then there was 10-year-old Christopher who had suffered beatings for years from his witch doctor stepmother. Now he was free and carried jerry cans of water for his dormitory brothers. There were thirty-seven others clambering for attention. "Aunty, I need soap," "Aunty, I need a new pen," "Aunty, I've lost my toothbrush," "Aunty, my slipper is broken."

At times, I felt overwhelmed, but mostly I was immensely proud of the commission given to me by the King of Kings, as I watched His plan unfolding for these precious lives.

The children would gather for morning assembly in our bamboo and thatched assembly hall, which looked like it belonged on a tropical island, not in the dusty back-blocks of Africa, and usher in the presence of God with a crescendo of drums and exuberant singing. As we followed the format of "ACTS"—Adoration, Confession, Thanksgiving and Supplication—the Holy Spirit would often lead us to shake the heavens with cheering and shouting, whistling and drumming, so grateful were we for God's protection and His presence. And then the children would pray, cry and groan for abducted siblings and friends.

One Monday morning in 1998 the mood was particularly solemn. Our children stood shivering in the cool morning air, their prayers dissolving into sobs as they wept for their relatives and neighbours caught up in the senseless violence. We had heard the most horrific stories from the villages: people being forced to kill their neighbours and eat their flesh; babies being smashed against stones; the ears, noses and breasts of frightened women being hacked off. One of our students told us he had seen many people killed and that he, too, was forced to cook and eat body parts. Mad at the devil, I stood in front of the 1,500-strong assembly and said, "Hands up if you've lost immediate family members" . . . only a few hands. Then I said, "Hands up if any of your possessions were taken?" Again, only a few hands went up. Suddenly, as if a light had been turned on, the children beamed and burst into rapturous applause, cheering as they realised God had protected many of them during the night. Our school children came to understand the symbolic meaning of their red uniform: that they were blood brothers with Jesus Christ and protected under His covenant promise. Most knew Psalm 91 by heart.

Spiritual warfare was always followed by prayer for CKS sponsors, donors and families whose unselfish giving had helped to build the sanctuary they enjoyed. Next, our resident preacher, Pastor Faustino would jump to his feet, pace the floor with his Bible in his hand and teach the assembly the word of God. Many children would look away ashamed as Faustino rebuked the traditional witchcraft practices I hadn't even recognised: shaving their heads in certain ceremonies, drumming a certain beat, throwing salt, water or seeds over their shoulder, attending funeral rites, using herbs or buying fetishes from a traditional healer. He taught them that all these superstitious practices must be replaced with trusting in the power of Jesus Christ; that His death on the cross had already paid for their healing, their rescue and their needs. The NIV version of Jeremiah 17:5–7 says, "Cursed is the one who trusts in man, who draws strength from mere flesh and whose heart turns away from the LORD . . . But blessed is the one who trusts in the LORD, whose confidence is in Him."

To lighten the mood, sometimes our morning assembly would be finished off with a Bible quiz where the winner got to choose a prize from the mystery box. Unused to the luxury of having choices, the child selected was gripped by lip-chewing indecision. Mostly they chose a visible prize: a story book, pen or exercise book. Sometimes a brave child would take the risk and cause a near riot as they withdrew the mystery prize from the box: a valued soccer ball or a despised mango. Assembly always closed with our school anthem "Victory in Jesus," and it is still sung today.

> O victory in Jesus
> My Saviour, forever
> He sought me and bought me
> With His redeeming blood
> He loved me ere I knew Him
> And all my love is due Him
> He plunged me to victory
> Beneath the cleansing flood.

Although the children couldn't quite articulate the words, they knew the power of proclamation.

After morning assembly the children would disperse to their classrooms or go to the field, collecting hoes on the way to plant maize, beans, sweet potatoes or millet. A queue would form outside the clinic where treatment for malaria, chest infections, stomach upsets and tropical ulcers would be dispensed by our team of loving nurses. Around mid-morning, our welfare officer would roam the classrooms, drawing out neglected children for special attention like hair cutting, bathing, and mending of clothes or extra feeding. Then at 10.30 a.m., queues of hungry 5-year-olds would gulp down mugs of porridge and powdered milk dished out by our village cooks from oversized pots with large wooden ladles. This process could take several hours, after which lessons would resume. In each classroom, teachers who were trained locals would attempt to teach our children the basics of literacy and numeracy. In the early days, without resources, the children used sticks to scratch letters of the alphabet on their skin.

Satisfied that all the classes were underway, I would head into my stiflingly hot shed-office and fight with a cantankerous typewriter. Too hot to continue, I'd often leave my desk and go to check on the builders' progress. The work was slow because the ground was baked hard as rock and materials were hard to come by. Workers often put their lives at risk as they drove our heavy Bedford truck—which at one point had been used by the United Nations during the Rwandan genocide—along village tracks in search of bricks, stone and rough-hewn timber. Moreover, our builders lacked some of the basic skills. Apart from David Livingstone and our building supervisor, Joel, the builders were unfamiliar with the construction methods needed to make permanent buildings. My job was to check the progress daily, to make sure the foundations and drains did not rise above ground level. During my time in Africa, this granny became a Jack-of-all-trades. I constantly prayed to God, "You have filled them with skill to do all kinds of work" (Exod. 35:35 NIV).

At lunchtimes our cook, Cecilia, would prepare the forty-gallon drum of maize dough over a hot fire. Teachers would help serve a seemingly endless queue of children holding colourful plastic bowls in their hands, waiting for their beans and *posho*. Once inside the shade of our newly constructed classrooms, the children would utter a beautiful prayer: "Jesus, as we break this bread we remember Your body which was broken for us. We thank You Lord and take into ourselves everything You have won for us: perfect health, victory over evil and life with You forever. Amen."

The hour and a half lunch break was spent eating, collecting water at the water boreholes, playing volleyball and skipping games. I could hear the children's voices in the playground laughing and squealing while I sat completing paperwork in my office.

Afternoon classes followed the Ugandan curriculum, with allowance for artistic expression, sewing, exercise, Bible stories and singing.

Late in the day I'd check food and medical supplies then walk the couple of kilometres into town to collect the mail. My daily stroll would give me the opportunity to enjoy the vivid African sunset of flame-coloured clouds set against a teal-blue sky. With each step I would thank God for the day and for the progress we were making, eventually reaching the school grounds in time for the evening prayer for protection.

Our prayers always intensified on the last day of each school term. The rebels knew that the children then returned to their village homes to help with food cultivation. In isolated communities they were easy targets. Often I would look over the school assembly at the thousands of bowed heads, their eyes squeezed shut and lips moving as they prayed for safety and a bountiful harvest.

From time to time, the children's soft prayers were drowned out by a witch doctor's hypnotic and very loud drumming just outside our fence. Incensed by this invitation to demons, I'd make my appeal, "Do you accept the enemy living in our town?"

"No," they'd all chorus. Small fists punched the air. These little warriors were ready to defend their territory.

"The angel of the Lord encamps around us, and he delivers us. We put our land and family under Jesus' blood. Jesus is Lord over Kitgum! Satan, in Jesus' name, leave our family, leave our land. You have no place here. Even the witch doctor, we put him and his house under the blood of Jesus. Jesus You died for him and Your blood purchased him—not Satan."

We would stop to listen.

Silence. The drumming had stopped.

A spontaneous cheer of victory would rise across the assembly. I knew God was training them to handle spiritual warfare back in their own villages.

"Lord," I would pray, "I commit every child here into Your hands. Keep them safe in the town and the country. Keep their going out and their coming in. Keep them from all evil." I was always reassured that God would guard each and every child until the school opened again.

At home time, the children would file out through the gates, satisfied in body, soul and spirit. There were some who were reluctant to leave, so we'd check their home situation to see if residential care was needed.

On school days, those who were in our residential care programme ate dinner together. This was usually beans. The continuing war put Kitgum under siege and there was no fresh food coming in. The only available flavouring was curry powder. So I'd pray 1 Timothy 4:4–5: "Everything God made is good. It is sanctified by His word and my faith." Sometimes the water tasted as sweet as juice and the beans like the tastiest meat pie. I would often close my eyes and imagine I was about to tuck into a hearty roast chicken dinner, but would be jolted into reality by the sloppy gloop placed in front of me. In the early days I can recall writing to Heidi, describing the food as bland and disgusting, but in time my taste buds adapted and I became used to eating what the locals ate—beans and *posho*. Now and again something different would be offered, but this was a rare treat.

One night, I was offered a bowl of pigeon soup, which tasted like salt water. I fished around until I found a piece of meat and began to chew it. Something sharp stuck into my tongue. When I examined the golf-ball shape in the moonlight, I discovered it was a pigeon's head, complete with eyeballs and beak.

Another meal eaten in Kitgum was stew using boiled-up meat bought from town earlier in the day. A trip to the butchers meant choosing a cut of meat from carcasses suspended from large metal hooks. Once the selection was made, the butcher would smack the meat onto a large wooden chopping block and then take to it with a hatchet, splattering blood and bone in all directions. I'd duck for cover. Beaming, the butcher would hand over a plastic bag containing splintered meat ready for cooking.

After the evening meal I'd really look forward to a cup of hot, sweet tea to wash it down. I remember one evening as I poured my tea from the flask it slowed to a trickle, and then a plump, wet thing plopped into my cup. I jumped to my feet and shrieked, "Oh yuck, a frog!"

The orphans who often studied in my caravan at night gathered around my tea cup, peering at the frog with puzzled faces. They exchanged glances and smiled at each other, then went back to reading their books.

From time to time, I'd fry up white ants for a snack. In the wet season, the white ants do a flying mating dance, then fall to the ground and crawl around, at which point, the children would catch them by their wings, fry them up and add salt—African crisps!

As a special treat one time, one of the children brought me a wild mushroom. It was about twenty-three centimetres in diameter and creamy white. I took it from his hand and began to break off the pieces, chewing it raw. "All this needs is a little bit of salad dressing," I said between mouthfuls. The children stood staring at me with open mouths. One of the workers, grabbed it out of my hand and exclaimed in horror, "Mama, look here, don't you see the little animals. Yuck!" The pleats of the mushroom were crawling with tiny worms, which I could immediately feel creeping around in my stomach.

When the eating was over for the day, it was time for hand-shaking and hugs. "Goodnight Aunty," the children would say, wrapping their bony arms around my waist.

Then I was alone. These were often the hardest times, and the moments where I felt the loneliest, except for fellowship with Jesus. Under the flickering light of a kerosene lamp, I'd read scriptures and write them in my A–Z notebook. Occasionally I'd scribble scripture on the walls of my caravan—a permanent reminder to enemies lurking that I meant business. When I wasn't reading my Bible, I would tune into the BBC news and listen to the announcers who would fade in and out warning of rebel activity. "Bus ambushed (satellite beep) sixteen people dead (beep, beep) ten students abducted in an attack in Dura" (about ten kilometres from Kitgum Town). Radio broadcasts often caused me to pray even more earnestly for the children.

Unfazed by the terror that surrounded me, I'd blow out my light, stretch across my bed and utter this prayer: "Thank You Lord Jesus. No harm shall befall me. No disasters come near my dwelling place. Goodnight Papa God, sweetheart Jesus, precious friend Holy Spirit. I love You."

He was an ever-present help in time of trouble, but from time to time, my faith was rocked.

31

BATTLEFIELD

KITGUM, 1998-1999

EVERY DAY, TANKS and war machinery passed back and forth through town. Mortar bombs exploded behind our fence and machine gun fire ripped across the night sky. The news reports confirmed our fears: Ten dead in Kitgum ambush; sixty LRA killed; more fighters from Sudan; war is the only choice. Daily life in northern Uganda was like a pendulum swinging from fear to faith.

I often asked God, "Why do I behave fearlessly, while my head is saying, 'Hide!'?"

In my spirit I could hear God responding to me, "Get mad Irene, how dare the devil disturb your rest!"

So I would quote scripture: "For in the day of trouble He will keep me safe in His dwelling; He will hide me in the shelter of His sacred tent and set me high upon a rock. Then my head will be exalted above the enemies who surround me; at His sacred tent I will sacrifice with shouts of joy; I will sing and make music to the LORD" (Psalm 27:5–6 NIV).

One evening after dinner, I heard gunfire. As I stepped out of my caravan towards our manager David's room, he met me in the dark.

"We're surrounded," he whispered.

"What's happening?" I asked.

"Shhh, be quiet," he hushed me, his eyes wide with fright.

We heard a fresh staccato of gunfire outside the compound.

"What's happening?" I persisted.

"Be quiet!" he hissed, raising his hand inches from my face. Pushing past, he disappeared into the blackness. My heart was thumping as I followed.

Lights flashed across the sky. Machine gun fire echoed across the valley. Then silence.

I stood motionless underneath a tree, my lips mouthing, "No harm shall befall me, no disaster shall come near my property . . ." I continued, praying in the language of the Spirit.

A shower of leaves fell over me. I looked up and gasped to see David silently descending from the tree. David's teeth flashed white as he spoke: "Hundreds . . . there are hundreds of rebels running alongside our fence!"

Outside the compound, rebels were invading huts, collecting children, roping them together, shoving them forward and forcing them to march towards Sudan. As the battering of doors abated, an angry silence engulfed the community. Eventually I fell into bed, unaware of the horror that would await me when I woke.

At first light, a shrill wailing pierced the dawn: mothers who were howling for their stolen children. My head was pounding. I tried to regain the oblivion of sleep until insistent tapping at my door caused me to throw the covers off and face a day of new challenges.

"What is it Peter?" I asked.

"The rebels have killed the father of one of the boys. His body was on the road."

I sighed. Peter's news wasn't a shock to me. I knew the rebels had a habit of forcing the children to kill their relatives after they had walked a few kilometres—firstly to traumatise the captives and then to make it impossible for them to escape back to home.

"Peter, this is terrible, is there anybody else?" I asked.

"Joel is missing," he replied.

My first reaction was to fret, but then I knew Joel, our building supervisor, was a man of faith, so I prayed fervently for his safety.

A few days later, Peter greeted me at the project site with some news.

"Good news Aunty. Joel has escaped. He's in the hospital. I'll walk you there if you're not too tired."

We found Joel with one leg heavily bandaged, sitting on a metal bed. He explained what had happened:

"On Monday night I ate supper with my family. We sang songs and praised God under the stars and then I went to sleep. At 11 p.m. explosions and gunfire woke me. I saw rebels across the valley firing mortar bombs over our land and into the town. When I heard the sound of footsteps running, I fled outside and hid in my banana plantation. An army officer who was nearby shouted to me, 'I can see the rebels; we will get the army down here to help you.' So I called out to my daughters, assuring them that the army was coming to protect us. Through the trees I saw some men in khaki running towards our compound. I squeezed into a tiny space in the banana tree. The men began pounding on the door of our home. My daughters were inside. I prayed that the girls wouldn't open the door.

"When no-one answered, the men left the house alone and began jabbing their bayonets into the garden. One spotted me and shouted, 'What are you doing there?' I couldn't answer. He prodded me to make me come out, then shoved me into a group of six youths and two elderly men. We were roped together and pushed along the path. Our captors were ten men and twenty child soldiers aged between 12 and 16 years. They were all dressed in army clothes and carrying guns with bayonets. We were forced to carry heavy loads on our backs.

"After a short while, my neighbour, a sick old man, fell down and couldn't get up. One of the youths shouted, 'This man is fooling us, what should we do with him?' Their leader replied, 'Take what he is carrying and kill him.' I walked away quickly so I wouldn't hear his cries.

"I began to cry and plead with Jesus to help the innocent children. We stumbled through the dark, until we reached Pinymunu. There we joined another group of rebels and teenage girls. There was another line of prisoners. We slept in a line all roped together.

"Before dawn on Tuesday, we were given a small amount of raw cassava to chew. The boy prisoners, including my 12-year-old nephew, John, were dressed in army clothes and warned that the government soldiers would shoot them if they tried to escape. My group was given two dismantled guns to carry. It took five of us to carry the barrel of the B-10. We walked all day, criss-crossing our tracks. The girls walked beside the men who had chosen them as brides.

"On Wednesday we remained hidden all day. I saw the abducted children threatened and forced into evil behaviour: they were taught to interrogate and beat the adult prisoners. I believe God protected me, as I was not made to take part in any of this. Nevertheless, it was terrible to observe.

"That night, when the rebels saw the lights of a vehicle heading towards Kitgum, they set up the gun in the middle of the road ready to ambush. Then they stood in a 'V' shape either side and waited. When the driver spotted the gun, he leapt from the vehicle and escaped. The rebels fired their gun, which annihilated the engine and cabin of the truck. People died on the spot.

"Later, we were marching towards Sudan to pick up an anti-aircraft gun. At noon we stopped and the rebels began to pray—some with rosary beads and some with Muslim prayer beads. I took the opportunity to talk to God. Peace flooded my heart. I could hear Aunty Irene's voice praying in tongues. I could hear my daughter's voice, saying, 'Daddy, why are you leaving us?' I replied to her in my heart, 'My daughter, don't worry, God is releasing me. Tonight I will not sleep with these people.'

"At 4 p.m. we were told to pack everything, as we were leaving. Still roped together, we were struggling to carry the big gun barrel, when army troops opened fire on us with bombs and bullets. One member of our group was shot in the foot and he fell down, pulling the rest of us down. We were all tangled up in the ropes and by now blood was flowing over us from shrapnel wounds. Bombs being detonated by the army exploded all around us; the rebels were running away. I cried, 'Jesus, please help us?' Miraculously, the rope attached to the injured man slipped undone and we managed to free ourselves. Although our feet were injured and bleeding, we began to run. If we ran to the soldiers, they would kill us, believing we were rebels, so we ran into the dark until exhausted. Hours later, I fell to the ground and slept.

"In the morning, I met some men making charcoal. They were startled and might have killed me. But I said softly, 'Please don't fear me! Please help me! I need to get to the hospital.' They borrowed a bicycle and carried me there."

Joel returned to work after his shrapnel wounds healed. Although he had a noticeable limp, he was able to supervise his building team and share his testimony of our all-powerful God who rescues those who love Him.

32

VISITORS

WAR-TORN UGANDA was not ranked as one of the world's top holiday destinations in the eighties and nineties, so it always surprised me when visitors chose to spend their annual holidays volunteering at Childcare.

In the early days of the work, many of our visitors were friends from C3 Church, Sydney—my home church for many years. Some came alone and others in pairs or larger groups. In 1998, a team from Sydney put on their spiritual suit of armour and visited Kitgum. They spent days teaching in the classrooms, helping the builders with the continuing construction of clinics, latrines and extra classroom blocks. They also enjoyed informal football matches and games with the children, blissfully unaware of the drama that was about to unfold.

One morning after breakfast, while our volunteers were happily assisting the project staff, a girl named Kevin turned up and begged to stay. For several years she had been the wife of a rebel commander, but had miraculously escaped and made her way to the CKS project site. She arrived battered and bruised, her legs and bare feet cut by thorns. After being given a wash and some food, she was able to rest.

The following evening, the whole community was panic-stricken and running frantically past the school grounds towards town. One villager, his eyes wide with terror, warned me, "Aunty, you had better run into town too. The rebels are coming for that young wife. You shouldn't have taken her in. They will kill you and abduct her again."

After hearing this, our visitors from Australia were aghast, wondering if they should flee into town. "Nah," I advised. "You don't need to run from the devil. We will be quite safe here. It's God's sanctuary. Proverbs tells us the wicked shall not enter the gates of the righteous; they will stand confused at their gates."

That evening, our nightly worship was cut short as everyone wanted to lock themselves in their rooms. Regrettably, our guest rooms were only partially constructed and the doors were not secure. This unnerved everyone.

Once the guests had gone to bed, I stood outside my caravan searching the heavens for some reassurance that we would be safe. Although I had displayed tremendous bravado with our guests, I did wonder if this was the night I was going to die. Stars glittered silently against the navy-blue sky. Wearily I entered my caravan, lit my candle and read from Leviticus 26:6: "You will lie down and no-one will make you afraid . . . the sword will not pass through your country."

Secure in God's Word, I blew out the candle and fell asleep—still wearing my boots, I might add. At midnight, I woke to the sound of an axe chopping through a wall. *Oh no, they are breaking into the dormitory,* I thought. As I lay there, my heart pounding, I wondered what I should do. Suddenly volleys of gunfire sounded. Then silence. Were the rebels outside my caravan?

Only silence.

I lay frozen but eventually drifted back to sleep.

At dawn's first light, I went into the dormitory block and knocked on the door of the room Kevin was in. She appeared dazed and pale among the other girls.

The girls gabbled excitedly.

"Aunty, we heard the rebels talking last night. They were confused and arguing. Some said, 'Let's get her now,' but others said, 'First we'll loot the market shop, get food, then pick her up on the way back.' The soldiers heard them smashing the market wall and started shooting, so they all ran away. But we fear that they will come back tonight."

"Kevin," I said, "catch the early bus to Kampala and stay there in my street boys' house until this war stops. Change your name to Patricia in case they follow you."

The visitors emerged from their rooms, their faces pale.

"How is your faith this morning?" I asked.

They hugged Kevin with relief and watched as I disguised her with a scarf, gave her the bus fare and hugged her goodbye. No doubt their faith had been tested and they would have a story to tell when they got back to Australia.

Patricia (formerly known as Kevin) went on to become house-mother to our forty street boys in Kampala. CKS sponsored her to do tailoring courses, and after five years she returned to Kitgum, married one of our teachers, and is now the proud mother of two. She is also a leader in CKS Community Church's women's group, teaching handicrafts.

❖ ❖ ❖

Another of our courageous visitors was Pam, a tall, blonde, 52-year-old artist, who made the long trip to the northern-most part of Uganda to spend several weeks volunteering with Childcare. We had met at a friend's house on the Northern

Beaches of Sydney while I was promoting child sponsorship. A short time later, she wrote and told me she was coming to stay.

Pam visited CKS several times. Her first visit was in 1997, at a time when the LRA were very active. Pam was the kind of person who liked to laugh and joke, but during her time at CKS I observed her joy disappear as the reality of the war sunk in. At night, after she had gone to bed in our guest quarters, at that time a tin shed, she would lie awake for hours paralysed with fear, listening to the relentless nightly drumming of local witch doctors.

The strain of staying in a war zone was clearly taking its toll, so to take our mind off the war I decided to take a week off so that I could travel with her to Bwindi National Park—home to the silverback gorillas.

The day before we left for our retreat, we drove to the IDP camp at Padibe to assess the living conditions of the Acholi people who had been displaced by war. As we walked through the camp and spoke with the women and children, we became painfully aware of their desperate fight for survival: women who were forced to make and sell their own illicit local brew to survive; young women who sold their bodies in exchange for food. Overwhelmed and a little disheartened, the staff and I left the camp discussing how we could start a new school in this area.

On our way back to the project site, I watched Pam's face blanch as we passed several burnt-out vehicles—cars and buses that had been ambushed by rebels with all occupants incinerated. She stared open-mouthed in disbelief at the charred remains. Although I was accustomed to seeing the rebels' calling card, Pam was not. She spent the entire night in her room fretting about our trip to Kampala the following day. At 4 a.m. I knocked on the metal door, with the words "Jesus is Lord" painted on it.

Knock, knock. "Pam, are you in there?"

No response.

Knock, knock.

Still no response.

I leaned in and spoke through the metal, reminding her we needed to leave quickly in order to avoid being spotted by the rebels who, at this time of the morning, would still be sleeping.

She opened the door hesitantly and peered with one eye through the crack.

"Irene, I don't think I can go," she said. "I am a nervous wreck and I haven't slept all night."

I looked through the gap into the dishevelled room and knew she was telling the truth. But time was ticking and the rebels would be stirring. I spent a few minutes reassuring her, and then loaded her suitcase onto our old army truck. We were on our way.

But minutes into our journey Pam began hyperventilating. Unfit to travel by road, I encouraged her to book a plane to Kampala from the local airstrip.

"It could take days," I advised. "But don't worry, Pam," I added, passing over her handbag and case, "God will get you there." And with that reassurance, we were off to Kampala, leaving Pam with the challenge of finding another way to the city.

That afternoon, after a hazardous twelve-hour trip through rebel territory, we arrived at the travel agency in Kampala and immediately called the CKS office for an update on Pam. No sooner had I picked up the phone and started dialling, than I heard a familiar voice behind me, "Hello there!" I turned around to see Pam grinning from ear to ear.

"You told me God would get me back, and here I am," she said, arms extended to demonstrate the enormity of the miracle. She told us that soon after we had left, she put her faith into action and prayed for a miracle flight out of Kitgum. Within minutes, she heard the distant hum of a plane engine, then looked up to see a Cessna single-engine fourteen-seat plane coming in to land at the airstrip. "Your staff took me to the field," she explained. "I found the pilot and begged him to take me to Kampala. And here I am! They even gave me a nice cold coke on board."

The following day, a tour guide picked us up at our Kampala home and drove us to Bwindi National Park.

After checking in to Pearl Lodge—a small white concrete building with a long verandah overlooking the jungle—we unpacked, sat on deckchairs and had a cup of tea. I was in heaven! After the first peaceful sleep we'd had in weeks, Pam joined the trek and came face to face with eight gorillas, while I sat on the verandah and read my Bible.

The following morning, I woke with a sense of anticipation. It was my turn. A small group of us tailed a tall, leathery-looking guide as he slashed his way through the dense foliage. Unlike the dryness of Kitgum, the national park was lush and green, with the smell of moisture in the air, not the smell of gunpowder. This trip was a welcome respite and so peaceful compared to the battle-zone we had left behind. Deep in the jungle, I was delighted to see several silverback gorillas happily munching on green leaves, oblivious to all my dramas.

The following day we packed up and headed to the Queen Elizabeth National Park. Observing the mating habits of lions—who looked like people wearing lion suits—was the tonic we needed to get us laughing and to refresh us for the journey back to Kitgum.

33

LIGHT IN THE DARKNESS

KITGUM, 1998-PRESENT

I'VE NEVER REALLY LIKED clichés and whenever possible have avoided using them. But there was one cliché that seemed to capture the essence of the season we had found ourselves in—every cloud has a silver lining.

Living in a war zone, watching the destruction of a community I loved deeply, the chinks of light peeking through the seemingly impermeable dark clouds of oppression were the miraculous stories that emerged.

One of these came unexpectedly.

Days before Pastor Faustino was due to take his first trip to Australia, his mother decided to deliver some gifts for his travels—home-produced peanut butter, some precious eggs and a chicken—gifts from a mother's heart to her only son, to wish him well.

The truck that would transport her to Kitgum stopped near her village, about sixty kilometres from Kitgum, and Nora was helped aboard and settled down atop bags of grain and drums of kerosene, alongside forty other passengers. Their truck led a convoy of five vehicles. Because of recurrent ambushes, they were anxious to reach Kitgum before nightfall.

Rattling up a narrow dirt road, the truck careered round a bend only to be confronted by the barrel of a rocket-propelled gun. It fired. Few saw it before they were hit by a ball of fire and metal that incinerated fourteen people on the spot and peeled the flesh from the faces and limbs of many others.

Nora cried out, "Jesus, save me!"

As the army brought in the corpses and the injured—those who were retrieved from the roadside—weeping and wailing filled Kitgum Town. Faustino examined each body to try and find his mother, without success. Meanwhile the wrecked truck, with passengers imprisoned in it, burnt for several days. With tears in his eyes, Pastor Faustino told his congregation that his mother's body must be one of those still burning in the wreckage. He planned to travel to the family village to hold a memorial service. I pressed $10 into his hand for the fare and said, "Don't look at the truck as you pass. She is not there."

On Sunday afternoon, with a heavy heart Faustino was packing his bag for Australia when a shadow fell across his doorway. His mother stood there in her best dress, glowing, without a scratch, a burn or even the smell of smoke.

"I made it son!" she exclaimed. "I'm sorry I lost the chicken and the peanut butter."

He watched, speechless, as she settled herself on a mat and went on to tell her story.

"As we were speeding along the road over every bump, I called out, 'Jesus, help me!' When the bomb hit us, fire was everywhere. I called out louder, 'Jesus, save me!' Although I was wedged in the middle of everything, God's arm reached down, pulled me up, and dropped me in the bush, right in the middle of the rebels. They took me to their commander who said to me, 'I see you are a woman of God. You'd better rest with us.' He gave me headache tablets, soap and $5. 'I don't want any of your things. I have my life in Jesus,' I told him. I spent a few nights there, and then they escorted me to the main road. My son, I am so happy to see you. Now you can go and enjoy Australia."

As Faustino told me this story, he said, "My mother should be called Abednego, because she survived the fire." At the time of writing, Nora is 93 years old and still living in the village with her grandsons looking after her. She isn't able to dig any more, but can still grind peanut paste and pray earnestly for the work of CKS.

✦ ✦ ✦

Another miraculous story was that of David Ocora.

David was one of our best students and lived with his grandmother in Kitgum Town. David was fed at our school, but his grandmother was starving. So one day, David rode his bike twenty kilometres to their sorghum field to harvest some food for her. He came across rebels squatting on the road, burying a land mine. The rebels saw him, broke his bike into pieces, tied David up with rope and took him to a large group hidden in the bush. There were 500 adult and 400 child soldiers. David's initiation was a severe beating across his chest, head and back with machetes and gun butts.

After the vicious assault, they dressed him in combat uniform and loaded him up with boxes of ammunition to carry on his back. For three weeks, he was forced to march for hundreds of kilometres into Sudan to collect ammunition and then bring it to Kitgum district. Several times, his group was required to ambush vehicles. One was a school bus. It was looted, burnt and many children were killed.

Weeks passed in a blur of hunger, beatings, exhaustion and religious indoctrinations. David's body was smeared with oil and incantations uttered that no bullet would touch him. He witnessed demonic power when a bomb landed in the middle of their prayer ceremony, sending splinters straight up into the sky.

David later told me: "When they pray over you and seal you into their army, they determine that if you ever escape, they will find you and kill you—even years later. They killed several adult escapees in front of our eyes. I was praying that God would help me to escape.

"One day, the rebels were trying to transfer ammunition and supplies across the river. People were struggling not to drown. When I reached the other side, I managed to get away and ran into the bush. I must have been about a hundred kilometres from Kitgum Town because I walked for two days before I found my grandmother's house. She was so happy to see me alive that she called the whole town to see me."

David re-joined our school and lived in our dormitory for a year. Sometimes he would sit and stare into the distance, perhaps reliving the horror of his experience, but his attention soon returned to the work at hand: his primary studies, the agricultural harvest, a soccer game or deciding which CKS vocational courses to pursue.

Every morning during worship, the presence of the Holy Spirit brought fresh healing to his wounded soul. His story reminded me of the Bible verse, "He delivered me from my strong enemy, from those who hated me, for they were too strong for me. They confronted me in the day of my calamity, But the LORD was my support. He also brought me out into a broad place; He delivered me because He delighted in me" (Ps. 18:17–19).

David's story, like many others, was testament to God's faithfulness in rescuing His servants from the clutches of the enemy.

◈ ◈ ◈

I believed in all sorts of miracles.

One day, our infant children were queuing for lunch, their faces eager with anticipation as they held out their bowls to receive a serving of *posho* and a ladleful of beans. For many waiting in line, this was the first meal of the day.

All of a sudden everyone scattered, as a pick-up charged across the fields towards them. Frightened children dropped their bowls on the ground as armed police leapt from their vehicle and stormed into the staff room. The District Inspector of Schools, a pudgy man in a dark blue suit, handed me a closing order for our primary school.

"You have failed to register as a private school. All children must leave the grounds immediately."

I was gobsmacked.

"But the children are having their lunch," I protested.

"Feed it to the pigs," he snarled.

"Did you have your breakfast?" I countered.

He motioned to the police official who advanced towards us, raising his gun.

"If you resist, I will put you in a cell. I want all the pupils assembled *now*!"

Buying myself a little time, I waved the registration papers in front of him and said, "Look, they're all ready. We were only waiting for your inspection report."

His bloodshot eyes glared at me.

"Too late, too late," he barked as he pushed me aside and strode to address the assembled school—1,500 confused and tearful children and twenty-five concerned teachers.

He began his tirade in Acholi, which the children later translated for me: "This school is closed. Every child must go and register with the government school before the census on Wednesday. Also, all teachers must register with government schools. You must leave immediately. Is that understood?"

A thin, gangly child feebly raised his arm. "Please sir, can we eat our lunch? We have nothing at home."

Unmoved by the request, the official simply said, "That is not my concern."

Inwardly I shook with rage as the officials made their hasty exit. But softly God whispered to me the words of Psalm 73:16 (NIV): "When I tried to understand all this, it troubled me deeply till I entered the sanctuary of God; then I understood their final destiny."

The next thing I knew, pandemonium had broken out. Plates of food were trampled underfoot. Spirits of rebellion and anger were gaining strength. Many students ran towards the gate. I headed them off, blocked their departure and, like rerouting a flooding river, directed them back into the assembly hall.

By the time I entered, the hall was an angry sea of hatred—many were being crushed and the noise was deafening. I clapped my hands and began to sing, like a puppet without any sound. In a faltering voice, I continued, "Jesus loves me . . ." I crossed my hands over my heart, "this I know . . ." pointing to my head, "for the Bible tells me so . . ." The noise began to subside as puzzled children stopped to gaze at me miming an old favourite I used to sing to them under the mango tree. I rocked my arms like a cradle: "Little ones to Him belong . . ." then dangling my arms, "they are weak . . . but He is strong." Thousands of little fists punched the air in victory: "Yes, Jesus loves me! Yes, Jesus loves me! Yes, Jesus loves me! The Bible tells me so." Without losing the beat, we moved into the school song "Victory in Jesus." The dear Holy Spirit transformed every heart, and pretty soon every face was shining with joy, leading into a time of praise and worship. Teachers crept in and were soon dancing and shouting to the Lord. A plea for the salvation of the officials was offered.

After several hours the children filed out. I saw their sad faces, heard their whispers, "Goodbye Aunty . . ."

I went into my caravan and cried.

A week passed and we were still waiting for the inspector's report to accompany the 400 documents needed by the education department in Kampala. I couldn't bear to see the pleading eyes of the children outside our fence. I could only give them into the Father's hands. Every morning the teachers prayed and sang in the assembly hall. As we began to sing and praise, the Lord gave us the victory. We eventually got our registration cleared for both primary and vocational training.

Once again the lunchtime queues were satisfied and the tailoring and typing classes were filled with beaming teenagers eager to learn and create for themselves a future and a hope. I learnt that no power, no force, nothing the devil can throw at us is stronger than the almighty power of the name of Jesus. This was yet another miracle.

❖   ❖   ❖

Sometimes our answers to prayer were more practical. In 1999 we were finally able to connect our first satellite phone/fax, which meant no more frustrations of isolation. By using the truck's cigarette lighter, I could call Australia on Mondays and Tuesdays. Now *that* was a miracle!

34

A FUTURE AND A HOPE

KITGUM, 1999

THEY HAD ONCE SAT under the shade of a mango tree dressed in ragged clothes, looking at me and scratching their itchy heads riddled with lice. Seven years on, these same children stood tall, dressed in crisp uniforms, proudly accepting their P7 graduation certificates. These were the first of our students to graduate from primary school—forty-nine in total.

It was an emotional time for me and for our teachers as we watched each child step forward in morning assembly, faces beaming as they received a piece of paper recognising their achievements. Against all the odds—cramped living conditions in small, dark mud huts, interrupted sleep on thin papyrus floor mats, and homework completed under a dim kerosene lamp on a dirt floor—they had graduated. As elated as I was, I couldn't help but think, *what now*?

While some young people would be lucky enough to go to secondary school, many would simply go back to their villages and face a hopeless future. Boys might become petty thieves and sit in video halls watching violent films—an unhealthy outlet for the anger and frustration they felt inside. Others might run bicycle taxis and never progress beyond that. Young girls with no occupational skills might end up as house girls, then concubines, sharing the few available men and risking AIDS.

God spoke to me about building a vocational training centre that would be the first private vocational school in our district.

Even before the purpose-built structure was complete, we had enrolled seventy pupils who were studying office skills, dress-making, carpentry and bricklaying in temporary classrooms. Having our own building would enable us to accept and to train many more young people for their future. When opening day arrived, we were expecting thirty new students to enrol, but were stunned when 300 young people showed up. As the only voca-tional school in Kitgum, we offered to train them in skills that would ensure them jobs in the district when they graduated. The students themselves excelled, and today we have many stories of student success.

The vocational training centre has continued to grow in strength and momentum. I thank God when I think about our students who were once recruited to the devil's army, forced to carry guns and machetes and participate in unimaginable cru-elty, and who are now conscripted to God's army. Armed with hammers and drills, a new generation of Ugandans are taking their skills and passion for Jesus and using them to rebuild north-ern Uganda.

35

HIS BANNER OVER ME

KITGUM, 2000

WHEN I AWOKE six years earlier clutching the tear-stained divorce letter from my husband, I was terrified. Here I was in my fifties, in the back-blocks of Africa with no family, no home and without any creature comforts. I was living in the middle of a barren, drought-stricken landscape, surrounded by thousands of desperate, sick and hungry orphans who were traumatised by war. Naturally speaking, the situation was pitifully hopeless. But for the grace of God I could have despaired at each new crisis.

At times I was emotionally needy—a legacy of my traumatic childhood. Nevertheless, I knew the old foe of rejection had been covered by the blood of Jesus. As I sought comfort in scripture, God revealed His intimate love letters to me. He showed me through Hosea 2:14 that it was His plan to bring me into the wilderness; that I would learn to sing there as in the days of my youth. Through Isaiah 62, He told me that I would no longer be called "deserted." He gave me a new name "Hephzibah," which means God's delight, God's pleasure, God's valuable one. In Isaiah 54:5 God convinced me that He was and will always be my husband, my champion—the one who would fight for me and who will love me unconditionally. So I embraced God as my husband.

One night, He gave me a beautiful dream:

I was led into a garden and delighted by its beauty. An arbour with smooth white limbs like snow gums arched overhead, heavy with delicate creamy pink flowers. Their petals fluttered down onto a carpet of pale green moss underfoot.

A soft breeze wafted a heady perfume over me. A fragrance unlike anything on earth, but so real it filled all my senses as I breathed. Pale yellow canaries sang with bursts of joy in the blossoms overhead. Some swooped down to bathe and preen in a small fountain, whose droplets sparkled with a myriad of colours.

Nearby, two large saucer-shaped chairs carved from mother of pearl shells and cushioned with pink velvet beckoned. Beside them a low table was set with plates of food and crystal goblets that tinkled in the breeze. I removed the covers from the food to find the most delicious fare. It was a setting for a bridal couple.

I looked around for my sweetheart. Shafts of sunlight shimmered through the branches arching overhead. I heard the call of a courting bowerbird on his joyful flight in search of treasures for his lady.

I heard my husband whisper, "Yes, our garden is filled with gifts I've hidden to surprise you."

A dewdrop sparkling within a petal was a diamond ring.

When I rested on a cushion, the fountain rose higher. When I moved, the water spiralled gently. Beneath my cushion was a dress of embroidered pale pink silk.

Again I heard my husband whisper, "This is where you wait for me when the days are grey. I will allure you. I have drawn you to me with loving-kindness. You are mine."

I woke from the dream ecstatic. All around, the African bush buzzed with insects and villagers sleeping fitfully. But I had breathed the fragrance of heaven. I had seen the mansion that my Sweetheart was preparing for me, full of unimaginable treasures. He had shown me my place of waiting for Him.

The line from Song of Solomon 2:16 leapt to mind: "My beloved is mine and I am his."

I was often lonely in my double bed, so I wrote those words in fluorescent chalk above my bed on the ceiling. They comforted me as I lay there reading them in the dark, never imagining that one day the words would save my life.

❖   ❖   ❖

A gang of armed thugs dressed in khaki began terrorising Kitgum Town every weekend. One Saturday, they strangled the local gas station guard because he wouldn't give them money. The following Saturday it was my turn.

I slept soundly until 2 a.m., when I was woken by the sound of keys rattling in the lock of my caravan door. I looked out of the small window and gasped to see nine armed men in my caravan annex. It looked like a scene from a Rambo movie: cartridges around their necks, AK-47 rifles and bayonets pointed, machetes and logs of wood raised. Seeing my face at the window, one snarled, "Open the door. Give me the money."

Unprotected and alone in the deserted school grounds, I could only scream. Their gun barrels began smashing through the windows. Horrified, I watched their heavy leather boots kicking in the aluminium door. They tore it from its hinges and threw it across the compound. Then all nine men crowded into my tiny room and pushed me onto the bed. They roared at me in Swahili.

As I lay there, my heart pounding, I thought, *I'm not going to get out of this alive.*

As I looked upwards, gun barrels, bayonets and demonic faces filled my vision. But above their heads on the ceiling, above the scowling faces, were those words from the Bible, "My beloved is mine and I am his."

A righteous anger filled me. How dare they intimidate me like this!

I sat up and pushed them away as I commanded, "Don't touch me. I belong to God. If you touch me, God will get you!"

They all leapt backwards, as if I had hit them with a blow torch. Their leader picked up my small bag and shouted, "Let's go!"

And then I was left alone in my caravan.

I pulled the bed covers over my shoulders and whimpered, "What sort of husband are You Jesus? I feel neglected and defeated."

God interrupted me: "Stop complaining Irene—not a hair on your head has been harmed."

"Hmm," I continued. "Well, Lord, I need something to comfort me."

I expected something amazing like a gold angel to appear, but I only heard His still, small voice, "Read Psalm 94."

I lit my candle and began to read. When I came to verse 17, my blood ran cold: "Unless the LORD had given me help, I would soon have dwelt in the silence of death."

Then Psalm 94 (NIV) continued, "When anxiety was great within me, Your consolation brought me joy . . . the LORD has become my fortress, and my God the rock in whom I take refuge. He will repay them for their sins and destroy them for their wickedness."

"Hmm," I mused. "How are You going to do that Lord? They are long gone."

The next day, one of the gang members entered the town of Lira in an attempt to sell my video camera, which was inside the stolen bag. As the potential buyer pressed the play button, the screen lit up with the children and me singing, "Jesus Never Fails." The buyer reported the stolen video camera, the gang were imprisoned and their reign of terror ended. The following Monday I paid my staff's wages from the $8,000 cash that had been piled up next to my pillow throughout the whole incident. God had been faithful to His promise in Psalm 94 and I learnt a valuable lesson.

36

GIDEON'S ARMY

KITGUM, 2001

MY CARAVAN OFFICE was always central to our school, which was growing exponentially. By day I was surrounded by 2,500 rescued children who were such a joy to see, running, laughing and skipping to the water borehole with basins and soap for bathing. From my office I could hear the shrieks of the children, I could see ducks waddling past on parade, goats and sheep that often nuzzled my dishes looking for some water, and turkeys strutting by fluffing their tail feathers. It was quite a spectacle and it was often hard to concentrate on all my paperwork.

Late afternoon, with the sun still blazing, a prefect would clang a metal rod against a wheel hub suspended from a tree and children would rush from their classrooms. I had trained them to exit in single file, fingers on their hushed lips, but the call of freedom was always too great. Freedom to escape the intensity of the classroom and splash in the soupy river, dig the sweet fertile soil of their *sambas*, stalk small birds with a catapult for supper, or collect firewood and jerry cans of water. Others would just play during the remaining two and a half hours of precious daylight.

By 7 p.m., when darkness fell, the scene was not so joyous. Outside, the road leading past our project site into town was crowded with small children balancing bundles of their worldly goods on their heads, all walking into Kitgum Town to find a sleeping place underneath the market tables, out of sight of rebels and thugs prowling through the villages. For nearly eight years, this bizarre migration of children between the ages of 9 and 16— later dubbed the "night commuters"—trudged into town each evening seeking safety from the rebels.

But town centres were not safe. Stories surfaced of harassment by armed men, rape and molestation. Returning from my evening walk, I would try and give a nightly blessing to these thin children, laden with pitiful possessions, emerging and then melting into the dark night. "Good night darlings, bless you as you sleep," I would say to them, trying to sound cheery. But inside, my grandmother-heart was breaking, as I remembered my own grandchildren's night-time ritual of sudsy baths, warm pyjamas, a good supper, a bedtime story and prayer. With lullabies unsung and Bible stories unheard, their white teeth flashed in the dark as they appreciated my night-time greeting—small comfort for the long, cold night that lay ahead of them, sleeping on the ground beneath a bamboo market table. I wanted to take them all in, but was warned that I would be putting all our resident orphans at risk if I did. I resented the families of the perpetrators of this war, who slept in peace while thousands of innocent victims suffered.

❖ ❖ ❖

One night, I studied the fields. Cloaked with black shadows, they were a hiding place for beasts and demons. Defiantly I declared "You will lie down and no-one will make you afraid . . . the sword will not pass through your country" (Lev. 26:6 NIV), and then hastily retreated into my caravan, which at the time was isolated in a deserted school yard. I searched for some matches and lit a candle. I preferred it to the kerosene lamp whose fumes made me sleepy. Weary from the day's work, I tried to connect with God. Writing down paraphrases of the Psalms was always comforting, but my candle melted faster than I could write. I remembered an old hint and that was to put the candle in the fridge before use. Of course, if I'd had electricity for a fridge, I would also have had a light switch and light bulb, but quotes for electricity connection from town had risen to $30,000. It wasn't going to happen anytime soon. I uttered my final prayer before getting into bed: "Father God, these children are Your creation. Protect them with Your armies. Give substance to their hopes and let them grow to the full potential You have planned for them."

At 3 a.m. a strange bump outside woke me.

As I lay there in the darkness, my heart thumping, I began to pray in tongues. A few minutes later I heard a scratching at my window. By now my eyes were wide open with fear, as a blood-curdling howl filled my ears. I looked through the window to see two wild dogs scampering away.

Well this is my last night sleeping here! I thought to myself as I pulled the covers over my head.

The next night I moved in to the concrete dormitory that we had built in 1999 to accommodate resident orphans. For a while, it was safer. Myriad stars glittered across the canopy of night, which hid the evil schemes of the desperate rebels. With a last gaze at the handiwork of God, which in other parts of the world would enchant, I closed my caravan door and walked swiftly across the dusty ground to the dormitory, slipping silently into a dark vacant room.

Denied the luxury of lamplight, which might pinpoint my whereabouts, I lay down on an iron bed and soon drifted into sleep. Several hours later, the sound of breaking glass shot me to my feet. I lit a match and looked at my watch—I could see that it was 2 a.m. I dressed hurriedly and peered through the cracks of the wooden shutter. Torch lights flickered in and around my caravan, then I heard men's voices. One of the voices was that of Robert, a visitor from Australia, who had decided to confront the thugs.

"What are you doing? What do you want? Go away, we do not want you here!"

I heard them reply, "We want Aunty Irene, now get back!" They advanced towards him and shouted once more, "Get back into your room!"

Holding a machete, the largest man moved towards Robert. Another man bent down and hurled a brick at him, which landed with a thud close to his feet. Retreating inside, Robert locked his door and prayed. The thieves stormed the verandah and battered down one of the twelve doors. I could hear their harsh demands.

"We want Aunty Irene. Where's Aunty Irene?"

A small boy, one of my residents, was whimpering, "Please forgive me. I don't know where she is."

Next, I heard the sound of furniture being overturned and then the next dormitory door was battered down. I slid to the floor and hid under a desk, desperately praying in tongues. *Surely, Lord; You hide me in Your sanctuary in the time of trouble*, were the words of my heart. Disgusted by my cowardice, I stood back up again, rose to my full height and said to myself, *I will go down fighting*. But as I put my hand on the door knob, God said, "No. Stay where you are Irene." I heard more furniture being overturned and then silence. Moments later, fists were thumping on a door. I could tell they were getting closer to my room. More thumping. *Dear God, remember us Your children. Can You see us under the blood of Jesus? Please don't let the enemy kill us.*

I strained my eyes to see along the shadowy verandah.

All of a sudden, huge floodlights beamed down from above, sweeping across the compound. A voice from a loudspeaker boomed, "You are surrounded. You must surrender." The loudspeaker blasted out a warning siren, followed by deafening staccato bleeping. Floodlights criss-crossed the compound and the fields. I looked up expecting to see a helicopter, but instead saw the shadows of five men running down into the field. Then silence.

One by one the children crept out like mice whispering, "What was that?"

Minutes later I heard David's voice, "You can come out now, they have gone."

He explained what had just happened, "Your boy, Willie Opoka, ran barefoot all the way to town after he heard the thugs breaking into your caravan. So we carried my portable floodlights and megaphone up the hill and along the ridge until we could cover your place. Then we ran down the hillside in gumboots. I hope we sounded like the army."

"Like Gideon's army," one child added.

"Thank You, Father God, that we are all safe," I said. "Now we can go back to sleep."

The next day someone overhead the village locals saying, "You don't mess with Aunty Irene, she is a white witch. She has the power to make a big noise and make lights come down out of the sky." I prayed they would understand, as all the children did, that the only power we have is because of our blood brother, Jesus. The red shirts of our school uniform were like powerful spots of His blood, as the children dispersed each afternoon to their surrounding villages telling their relatives stories of victories through Jesus.

37

LESSONS IN
THE DARKNESS

KITGUM, 2002

HOT DUSTY WINDS blew across the scorched playground as gravelly dirt invaded everywhere. My Bible was full of dust. My clothes were scratchy with grit. My hair was stiff and sand stuck to my sunblock. I chewed dust every time I ate.

"What did I do?" I complained to God. "What a terrible place this is. Why do You keep me here God? Can't You get someone else to stay in Kitgum and let me do office work in Kampala?"

Did God answer me? No. He was watching and waiting.

I noted the children's condition had deteriorated over the summer "drought" holiday—their bodies were thin and their red T-shirts were in rags.

As the new school term began in January 2002, the assembly hall was once again filled with suffering humanity. One by one they arrived: people on crutches and others bandaged. Leathery grandmothers sat outside in the dust and waited; brazen women wearing hard-won jewellery pushed their children to the front. All were waiting for their children's names to be registered. As usual, more children registered than we anticipated. On our first day, 2,000 new hopefuls applied! Unwilling to send anyone away, I considered holiday classes under the trees.

A week later, applicants for the vocational training classes also crowded into the assembly hall—400 applied for 60 places. These were fine young people—many of them former child soldiers who were desperate to escape the horrors of their past. It was impossible to leave them to a future without Jesus, without training, without hope. God gave me the idea of holding half-day classes to absorb most of the youth.

Although I felt overwhelmed by the increasing need, I walked around the project site heartened to see the many familiar faces—children and youth who greeted me with huge smiles and sticky handshakes, eager to begin studying for a future outside their troubled villages. Many would tell me they were saddened by the disintegration of village life. After years of war and having to live in "protected people's camps" the fabric of Acholi life, which once revolved around communal respect and honour for elders, had been reduced to cruel indignity.

Destitute widows were now selling their bodies for a pittance in order to buy salt or soap or for any trinket that would cause their thin, pale children to smile. Unaware of the resources they had available to them from their heavenly Father, they used their own means to survive. Most huts in the district were filled with the sickly smell of fermenting peelings or corn sprouts, which became a poisonous "brew," numbing enough to transport the few remaining men into a temporary oblivion where the "Why?" questions were silenced. Receiving the brew as payment for digging fields, building huts and other manual work had resulted in a population of inebriated adults attacking each other viciously. Children would watch and learn that anger and violence is the normal response to injustice. We had come so far, and I was determined not to let the devil rob this region any more.

In our bid to change the spiritual landscape, we prayed. Every Tuesday, the children would fast from their breakfast and earnestly pray for their unsaved and sometimes drunk and violent relatives. It was such a humbling experience to see a child pound the wall, crying for their mother and siblings, and then to see another child raise their arms to heaven, tears pouring down their cheeks, before dropping to their knees with their head on the dusty ground and pleading with God. Many times I cried also, because I believed these children knew God better than I did. Stripped of everything, God was their only hope. They prayed for their older siblings—those teens who had lost both parents and who now carried the weight of family expectations. I saw many teenagers seek oblivion in each other's arms during long, dark nights. For some, having a baby was a distraction from the relentless slog of simply surviving.

Despite the undercurrent of hopelessness that existed, we persevered throughout the year, teaching these children and teenagers, whenever we had the opportunity, that they were precious and that God had a plan and purpose for their lives.

As the September school holidays approached, I had a sense of foreboding. I knew that most of our children would be visiting family in remote villages during the break, which often turned into a time of hunger, sickness and fear. Nevertheless, these red-shirted children were tiny messengers of Jesus in a battle-scarred land.

It was as I suspected, when the children again returned from their holidays their condition had deteriorated and a spirit of fear had crept in. They fought in the food lines, requiring the cooks to increase the quantities to feed almost 3,000 hungry children daily.

Outside the project centre, tanks began moving through town—ancient ugly tanks with their barrels swinging around wildly, depressing signs of war ready to escalate at any time. At night I tried to pray, but the sound of tanks growling through the darkness stopped me praying. I could only complain, "Now everyone's lives will be disrupted. I'm not ready for war again. What a terrible place. Take me home, Jesus."

Our generator kept blowing up.

Staff were absent because relatives were dying.

I was fighting the builders because of unsafe buildings, fighting the cooks for wasting precious firewood, and fighting the stress of being crushed beneath an avalanche of requests for assistance.

Then I got sick.

As I thrashed around in pain, my ears could dimly hear the school children shrieking and running outside as they enjoyed their lunch break. This malaria attack was too stubborn. I looked at the cross of our beautiful Jesus who two millennia ago bore our pain.

Through weary eyes I saw God's minister Lois Ford, a missionary to Sudan, heading purposefully across the school grounds to my caravan. With troops gathering on the Sudan border, she had been turned back to Kitgum. Her gentle voice was balm to my soul.

"I'd better take you in for tests," she said.

An hour later, the trainee doctor confirmed typhoid. He dispensed a course of huge "horse tablets" and warned me that the treatment can be as dangerous as the sickness. Over the following week, the symptoms abated, but my heart started having violent spasms which frightened me.

One night I sat in the darkness barely able to breathe, with my heart shuddering—I thought I was going to die. But I was not ready; there was still so much to do. I called out to God, "Because I care for the poor, You God will preserve my life from danger. You will raise me from my sick bed" (from Psalm 41). Then I added, "But God . . . why does my service have to be in this contagious, disgusting place?" In my mind I was thinking, "The moment God takes His hands off this work I am out of here and back to Australia." It was getting too hard.

In the dark He spoke into my heart, "My child, My soldiers should not despise their commission. If you want to dwell in the deepest place of God and if you want to sit with Jesus on His throne of love, you will not be there alone. You will be in the company of the unlovable, the despised, the diseased, the dirty and the despairing—all the casualties of Satan's war against God's precious humanity. That's where My heart is. The heart of God is not always reached by preaching from a flower-filled platform or singing love songs to Me into a microphone in front of a beautiful congregation. Whatever you do for the least of these brothers and sisters, you do for Me. When you neglect them, you neglect Me."

Still I brooded and fretted and continued to complain to God, "How much longer in this uncomfortable, inconvenient place?"

His voice was soft, "Patience, My beloved. Just a few more precious wounded to be rescued then, in the twinkling of an eye we will be taking our seats at the grandest feasting table. The angels are preparing the wedding feast now."

My heart was filled with joy. He had come down to visit me in the darkness. What a privilege. What a royal commission. Whatever came from that point onwards, I knew that I was vitally involved in the interests of God's heart. I read scriptures that reinforced this: "Whoever listens to me will live in safety and be at ease, without fear of harm" (Proverbs 1:33 NIV); "Great peace have those who love Your law, and nothing can make them stumble" (Psalm 119:165 NIV); "You will fill me with joy in Your presence, with eternal pleasures at Your right hand" (Psalm 16:11 NIV).

For the time I remained bedridden, God's Holy Spirit taught me some crucial strategies for dealing with the challenges that were to come. These were strategies I now planned to broadcast to the whole of northern Uganda.

38

PROCLAIM THE LORD

KITGUM, 2002

MY OLD CASSETTE PLAYER often spoilt my mornings. Too leanly fed from a boiled-up solar battery, my precious worship tapes and teaching tapes—my "heart starters" for the day—were being s-t-r-e-t-c-h-e-d and scrunched and chewed.

By the middle of 2002, after a season of whinging to God, something was different. The world seemed brightly coloured: the sky was a clear sapphire blue; the earth's rusty ochre was flanked by grass stubble that was golden and glowing.

As I flicked the switch on my radio and turned the dial to Peace FM radio, God's music blasted out. This was Kitgum's newest radio station—a humble operation that began with a vision, much prayer and the support of two Australian businessmen. It meant that I could feast on every style of worship from Hillsong to Carmen, German nuns' choirs to cellos—a veritable smorgasbord of spiritual food. Now we were able to spread the message of Jesus Christ through beautiful Christian music and preaching.

On this particular morning, the heavens and the *sambas* echoed with a song from Hillsong Australia. I turned up the volume and smiled as I thought back to discussions with our manager, David Livingstone, two years earlier, when Peace FM was just an idea that had been planted in our hearts at a time when no other Christian FM stations existed in Kitgum. Occasionally I would pick up news reports on the BBC via satellite, but nothing on the airwaves that was going to change the spiritual landscape of a country sinking deeper into a sea of misery.

Every day I heard heartbreaking stories of despairing mothers in IDP camps who were committing suicide because of the sheer hopelessness they felt in not being able to provide for their children. David and I would often talk about a more efficient way of reaching them with the good news of Jesus Christ. With 80 percent of the population either owning or having access to a transistor, radio broadcasting seemed to be the most effective medium. At a cost of 12,000 Ugandan Shillings ($6), transistor radios were both affordable for those who lived in chronic poverty, and a distraction from the drudgery of everyday survival. After months of prayer, and with equipment donated by an Australian who had prior experience in establishing radio stations in the Congo, we launched Peace FM. It began humbly in David's backyard with a transistor, antenna, console and two microphones. Several years later, we built a multistorey building on a hill overlooking David's home.

Over time, the radio changed the spiritual climate throughout the Kitgum district of half a million people. In the mechanics' and welders' workshops in town, young men worked to Christian music. In fields, as villagers stacked handmade brick into kilns, God's words and music lightened their work and soothed their spirits. Every workshop, market, and compound in Kitgum reverberated with voices worshipping or preaching the word of God.

At night in my caravan, when I was tempted to feel sorry for myself or grumble and complain about being without a husband, missing my family or not having enough resources to meet the growing needs of the children, I'd tune in the radio to Peace FM and allow myself to be encouraged and strengthened by the preaching and the worship. I can remember one evening, sitting in my caravan annex looking up into the coal-black sky pierced with glittering stars. In the background, the heavy drumming of a witch doctor disturbed the peaceful brilliance of God's handiwork. He beat an empty gourd with a wire brush, and his frenzy increased as he called all in the vicinity to come and watch the devil's entertainment. But no-one was responding. Looking around the project site, crowds of young people would briefly glance across the fields in his direction, then huddle in a circle around a tiny radio. The drumming would grow dim as Pastor David's gentle voice touched every heart. "I have been where you are," he'd say. "I, too, have buried loved ones. Together we have survived to reach this moment, and together we will go on. I give thanks to God for this blessing to the community of Kitgum. Let's close our eyes and thank him together . . . Now let us pray for those who are hurting . . . children who need school fees . . ."

More effective than a crusade, more far-reaching than pastors on bicycles, more compelling than books, the preaching by Pastor David five times a week encouraged, taught, corrected, and began to wear down rebellion and superstition with the power of the word of God.

And then as the moon set at 11 p.m., Pastor David would close down for the evening: "I know you've enjoyed your day with Peace FM Christian Radio. We are bringing you the best in worship and preaching from all around the world, as well as in our local dialect. We are a no-compromise Christian radio station believing in the blood covenant we have with Jesus Christ. Not the blood of goats or chickens, but the all-powerful, all-protecting blood of Jesus Christ. Knowing this, I pray God's protection over all our listeners as we rest tonight. God bless you and goodnight."

Each night in my caravan, I would say "Amen" to that, blow out my candle and curl up for the best night's sleep in years. When the power of Jesus' protective blood has been proclaimed over the district, who could challenge it? Of course, the devil thought he'd try.

❖   ❖   ❖

One night, I noted the spirit of fear weighing heavily over Kitgum district, which had been fuelled by the ongoing reports of killing and rebel activity. We even heard reports that the rebels were coming to blow up our radio station. As the usual exodus of "night commuters" began, dense black clouds rolled in to add to their misery.

Unexpectedly, there was a volley of shots.

The procession broke up and charged along the road. Police and army tore off their uniforms to avoid detection. I was proud of my dormitory girls, who continued to sing their evening worship songs. However, they did end up cutting them short to lock themselves in their rooms. The storm passed over without rain, but the menacing darkness continued to descend over everyone like a shroud. The stench of evil was tangible. I turned my radio on, but only got static.

Meanwhile, half a kilometre away in his house, Pastor David was restless.

"This waiting . . . this silence," he said to his wife, Cathy. "The rebels wanted to preach on radio! No way! We've got the radio and I'm going to preach."

Cathy looked at their sleeping baby named Peace and murmured, "David, please don't bring trouble to our home."

David hurried into the black night and kick-started the generator. He opened the radio studio, sat down and pulled the microphone close.

"Good evening, listeners. I love you so much and God loves you so much. We have nothing to fear except the spirit of fear, and right now I bind it in chains with the full authority of Jesus Christ. I command the spirit of fear to leave the district. Now listeners, we'll have some music and I'll be back to read God's word to you."

Before the first song finished the mood of the district began to change.

I could hear movement inside the dormitories as, one by one, our young people turned up their radios.

David began preaching. "It's times like these that our God wants to show that His strength and protection is there for His children. The battle is the Lord's. Peace doesn't come through the barrel of a gun. We won't find peace either by running everywhere, carrying our possessions. How far can you run away from death? People are getting hurt, falling over in the dark. When God is living inside you, where are you taking Him?

"In the time of Moses they had a similar problem. Know what God told them to do? He told them to stop being afraid, to stand still, look, and see the rescue of the Lord which He would bring about that day. He will fight for you, and you will know peace. Let's hear what Psalm 27 says in the NIV translation: 'The LORD is my light and my salvation—whom shall I fear? The LORD is the stronghold of my life—of whom shall I be afraid? . . . Though an army besiege me, my heart will not fear; though war break out against me, even then I will be confident.'"

He continued reading, ". . . I remain confident of this: I will see the goodness of the LORD in the land of the living. Wait for the LORD; be strong and take heart and wait for the LORD."

For several hours David read the Psalms, piercing the fear-filled silence of Kitgum district and depositing the living word of God into almost half a million trembling hearts. By the time he got to Psalm 64, where God Himself promises He will shoot the enemy down, the dark oppression had lifted and thousands of God's children prayed "Amen" and slept soundly.

The radio continued to deliver a powerful message of hope.

In October, 2007, we started building another radio station on a hill overlooking the CKS project site. This station was called Mighty Fire FM, which today transmits the good news throughout northern Uganda and southern Sudan, and has more than a million listeners.

We were taking some serious ground. But the enemy was not going to give up without a fight.

39

CONFUSION
IN THEIR MIDST

KITGUM, 2002

NEWSPAPER HEADLINES blared out their warning as I stepped off the plane at Entebbe, after a much-needed break in Australia. With the resurgence of war, 2002 had been a traumatic year.

Memories of a refreshing holiday alongside Sydney's sparkling waters and calmed by the love of my family and church soon faded as the seriousness of the situation in northern Uganda became apparent.

Several months earlier, Sudan had invited the Ugandan army across their borders to fight the rebels in Sudan's mountain hideouts. The army was decimated when it met Joseph Kony's rebel LRA, who were equipped with the most advanced weapons of war. Now the LRA were on their way back; the terror was about to resume. Reports had claimed that over the past four months, sixty soldier casualties a day were being carried back into Uganda, either dead or dying. Kitgum was without defence.

On the road back from the airport I took a deep breath, saluted the General of the Armies of Heaven and set out on the long trip back to Kitgum, ready to get back to work. David Livingstone had come to pick me up and was determined to reach his home before nightfall. Another courageous fellow traveller was my grandson, Jay, who had chosen to give further purpose to his life by spending some time in Kitgum helping locals by sharing with them his electrical and mechanical skills.

We drove for several hours through the banana plantations that skirted Kampala and past bamboo market stalls selling piles of tomatoes, cakes and dried fish, until we reached the army checkpoint at Karuma Bridge. They waved us on. Below the bridge, the mighty Nile River thundered over rock shelves as it raised unbridled white plumes on its long passage to the Mediterranean Sea.

As the car climbed the hill on the other side, my grandson was mesmerised by the dog-faced baboons that came alongside the car, begging for bananas. Mother baboons sat in the shade, warily shielding their infants. It was a momentary distraction from the fact that we had now entered rebel territory.

An army barracks built of grass houses looked deserted. It had been attacked a week earlier. We passed two burnt-out vehicle shells.

"When did that happen?" I asked David.

"Two days ago," he answered.

An oncoming vehicle swerved to a stop in front of us. David and the driver conversed in Swahili.

"What did he say?" I asked.

David focused his eyes ahead, put his foot down hard on the accelerator and muttered above the roaring engine, "Two ambushes today."

I could see he was in no mood to chat. I held on to the words of John 19:11, that the devil has no power except that which God allows him.

Approaching a large trading centre, we were flagged down by an old man. He was a traditional elder who had been in talks with the rebels. He handed David a handwritten letter from the rebels addressed to the manager of our radio station. It contained accusations of partiality towards the government and threats against the radio staff and station. What was more disturbing was that our car and travel plans were obviously common knowledge. We still had a long way to go.

Stopping for diesel in Gulu, the authorities warned us not to go any further. The day before, an armoured vehicle loaded with soldiers and rocket-propelled guns had been ambushed on the road to Kitgum. The whole truck exploded in an inferno. In light of this advice, I suggested we stop for soda and think about our options.

Undeterred by my concerns, David retorted, "We're leaving now!"

With that, we continued our journey, bouncing over potholes and leaving clouds of red dust in our wake. Our eyes strained towards the forest on either side. No-one spoke.

Suddenly, the ashy skeleton of the army truck loomed in the centre of the road, blocking our way. Wisps of smoke drifted upwards from the incinerated troop carrier. As we drove past, tipping sideways into a ditch alongside it, I could picture in my mind the cries of the passengers just twenty-four hours earlier. But I was confident that this was not my day of departure. Carrying the Holy Spirit within me meant that I could not be snuffed out at the whim of the enemy. My exit day would be by royal decree, because I serve the Sovereign God and His purposes.

A man darted across the road in front of us. David told us that it was the rebels' informant. If we'd had an army officer in the car, they'd be waiting for us further on.

As the long dirt road stretched out behind us, our tension eased. Eventually we reached the Lacekecot army checkpoint where a heavy tree was blocking the road. On the other side, the bus from Kitgum had been stopped and was waiting for clearance. At first, the army commander didn't want anyone to proceed but we assured him we had made it through and it was now safe. One of our staff members, John Paul, waved to us from the bus windows. They had been delayed for two and a half hours. It was 1.30 p.m. and he still had ten hours' travel to reach Kampala for a dental appointment. As we waited, I told a Muslim soldier who was standing on the side of the road all about Jesus. I said to him, "If you're in danger, call out to Jesus." He smiled and said, "Yes, I believe in Him," and waved us on. Later we heard that the barracks had been attacked by rebels. Many soldiers had been killed and injured. I wondered if I'd meet the Muslim solider in heaven.

We arrived back at the project site, had supper with the children and went to bed.

At midnight I woke to the sound of splintering wood as rebels kicked in doors along the road outside the project centre. Smoke billowed as fifteen thatched roofs were set alight. Terrified children spilt out. They were roped together and dragged off into the darkness. Anyone who whimpered was clubbed. Three young men were axed to death.

Eventually the army was alerted to the kidnappings, and so began a barrage of bombs and gunfire. Brick walls and wooden doors do not stop bullets, so I lay on the edge on my bed praying in tongues. My grandson, Jay, who was sleeping in the same room hissed at me in the dark, "Shh Grandma, they'll hear you!" I prayed even louder. I was not going to give the devil any ground. I fell into a fitful sleep, while my heart continued to plead with God on behalf of His precious children.

At dawn we checked and were relieved to find that all of our resident children and adults were intact. However, our empty gatekeeper's house had been shot through eight times. This was the only damage God had allowed. A child from the district who had escaped the clutches of the rebels told me what they had said to her: "We're going to Aunty Irene's. We want her solar panels." The child warned them, "Her place is full of soldiers." But by this time they were at my gate. "Is that where they hide?" they barked, spraying the gatekeeper's shed with bullets. Normally they would have entered. Certainly they would have looted the vocational training centre. I imagined that God had terrified them with soldier angels. God is great!

Around 7.30 a.m., weary children gathered in the assembly hall. Their teachers stood next to them solemn and tired. When I entered the assembly hall with Jay they cheered and applauded. God's family had survived the night and we were together again. As I read them the prayer of Jehoshaphat in 2 Chronicles 20, where his community was also under attack from armies too big for them, the children joined me in praying, "We have no power to face this vast army that is attacking us. We do not know what to do, but our eyes are on You, God."

I called three song leaders out and we praised and worshipped our God, confident that He was setting ambushes against the enemy and causing confusion in their midst. We wrote on a giant piece of paper the names of the sixteen CKS children who had been abducted and earnestly prayed for them. Days after our prayer, fourteen escaped and gave great testimonies to the rescuing power of their Father God.

40

LET GOD ARISE

KITGUM, 2002

I WAS EDUCATING, feeding and providing medical care to thousands of children daily and now God was asking me to do something else—visit the local hospital.

I questioned God. I told Him I thought I'd done enough, but He responded by showing me that the hospital was "the devil's playground" and that I needed to take God's presence to those who were without hope. And so I obeyed.

The first few weeks of my hospital ministry were extremely challenging. I would stand at the doorway looking at Satan's victims—a scene of horror—and take a deep breath before I entered. Diseased, emaciated patients lay on dirty iron beds. On the floor between each bed, skeletal figures lay on plastic mats. The air reeked of death. I held my breath and began to drag my feet, murmuring, "Though I walk through the valley of the shadow of death, I will fear no evil."

Many of the children in these wards were victims of ambushes—the suffering of the amputees often brought tears to my eyes. One time I saw a small boy who lay there listlessly in his grandmother's lap. His arm was a bandaged stump; his face was lacerated and swollen. The nurse whispered to me, "His mother was burnt in the ambush, but he survived."

The grandmother smiled sweetly as I gave them the gifts: a piece of soap, a small toy and a Christmas card picture of Jesus and Mary. The boy struggled to sit up and look at the picture. "*Mego*," his grandmother pointed to Mary. "*Latino*," she pointed to Jesus. The boy smiled weakly and then he held the picture close to his chest and closed his eyes and went to sleep.

I asked the grandmother if I could pray for him. What can you pray in the face of such terrible suffering? I lifted him up to God.

In the next bed was Brian, a small boy whose arm was swollen to the size of a football as the result of a snake bite. It was as hot as fire and gangrene had set in. Amputation was expected. As I prayed, I visualised sin and sickness nailed to the cross. Jesus was taking Brian's hand and walking away with him.

The following week I was amazed and delighted to see that Brian's arm had gone back to its normal size and he was wheeling the toy car I had given him. God whispered, "You see, obedience brings Holy Spirit anointing. I will do miracles through you, Irene, as My surrendered vessel."

Eager for prayer, women waited expectantly beside their children's bedside. As I prayed for every precious child, I handed them a Nativity card to show them the source of healing power.

The adult wards were filled with soldiers wounded in battle. As I approached one patient wrapped in a blanket to pray, I realised it was a corpse. I quickly decided to start ministering at the other end of the ward. Thankfully the bed was empty by the time I reached it again.

A young man was writhing against his brother's chest. Shot in the stomach, he was howling with pain. I laid hands on his shoulder, looked heavenwards and sighed, "Oh, please God, help this poor man."

As I left the ward, I turned to see many smiling people waving to me. God reassured me, "You see how much I can do with the little you give Me."

Several days later, while I was driving, I saw a man on crutches. I offered him a lift. He gratefully accepted my offer and got into the car. Then he said, "You don't remember me, do you?" I shook my head. He smiled. "I had been shot in the stomach. You prayed for me, Jesus healed me and the hospital discharged me!"

I was often accompanied on my weekly hospital visits by long-term volunteer visitors to Kitgum. On one occasion, when Jacky Martin was with me, a gaunt man, a victim of war, lifted his ribcage off the grey blanket. His leg was stretched out with a bolt and screw through it. Staring through me, his glazed eyes were blind to all else except the spirit of death beckoning him. After praying for this man, I looked over at Jacky. She was smiling as she laid hands on a man with an amputated leg and prayed, "In Jesus' name, I command bad images to leave his mind. Jesus, let Your peace guard his mind."

I went outside for fresh air and met an army man sitting in a wheelchair. The stump of one leg was heavily bandaged. "We were bombed by the rebels," he explained to me.

"Can I pray that Jesus comforts you?" I asked him.

He told me he was a Muslim, but eagerly accepted my prayers and a pocket Bible.

Sitting nearby, another man pleaded with me: "I was shot a month ago and the rebels burnt my house down. My wife and son here . . ." he gestured towards a baby burrowing into his mother's dress, "have nowhere to live and no food. We are all starving." This story repeated itself in thousands of Acholi lives.

I prayed with him, "God we don't know what to do but our eyes are upon You." Then I said, "Young man, God cannot help you until you give Him permission to rearrange your life. Can you ask Jesus to be boss of your life?"

He nodded and prayed a prayer of salvation.

I continued, "Now your heavenly Father will supply all your needs. You can even laugh at war and famine. You read Job 5:22." I handed him a Bible.

On another visit I met a man called John Ochola, who had made headline news. This young man was on the brink of adulthood when rebels captured him, cut off his ears, lips, nose and hands. They wrapped the parts in paper and posted them to government officials with a letter threatening that this would happen to any government sympathiser.

As John sat looking at me, his eyes bright with anticipation, I floundered for words. I asked him if he was angry with God.

"No, no," he answered. "I love Jesus."

I reached into my bag looking for a present.

A mirror? I put it aside.

A toothbrush? I looked at his stumps. How could he hold it?

I placed a piece of soap on his bed and said, "As soon as you get released from hospital, come down to my school. We have 3,500 children who want to meet you and hear how Jesus keeps you happy."

When he was discharged from hospital, John's face was still raw and the stumps of his hands still bandaged. For two weeks he sat in our church listening to the preaching, his face aglow.

"Our Bridegroom is coming to gather His own," said the preacher. "He has been building us mansions in heaven. Soon He'll come like a thief in the night to take us away. There will be no more pain. We will dance with the Lover of Our Souls. Ask the person next to you to get clean and ready to receive His new strength."

Visibly moved to tears, John walked to the front of the church and knelt down. Eyes closed, he lifted his bandaged stumps to heaven and asked Jesus to take control of his life. Rising to his feet, his eyes shone with new hope. In John's weakness God's strength would be made perfect.

Several Sundays later, a happy procession of about 500 people dressed in their Sunday best clothes strolled down to the riverside. Many carried multi-coloured umbrellas to shield themselves from the fierce midday sun. Some street urchins ran alongside, crashing through the withered maize stalks. As an elder stood chest-deep downstream to catch any who might be swept away, pastors David and Alfred submerged each believer one by one in a glorious celebration. Each leapt up from the water, arms lifted to heaven and faces shining.

Despite bandaged stumps, John Ochola wanted to leave his pain, his old man, under the water and come out renewed. Romans chapter 6 promises that the enemy would no longer have any power over him. Doubtless the devil gnashed his teeth as John rose out of the water, waving stumps towards heaven. His beaming face gave witness to the Spirit of God now living in him. A song of warfare swept through the onlookers, "Let God arise and His enemies be scattered."

The following Sunday John brought his beautiful wife, Grace, and infant son, Alfred, to church. We thanked Jesus for making a way for us out of any pit, through His broken body, and into the throne room of our loving Father (see Heb. 9:12). Having escaped the enemy's control, we knew this family had a future. We enrolled John in the CKS Vocational Business Studies course and he has now been employed for ten years with CKS as a primary school office clerk.

41

I WILL BUILD
MY CHURCH

KITGUM, 2002

CHURCH HAD ALWAYS held a special place in my heart. As a teenager, I loved to sneak into the back of my local Catholic church, sit quietly on the wooden pews and observe the liturgies and prayers.

When I was converted, at the age of 37, I became inextricably woven into the fabric of a vibrant Pentecostal church in Sydney, which, for many years, actively supported and promoted the work of CKS.

Being part of a local church was a non-negotiable. Our mission shortly after settling in Kitgum was to find somewhere we could worship. One morning, Jeff and I were walking through Kitgum Town when we heard boisterous hand clapping and exuberant singing wafting out from the doors of the primary school. Pentecostal Assemblies of God Church was holding a home fellowship meeting in one of their classrooms. From the moment we stepped inside, we knew this church would be our African home. Within weeks, Jeff started preaching and I started helping out at children's church.

Throughout the ups and downs of my personal life and my ministry, it was Pastor Faustino and the PAG church leaders, along with other local pastors, who supported and encouraged me during my most vulnerable times. I loved my local African church, but in the late nineties, God began moving CKS in a different direction.

In 1999 whilst on a visit to Australia, David Livingstone and I went forward for prayer at the end of a C3 evening service. As was customary, Pastor Phil would lay hands on us and pray a prayer of protection and blessing over the work of CKS. As we were walking back to our seats, Pastor Phil pointed to David and said, "When you go back to Uganda, I want you to plant a C3 church." David saluted him, smiled at me and sat down. This was a dream God had already planted in his heart.

Several months later, Salt and Light Kitgum, which later became known as C3 Salt and Light, was established in Kitgum Town and later moved to the CKS project site. The church flourished.

Our congregation was mainly made up of orphans, children who attended our Childcare schools, local community members and staff. It was led by a faithful band of local pastors who also worked for CKS. Our worship leader at the time was a previously abducted girl called Concy.

It was rare to find a song leader like Concy. Her dress was worn thin, but washed and ironed with a clumsy charcoal iron. She'd stand in front of the congregation, her eyes tightly closed, beads of sweat on her brow and sing. And as she did, her face and body would passionately implore God, pleading for His presence in our midst. In that moment, the heavens would open to receive the chorus from the motley crowd of assembled saints. The Holy Spirit filled us with His joy and peace.

Concy had been brought to CKS in 1995 when she was just 11 by her invalid uncle. Nobody knew the whereabouts of her father; her mother was insane and often needed to be chained to stop her from wreaking havoc in the village. The rebels were active around the area where she lived with her uncle and he feared she would be abducted, so he brought her to us.

This young woman was articulate and had good organisational skills. She studied hard and hoped one day to become a teacher. Although she was plagued with a serious skin disease, which we treated with a long course of medication, the memory of her miserable past and her long-term sickness would be cast aside as she earnestly sought the Holy Spirit's presence. As a worship leader, she took us to a place where together we would soar above the present troubles.

For me it was always so humbling to live among these brothers and sisters and see how they rose above the lack, the thorns, and the horrors of this fallen world. Oh, how they knew what it meant to mount up with eagle's wings. How they could dance along the mountaintops. Why do we so often allow disappointment and discontent to keep us bound?

By the end of 2002, C3 Salt and Light had more than 1,000 members. Our youth group had about 250 members who were active in community ministry, visiting prisoners and former child soldiers, and holding outreaches in village markets and IDP camps. They undertook house repairs for the aged and those who had been orphaned. Many of the villagers saw the practical love of Jesus in action, demonstrated by our young people—which in itself caused a radical change in the community. Many people gave up consulting with witch doctors, slashing children with razor blades and other cruel treatments. Around the same time, a large women's group from our church took on some income-generating projects such as sewing and agriculture. They, too, demonstrated the love of Jesus by offering help and support to widows in the community.

Sunday church became the social event of the week and lasted all morning. The assembly hall resounded with music from *adungus* (Ugandan harps), drums, whistles and tambourines. Africans certainly know how to dance! Often the prayer lines were crowded with villagers seeking deliverance from tormenting spirits. The congregation frequently spent all day on a Saturday fasting and worshipping. It was not uncommon for passing villagers to be thrown onto the ground shrieking as demons battled for control of their souls. One teenager who was on her way back from the water borehole threw her jerry can aside and ran into the meeting screaming for deliverance. Pastors and elders were kept busy casting out demons in Jesus' name, while the church continued singing about the delivering blood of Jesus.

Late in 2003, I heard God telling me it was time to construct our own church building. The scripture He gave me was Haggai 1:4, 8 (NIV): "Is it a time for you yourselves to be living in your panelled houses, while this house remains a ruin? . . . Give careful thought to your ways. Go up into the mountains and bring down timber and build My house, so that I may take pleasure in it and be honoured."

We took up a collection from the congregation and soon afterwards, CKS builders began the foundations for a fifty-metre-square slab. At that time I was called to Kampala, so I left them smashing the granite foundations, with instructions to provide for fifty-four pillars to hold up the roof. When I returned, I was pleased to see a solid floor, but shocked to see no provision for pillars.

"How will we hold up the roof?" I cried.

A Dutch engineer in Kampala designed a steel framework for a gable roof suspended over the gigantic space and quoted

$300,000. I told him there was no way we could raise that kind of money. I was very disappointed and complained to God, "Well, it's Your church. It's beyond me!"

The following week I received a message from a friend in Australia who told me they'd sold some property and wished to donate $300,000 to be used at our discretion.

"Yay, God," I cheered, "that's Your church roof!"

By the end of 2007, C3 Salt and Light, under the leadership of David Livingstone, had expanded its reach to other parts of the region and moved to another location, but we continued building a community church on the project site—an expansive building that some say resembles an aeroplane hangar. The stunning gabled roof casts a natural light onto concrete walls painted with colourful frescos. Everest, our resident artist and former student of CKS, hand painted murals depicting the gospel of Jesus Christ in pictures. Many Acholi don't speak English, but fall on their knees in repentance when they study the stories showcased on our walls.

Nowadays, our community church, run by C3-trained pastors and leaders, operates a discipleship school and has developed a strong youth and children's ministry. Our prison and hospital ministries continue and, even today, evangelistic crusades are held throughout the region, seeing thousands come to know Christ.

42

HE NEVER FAILS

KITGUM, 2003

I WAS CONSTANTLY in need of God's help. With thousands of children to feed and educate, buildings under construction and donations to gather, I knew I couldn't do this alone. On the morning of the start of the new school term in January 2003, I sat down quietly at my annex table and opened my Bible. Facing the day with confidence was only possible with God's promises to comfort and strengthen me. I read several verses in 1 Chronicles 28:

> "The LORD has chosen you to build a house for the sanctuary . . . Be strong and of good courage, and do it; do not fear nor be dismayed, for the LORD God . . . will be with you. He will not leave you nor forsake you, until you have finished all the work for the service of the house of the LORD . . . every willing craftsman will be with you for all manner of workmanship, for every kind of service; also the leaders and all the people will be completely at your command." (NIV)

Fortified, I stepped down from my caravan and walked through the school grounds. I felt peaceful.

By 7.30 a.m. a throng pushed at the gate, waiting for the gatekeeper to open it. Enrollment had taken place the previous week and now they had all arrived. In preparation for the increasing numbers, we had built five new classrooms, employed fifteen extra teachers and more kitchen staff to cope with the massive task of feeding 3,500 children. This of course meant extra toilet blocks needed to be constructed and additional medicines were needed for the clinic, which was being managed by volunteer nurse Libby Williams. Classrooms were filled to capacity, but many more came than were registered. To stem the tide, staff tried to turn away those who were not registered.

Facing the shouting and pleading crowd, I calmed them down, then decided we must not reject any of these precious souls. Instead we would build more classrooms. I turned to see if the headmaster could talk with them. A teacher told me he was at home burying his brother who had been killed the day before. So then I asked to speak with the deputy head. I was told that he had been visiting a family in another district when there had been an ambush with many killed, and he may have been one of the casualties.

John Paul, the chief administrator, appeared looking shaken.

"The guardians of the children are storming the classrooms," he said. "They want their children enrolled, but the classrooms are packed full."

"Do we have enough food?" I asked.

"Yes, World Food Programme (who provided us with food during wartime) delivered last week, so we have enough for just a month. It's God's provision."

"It would be heartless to send them away," I said. "Let's enrol them, teach them about Jesus and feed them well. God will provide . . . Oh, and then we'd better have a builder's meeting to discuss more classrooms."

We rang Paul Zagorski in Australia. He and his wife Alice had supported our work from the very beginning and Paul was now President of CKS.

"I can hear those hungry kids in the background," he said. "I've known hunger. I was one of nine migrant children growing up in the outback. I was 6 years old when I gave my life to Jesus. God answered my prayers with miracles. I'll start ringing around after I've prayed."

In his lounge room in Sydney, Australia, Paul got on his knees and began to call down heaven. "God, they are Your children, but we are on our knees calling to You. They are starving and need Your help. And I need Your help to rally prayer and finances. I know Your favour is on all our efforts. Holy Spirit, control my tongue, so I won't speak out my words, but Yours."

Paul started making some phone calls. As he called donors who had supported us for many years, church pastors and other generous supporters, finances began to roll in. By the end of the day he had raised $65,000.

Now we faced an even greater challenge—how to stop the rebels from looting the food on route to CKS. Without wasting any time, Paul booked a flight to Kampala so that he could personally escort the food to Kitgum.

I met Paul at the airport, and then we headed to the United Nations office in Kampala to request food. The response was not what we expected.

"There is nothing allotted for you," they informed us, checking their paperwork. "Besides, there is a war going on and we don't think you will make it to Kitgum with the food."

Dejected, Paul and I went back outside to consider our options. Paul turned to me and said, "You know what Irene, we went in there without praying first." He was right. So we sat down and called on God and then went back in and approached the counter. It was the same person we had dealt with before.

He looked up and smiled, "Sir, what can we do for you?" Apparently, he was unaware of the conversation we'd had with him a few minutes earlier.

So Paul explained that he had travelled all the way from Australia to pick up seven tons of food for the children.

"I am sorry sir," the man replied. "We can't give you any food. There is a war and transporting it would be too dangerous." He paused, and then added, "It's a long weekend and we won't be back until Tuesday."

Paul was fuming. "You see that chair over there?" he said, pointing to the chair in the corner. "I am going to sit right there, and when you get back on Tuesday I'll still be here waiting for that food."

I said nothing. We sat and waited.

After an hour, and close to closing time, one of the staff approached us and said softly, "Have you got a van to transport the food?"

"Yes, it's out the front," Paul responded.

"Well then," the man said, "take it to the depot and we'll fill it up for you."

Paul and I looked at each other. On the outside we were composed; on the inside we were screaming for joy. But now more prayer was needed for the journey back to Kitgum.

We held on tightly to key scriptures and proclaimed victory over the enemy.

The evidence of the devil's handiwork was all around us as we travelled: there had been several ambushes that week and we quietly passed burnt out shells—a grim reminder of the horror that could have been lurking metres away in long grass.

Victoriously we entered Kitgum with our supplies. Arriving through the school gates, we received a joyous welcome from the children, happy to see the safe arrival of Aunty Irene and "El Presidento" Paul from Australia (his second visit).

❖ ❖ ❖

Weeks later, David Livingstone and I decided to brave the journey yet again, this time to collect hospital beds for our AIDS hospice. The day before leaving, we were both hit with doubts. Although my mind was convinced that we served an amazing God and that it was He who had commissioned us to complete this exercise as a testimony of His power against evil, my emotions were troubled. For the first time I could remember, I was overwhelmed by the spirit of fear. The enemy flashed visions of dreadlocked rebels swarming across the field and firing RPGs at our vehicle.

If we were going to continue, we needed to muster up some strength—for the journey ahead and for the task of convincing the government to waive the taxes. Already we had seen answers to our prayers on this particular shipment, as months earlier listeners of Sydney radio station 2UE had generously donated the money we needed for the shipping costs. Once again, God didn't let us down and granted us safe passage.

The next job was to find a truck to transport the beds to Kitgum. No-one wanted to risk an ambush with their modern trucks. At the container yard, we prayed for God to help us. A short time later, a modern Scania truck positioned itself beneath our 4.5-metre container.

The driver, a Muslim called Hussein, beamed at me. "Lady, you have your miracle from God. I was going to do a run to Mombasa, but God changed my mind. So now I'm driving you to Kitgum. Climb up, we are leaving immediately."

We gathered around the truck to pray, as we would never attempt a trip like this one without spiritual preparation. So we prayed Isaiah 35:8—the highway of holiness. With our spiritual safety belts in place it was time to once again face the challenge of bumpy roads, strewn with the wreckages of this week's ambushes. Feeling very peaceful, I realised that I was wrapped in a shroud of prayers. This was yet another protected trip.

That night I apologised to God for doubting Him and for allowing fear to grip me so tightly. He gently reminded me that He had continually protected me over the years, as we made many perilous road trips and suffered late night attacks. And then He reminded me of the miracles experienced by our students.

He reminded me of the extraordinary story of Mary, who in 1993 had rebels visit her compound. They tied her up, along with her cousin, and told her she would become the commander's new wife. For several days they walked in the blazing sun. All the while, Mary sang praises to God.

"Let's see what your Jesus will do for you," they snarled.

On reaching the camp, they took her to the commander's tent, where he was keeping eight other women and their children. A few days later, the commander got a phone call from Joseph Kony instructing him to go to Sudan for more ammunition. He told Mary he would be back for her and put a guard in charge. Then he raped her. She later shared that God cried with her.

The following day, they began their trek in heavy rain compounded by the cold night and their hunger. There was no food for abducted children and many of them began to show signs of weakness. The group was forced to loot villages and watch as villagers were killed in the most barbaric ways. Some were hacked to death; others were forced to kill and eat each other. When some of the children, particularly the smaller ones, cried "We are tired," as a child does, the rebels would turn to them and

say, "We'll give you rest." Then they would force the other children to kill them on the spot. Mary watched in horror as eight
children were killed this way. Another six children were stoned
with rocks as a punishment for trying to escape.

Weeks later, another rebel wanted Mary as his wife and a
fight broke out. She was told that if two men fought over a woman, she would be the one to die.

They plotted to kill Mary: "We'll send her away," they
planned. "Then we'll kill her and say she was trying to escape."

God assured Mary that He would protect her.

One evening, the commander directed Mary to "go and cut
grass." But Mary knew what that meant and kept a close eye on
the camp. At one point, she looked across at the camp and saw
six men all heading her way with machetes and hoes. She knew it
was time to flee. So, lifting up her skirt, she ran and ran.

Voices in the distance yelled, "She's escaped—spread out and
get her."

She could see their torches flashing and the sound of their
boots as they followed her tracks. But it started raining and her
footprints were washed away.

The next day she spotted a school, but God told her not to
stop as rebels had been there. He warned her to keep moving.
Eventually she ended up in a field, where two compassionate
farmers took pity on her and brought her to CKS.

This was another reminder of why God had put me in this
place. On the days I felt discouraged and overwhelmed, God
would gently remind me of the miracles that had already taken
place.

"Keep going Irene," he would say. "A new generation is about
to make an impact in this war-weary land."

43

BLESSINGS FOR HIS CHILDREN

KITGUM, 2004

THIS WAS NO ORDINARY morning assembly and the children knew this. They sat in rapt attention waiting for me to speak. The excitement was palpable.

Above the din I began, looking over a sea of red into bright-eyed, smiling faces, "God really loves you, children. Imagine Christians in Hong Kong—which is a long way from here—who have never met you but who have been collecting clothes, bags, shoes, toys, school desks and even hospital beds, washing machines, refrigerators and blankets to send to you."

The children's enthusiasm and volume increased. I motioned with my finger for them to quieten down. "They have worked so hard to pack everything into two huge twelve-metre containers. There is even three tons of playground equipment!" The children roared with excitement. "Now everything is waiting in Kampala and I'm going down to escort it up here." I knew from experience what that was likely to entail!

Thousands of faces beamed with delight as they prayed for my mission to be safe and successful. I needed prayer for protection and divine favour, as this is Africa and from past experience I knew only too well that approval is not easily given. For three weeks I ran up and down the stairs of office blocks in Kampala, trying to get the containers released with a promise that the Ugandan government would pay the $12,000 in taxes due. My frustration was exacerbated by the absence of the right officials who I was told were on leave. Discouragement and exhaustion accompanied me in the process. But, like Jesus, I tried to imagine the joy that was set before me— the faces of children when they discovered the treasure held inside these containers. My goal was to get the containers to Kitgum by the start of the new term, but it wasn't looking good. Late Friday afternoon, I was told the final signatory was unavailable. I stood in his office, speechless. My eyes welled with tears.

"Well go and see the big man yourself," someone suggested.

"Can I take my file from the secretary's desk?" I asked.

"Why not?" they said.

Praying for God's favour and a change of heart, I entered the big man's office. He looked at me sharply, then pushed his half-eaten doughnut aside and beckoned me in. After the mandatory exchange of greetings, I launched into my tale of woe about having to chase my file from office to office, collecting signatures for three weeks. School starts on Monday and 3,500 children are waiting for their aunty, and I have a 450-kilometre journey to escort the children's things through rebel territory."

"You go with the containers?" he asked incredulously.

"Of course," I said. "They could be stopped and looted otherwise."

"But don't you fear for your life? You must travel with soldiers?"

"Oh no, we fast and pray and God protects us and our possessions from ambushes along the way," I explained.

"Come back in two hours," he said. "All your documents will be ready."

Yet again, at the eleventh hour (5.30 p.m. Friday afternoon) all the papers were in my hand.

On Saturday at 8.30 a.m. my development manager, John Paul, and I arrived at the goods yard only to be disappointed to hear that no drivers were willing to take their trucks through rebel territory. As I sat praying in the hot tin-shed canteen, gulping down a much-needed caffeine hit of Coke, I heard the forklift roaring as it loaded our containers onto some trucks. My prayers had been answered.

"Madam, your trucks and drivers are ready," the staff informed me. I walked out into the glaring sunlight and gasped. Both trucks were pre-1940 vintage and one cabin was leaning over where its suspension had broken. I rejected it. The boss argued, while curious workers gathered around. But visions of the cabin, with me in it, lurching off a bridge into the boisterous Nile made me stubborn.

"An old lady like you," said the driver, "should not travel with us."

It was a remark loaded with innuendo, as I later discovered. Eventually they agreed to unload one container onto a different truck.

With John Paul in the other truck, we left the yard at 4 p.m.; I was elated to be on our way. A few minutes into our journey the driver passed green weed to his young sidekick. Both of them began chewing furiously and laughing wildly.

"Is this all insured?" the driver asked me.

I eyed him suspiciously.

"No."

My answer made him chew even more rapidly.

As night came, headlights hurtled towards us like asteroids out of the blackness. I shuddered and wondered whether we would ever reach Kitgum. I uttered a silent prayer, "Thank You Father that Your angels are protecting us."

For three hours the ancient trucks careered at full speed into the dark countryside until the lead truck suddenly screeched to a halt on the side of the road. We pulled over behind it. My driver turned the motor off and opened his door.

"Mechanical problem," he said as he climbed down, taking his torch and bag with him.

Outside, the African night was abuzz with the songs of insects and frogs. I strained to see what was going on, but apart from the occasional torch flash and the clunk of metal, there was nothing. After half an hour the turnboy opened the door and pulled out a sleeping mat.

"What is the problem? What does the driver say?" I asked.

The boy chewed his gum.

"The drivers have gone back to Kampala," he said.

"What! What for?"

"To get parts," he replied, slamming the door and disappearing into the black night.

There is a certain tune sung by the pig in the movie *Babe* that I often sing: "lu lu luloo." That was my lullaby that night. Perhaps the song was my way of relieving the anxiety. I had an awful feeling that this was a set-up for highway bandits. Sitting bolt upright for the next four hours, because the cracked plastic seat was no place to lay my head, I witnessed several empty trucks stop adjacent to the end of the container, turn all lights off and wait. Only the murmur of voices and torches flashing revealed there was any activity in the darkness.

I was angry that anyone would rob orphans, but also aware that the value of the precious cargo would more than justify the disposal of one interfering old lady in the bush. After all, the drivers had their alibi and were probably getting themselves drunk in some very public bar as evidence. All I could do was sit still and pray. I proclaimed Job 5:19–24 and Malachi 3:11. Eventually, I was able to lean my head against the window and doze for some time, repeating, "You Lord, command a blessing and You add no sorrow to it."

Rain dripped through a broken window. Mosquitoes buzzed all over me. My blouse was damp and I was cold. I looked at my watch, which read 3 a.m. I stuffed an oily rag in the crack of the window as the rain pelted down. *Is it possible for me to be more miserable than this?* I thought.

My thoughts were interrupted by a tapping on my door. The locks were broken, so it opened easily and a very wet young man climbed up into the passenger side. I squeezed myself behind the wheel as he removed his boots and stretched his feet across the windscreen. The smell of the weed he'd been consuming and foot odour was nauseating. I had the choice of opening the window and getting soaked or inhaling a cocktail of stomach-turning vapours. *Hmm, yes, I can be more miserable.* Oh the indignity of sharing my sleeping place with one inebriated, smelly young man! Doubtless he was suffering his own disappointments.

Morning couldn't have been more welcome. At daybreak, I was excited to see that I had survived the night and that the containers' seals were still intact. Praise our mighty God! I called John Paul and his turnboy down from their cabin and we wandered up the road a few kilometres to find some tea and chapattis at a small market. Large pastel pink pelicans flew overhead—a morning gift from God.

The drivers finally returned in the late afternoon. They had not been able to get any spares, but were looking clean, well-showered and wearing new clothes, albeit a bit bleary-eyed. Those of us who had been left behind, on the other hand, were feeling very grotty and hungry. We didn't challenge them about their long absence. Our hope at this point was to get to Lira before the army closed the bridge at Karuma. We were just hoping, not desperate. We had survived one night in the bush and we could survive another. With the necessary parts finally procured, I continued to pray as the trucks embarked on the next leg of the journey.

God is kind and His hand was on us. At 7 p.m. with darkness closing in, soldiers recognised me at the roadblock and waved us through. The trucks groaned as we began our tortuous descent, and we continued to pray as we cautiously crossed the bridge, observing the red and yellow warning flags—a mute memorial to the bus and its passengers who had driven over the edge several months earlier.

Late into the night, we reached Lira and checked into a Christian guesthouse. We were too late for a meal, but the shower (albeit cold) washed two days' dirt away and the bed sheets were clean and the pillows soft.

On Monday morning the soldiers waved us out of town and onto the Kitgum road. Smiling, I waved back, reassuring them that with our faithful God there was nothing to fear.

Finally, on Monday afternoon we made our triumphant entry into the CKS project site. The children watched the procession from their classroom windows. They smiled, waved and cheered. God had not forgotten them and now His blessings had arrived because of the love and sacrifice of His precious servants at Crossroads, Hong Kong. Even today, visitors sleep in our beds and sit in our chairs, unaware of the perilous journey involved in getting them to the site.

The following day the children squealed with excitement as they helped me unpack the containers, which also included seventeen brand new bikes that would be given away in a few days at our annual birthday party.

44

CELEBRATING
BIRTH-DAYS

KITGUM, 2004 TO PRESENT

MANY CHILDREN in Kitgum have no record of their date
of birth. They don't know how old they are and never celebrate
their birthdays. Most parents and guardians don't understand the
importance of recording a child's birth. Moreover, in an isolated
region shackled by war and absolute poverty, it is near impossible
for villagers who don't have transport to access services where
registration might be taking place. Not surprisingly, Uganda has
the lowest rate of birth registration in the whole of Africa. To
compensate, each year we would throw a communal birthday
party in our school assembly hall. It was a joyous occasion.

At our annual party day on a crisp, clear morning in 2004
the children began arriving at 7 a.m., scrubbed clean and excited.
They packed the assembly hall—wall-to-wall children dressed in
red shirts. They all listened intently as I talked about God's vision for their lives, quoting Psalm 139:13–18. Although war had
prevented their birthdays from being recorded, God marks even
the moment of conception and has a wonderful plan to bring
each one to Him, to spend eternity with Him. After my exhor-
tation, it was the very tangible blessings of gifts, prizes and good

food that helped each child to see that the Lord is very good.

One of the first blessings was a surprise cheque for $2,400 from the Ugandan government for our school. Government officials honoured the children with their presence. After many long speeches from dignitaries, in ascending order from the least to the greatest, the Resident District Commissioner, the President's representative, stood up to address the crowd.

But I could see the children were growing restless. They had already been sitting through two hours of speeches. Without thinking, I rose to my feet, looked at the children's faces and said, "This is your birthday children, and it's time for a song. Let's sing one of our favourites . . ."

As I sat down, I could see that the Commissioner was unimpressed. "Aren't you the Director?" he asked. "You should have introduced me and let me speak. It's about protocol my dear."

"Oh, please forgive me," I blustered. "I am Australian and we often do things upside down. Sorry."

Graciously he accepted my apologies and we continued on with the day.

After a special lunch of meat and rice, we went outside for games like sack races and human pyramids, and class presentations. The final event was a draw for the seventeen bikes donated by Crossroads. Children and staff crowded around me. Their faces were tense as each little hand held on tightly to a grubby ticket, which they had somehow kept safe all day.

"Sit down. Sit down," I said, motioning with my hands. Small faces grimaced as bigger children leant on them. The crowd squirmed and pushed until everyone had a patch of ground.

"We have seventeen bikes and fourteen consolation prizes," I told them. "So there will be thirty-one happy people. Some of you will not get a prize, but we've all enjoyed meat, we've all enjoyed games, and everyone will get a bar of soap to take home.

Now God is deciding who will win. Proverbs 16:33 says that every winner is decided by God. So let's invite Him to choose."

As I read out each winning ticket, the hand of God was evident. James Ayella, our limping water boy for the builders, was the first. Next was little Robert, who only has one eye, then Alex, one of our teachers, then Stephen Otema, a crippled boy on crutches, Francis Oketta, an undersized boy with a terminal illness, Labele, our deaf and mute porter, and Lucy, our over-worked cook and house-mother.

The day passed in a kaleidoscope of smiles, songs and joy—a testament to the goodness of our God.

45

LIVING IN
TWO WORLDS

2004

AS THE EARTH'S equatorial belly turned, and northern Uganda faced 45°C heat (113°F), I fled to Australia for some respite. Every year since moving out to Uganda, I had travelled back to Australia to catch up with family and raise much-needed funds for the work. My faithful friend Alice Zagorski would line up meetings for me at friend's houses, churches and schools, where I would share my stories from the mission field and God's heart for the poorest of the poor.

Africa had become my almost constant focus. So much so, that an event almost slipped off my radar—my sixtieth birthday. Although I had almost forgotten, my family hadn't. On 30 December 2004, while staying at Heidi's house, I woke up, rolled out of bed, walked over to the main house from my converted garage bedroom and made myself a cup of tea.

Clay, Heidi's husband, was in the kitchen. "Morning Grandma," he said chirpily. "Happy birthday! How about I take you out for breakfast this morning to celebrate?"

"Where is Heidi?" I asked, putting my bread for toast back into the freezer.

"Oh, she had some errands to run—she'll be back later." He sounded a little too dismissive.

Although I was disappointed at my daughter's absence on the morning of my birthday, I was thrilled that Clay had offered to take me out.

An hour later, we drove into Manly, a cosmopolitan seaside resort seventeen kilometres from central Sydney. We pulled up in front of a fancy ocean-front hotel.

"Wow Clay, this looks very nice!" I said, grabbing my handbag and straightening my skirt.

Walking through the main doors and into the restaurant, I spotted some people I knew heading through the lobby. *I wonder what they are doing here*, I thought.

And then I saw all my children—Heidi, Shelley, Maree, Greg and all the grandchildren sitting at a large table in front of a giant glass window overlooking the ocean.

"Surprise!" the group yelled.

I was momentarily speechless. I don't usually cry, but on this occasion, I did. I was overwhelmed. Beaming at me were the faces of my children, grandchildren, key people from my church and good friends.

"I feel like I am in heaven," I said, wiping the tears from my eyes.

My "missing" daughter, in consultation with Alice, had organised a surprise buffet breakfast for me. Catching up with family, eating a delicious breakfast and sharing stories and jokes, reminded me of how much I had missed Australia and, in particular, my family and friends. I was tempted to stay.

Then God reminded me that I had a job to do.

"Yes Lord, but today I'll enjoy fresh fruit and eggs."

When in Australia I was often asked, "Do you ever get disgusted with the extravagance of Australian life?"

"No," I'd answer them honestly. "I enjoy wherever I am to the fullest."

So I enjoyed fine foods, beautiful beaches and the sane, predictable life Australia offers. I loved spending time with my children and my grandchildren, and for a brief time doing what any grandmother would do. Then, with my soul fattened by the loving-kindness of family and friends, and my body plump with choice food, I would once again raise my palm and quell the rising tears of my children and grandchildren. In my spirit, I would get down on one knee, bowing humbly to the royal commission, then set my face towards Africa.

As my plane climbed, I would gaze through the window as the waters of Sydney beaches shimmered in the moonlight, until they were obscured by cloud. I was enclosed in an aeronautical time capsule, travelling through different time barriers, until I emerged in a different, more primitive time zone—a zone where trauma and persecution are balanced against God's presence and power clearly demonstrated in everyday life; where desperate prayers are answered.

This was a different climatic zone, where memories of warm ocean breezes dissipated before hot dusty winds, which often invaded my zippered Bible, making the pages gritty and stained brown; a zone where heat-bedevilled termites built soggy mud tunnels up bedroom walls, and spiders spun black ash-laced cobwebs to furnish rooms in gothic décor.

It was a different sensory zone, where bodily comforts were rare. Beans were chewed dutifully and washed down with borehole water; pungent smells of human waste were tempered by the amusing sight of cows standing, chewing their cud atop mountains of rotting garbage—an improvised roundabout for town traffic.

It was a war zone, where a man could hardly dream of a future, but fought day and night for survival: for himself and his beloved spouse, children, parents, cousins; relatives starving to death and restricted to the barren grounds of displaced people's camps until war-weary soldiers could drive the rebels back into Sudan.

It was a different communication zone where landline phones, faxes and emails still did not reach us. Such isolation strengthened rumours of imminent rebel attacks.

Travel to this part of the world was not "romantic," as portrayed in *Out of Africa*. Journeys were long, tense, uncomfortable and very dangerous.

46

LORD OVER KITGUM

KITGUM, 2005

BEATRICE O. AGENORWOT was 14 years old and had reached Primary 5 in Childcare's main primary school. Good feeding had made her body healthy and strong. She was also very confident and had a strong Christian faith. She played an instrument and sang in our church choir. Her older sister, Acayo Dorine, who was 15 years old, was quieter and more fragile in both temperament and in body. Her large brown eyes stared into the distance as her sister talked. The tragedy of war had deprived them of their parents, so cooking and washing became their life as they both cared for six younger siblings living in two huts in their compound. Their uncle lived in a third. Abducted by rebels and held captive for four years until he escaped, his mind was so tortured by memories that he sought oblivion in the toxic local brew. During these binges he became aggressive and abusive. The children hid in fear.

One Friday afternoon, the girls waved to me, as did many of the children passing through the school gates. "*Lubanga omedi gum*. God bless you. See you Monday," I said as usual. I knew the girls and most of the children would spend their weekend doing chores: collecting firewood, queuing for jerry cans of water, fanning flames in order to cook beans and maize, digging their *sambas* and attending our four-hour church service.

By Sunday night, Beatrice and Dorine's school uniforms had been washed clean in the river, and ironed with a heavy charcoal-filled ironing box. The girls lay down together on papyrus mats on the earth floor of their mud hut.

The night darkened and filled with strange sounds. Rebels prowled the outskirts of Kitgum Town, seeking their prey. At 2.30 a.m. I sat bolt upright. *Someone needs prayer,* I thought. I prayed in tongues and asked the Holy Spirit to intercede according to the will of God. After half an hour I snuggled down and slept. One of our pastors, Denis, had also been woken by barking dogs and had been prompted to pray.

Dorine and Beatrice were wakened by torches shining on them through the window.

"Open the door," a gruff voice demanded, "or we'll shoot you."

As they opened the door, hell's legions swarmed inside. Dirty, unkempt rebels with cartridge belts over their shoulders waved guns in the frightened girls' faces.

"Get outside," they commanded.

While the little girls cowered outside, crying, the rebels stormed the hut and looted whatever they could. One rebel kicked at a locally made instrument with beans inside. "What's this?" he snarled.

"We use it for praising God," Beatrice answered quietly.

The rebel sneered at Beatrice. "What's your name?"

"Beatrice Agenorwot (meaning 'I trust in the Lord')."

The rebel mocked her. "Ha! What Lord can save you now?"

Outside the hut, nudged by guns, the girls were roped to thirty other children and forced to march. Passing a small shop they were ordered to loot it. The noise attracted soldiers, and machine gun fire reverberated around them. Running blindly in the dark, Dorine whimpered, wondering if she'd be dead by morning.

Thorns ripped their bare feet as the bedraggled, terrified children were forced to march. They waded through a waist-deep swamp and eventually emerged in another district, far from any hope of rescue. Beatrice was singing to God in her heart.

Their captors began whistling like night birds.

In the darkness, other rebel gangs joined them until seventy gun-wielding rebels were harassing a hundred terrified children.

A commander barked out orders: "Are you a student?" "Can you write letters?" "Sit over there."

Children were separated. They all started to cry.

Dorine trembled as a rebel with dirty dreadlocks that hung around his face hauled her to her feet. Her heart repeated, *I will surely die tonight.*

"What about you?" the commander eyeballed the two sisters. "Are you pupils? What school do you go to?"

Dorine murmured, "Childcare Kitgum Primary School."

The commander frowned. "Are you from Aunty Irene's school?"

"Yes," the girls nodded.

"Any more from there?" The commander scanned the children's faces.

"These are disruptive people," he said "We don't want them. They will only disturb us. Praying. Praying. Praying. Always disturbing. Send them back. Here, take this old mother with you."

He pushed a 70-year-old grandmother towards the girls. "Don't look back. Just keep walking."

With one last lingering look at their neighbours, the girls and grandmother began their journey back through the swamps and black bush.

After their traumatic night the girls appeared at the school gates at 7.30 a.m. grubby and wet, but victorious in Jesus. They stood quietly as Pastor Denis told their story before the packed school assembly. Many children sat with their mouths open. Doubtless the long nights were full of terror for them also, as they curled up like animals sheltering in the bush.

As Pastor Denis related the way the commander had responded when he found out which school the girls were from, the school assembly cheered and whistled. I recalled my 2.30 a.m. prayer.

Pastor Denis interrupted my thoughts. "Do you have anything to add, Aunty?"

I looked out over those beautiful children. "The devil made a fatal mistake," I said. "Two thousand years ago, he killed the Lamb of God. Now he lives in fear and torment because he must bow his knee to the blood-bought children of God. We know our rights. We know the Lamb's blood set us free from the devil's plans. Let's disturb him every day. Let's not say, "Pray." Let's say, "Disturb the devil." Let's sing a song that disturbs him now: "I'm gonna walk/sleep/dig right under His blood where the devil can do us no harm." Their eyes shining, the children sang at the top of their voices.

I continued, "Revelation 5:9 says Jesus was killed and with His blood He bought me and you, and people from every nation—not to serve or be victims of Satan, but to be kings and priests to our God. And that includes the abducted children, and even the rebels. Let's pray for them right now. God wants the rebels to be saved and the children to come home safely."

I knew the devils were disturbed and I knew our songs and prayers spoilt their plans.

I asked Dorine and Beatrice later, "Are you too worried to sleep at home? Do you want to stay in the dormitories here?"

They both smiled. "We don't fear. God is able to protect us. We have to stay there and look after our brothers and sisters."

Rallying to the call to "disturb the devil," more than 1,000 children began gathering in the assembly hall every morning at playtime. Each time I entered the hall I was overwhelmed. A gigantic, hot crowd of children were kneeling and praying to their Father God that the devil would leave this district, so that they could return to their families' lands, plant their gardens, and climb mango trees as they used to do.

It was an emotional experience as I joined in the worship with these children who were lost in happy communion with God. Dusty faces streaked with tears, they lifted thin arms and sang with the angels, "Nothing I desire compares with You."

"Dear God," I prayed, "Father to these orphans. They have been patient for so long. End this war. Be Lord over Kitgum. Be Lord of all. Amen."

A year later, peace talks began and abductions stopped.

47

ETERNAL HOPE

KITGUM, 2003-2005

OVER THE YEARS, I had heard God speak to me many times about our building works. He was the master designer for the CKS site and I was the project manager.

One hot afternoon I recall watching a rickety barrow creak its way through the doors of Kitgum hospital and out into the blazing sun. The young man who was steering it looked at me with incredibly sad eyes as he pushed his load. The pile of rags inside shook with the movement. I could see that it was a woman. She was emaciated and unconscious. I mouthed the question to the boy, "Your mother?" He nodded, then proceeded down the dusty road. Eventually he would find a wasteland, far from rebel activity, dig a large hole and bury his mother—alone.

On another occasion, a young man wheeled his bike into my compound. As he did, an old man fell from the luggage rack and onto the ground, gasping. I was shocked. It was David, our duck keeper.

"It's tuberculosis," his son told me.

Tears filled my eyes as I laid my hands on his heavy chest and prayed for God's comforter to arrive. That's when God told me to start raising funds so we could provide palliative care: a sanctuary where the sick and dying could be treated with dignity and love;

a place where children would be relieved of the burden of caring for their dying relatives in primitive dwellings. Already we had been given ten hospital beds by Crossroads—now it was a matter of drawing up the plans and hiring builders to carry out the work. The hospice would provide dignity, comfort and an eternal hope for AIDS sufferers in particular. In northern Uganda rates of HIV and AIDS were significantly higher than anywhere else in the country. This was partly due to the practice of polygamy and partly a result of war. Many of those who had been displaced found themselves using sex as a means of making money. In the IDP camps HIV/AIDS was one of the most common causes of death. Rape, defilement and prostitution were all hallmarks of a place where human beings had lost self-respect in their quest to survive. Most disturbingly, parents would encourage their children to become self-sufficient, which might involve having sex as a strategy for survival. With a weakened immune system and no access to life-saving drugs, many would lose the battle with malaria, cholera or typhoid.

It took three years to build our AIDS hospice, which we named Gloryland Junction, but eventually we were ready to accept our first patient who, actually, didn't have AIDS.

One warm evening in June of 2005, Joachim and his brothers stood at my door looking miserable.

"What's up?" I asked them.

"It's our mother. They sent her home from the hospital on a *boda boda*. They can't do any more for her. She is worsening. I will have to leave school and look after her." Joachim's eyes filled with tears.

"She must be alright if she could sit on a bicycle," I countered, reluctant to have to deal with a cancer patient.

"No, they tied her on and that's how they sent her home, armed with a small bottle of morphine for the pain. Now she is getting worse."

I consulted my visiting nurses.

"I know you leave in forty hours, but can you fit in a visit to-morrow? I need your wisdom and experience to assess her. I think she will be our first patient at Gloryland Junction."

The following day, directed by Joachim, we bumped along a stony track until we arrived at a dilapidated hut on an arid hillside. As Gill, Leonie and our three Ugandan medical staff disappeared into the hut, a swarm of flies flew out. I hesitated before entering this hell hole, wrestling with a strong impulse to turn and run. Many years earlier, as a 14-year-old, I'd had to leave school in order to care for my mother who was dying of cancer. The trauma of my transition from classroom with friends and laughter to the isolation and smells of a sickroom had left memories I would rather have kept buried.

There is no way around unpleasant duties, I told myself. *Irene, you have to get over it.*

I gritted my teeth and entered the chamber of death.

Lying on a grubby mattress on a dirt floor was the withered body of a 40-year-old woman. Mercifully, her wounds were hidden beneath a threadbare grey blanket. With one bony arm bent over her forehead, she sucked in her breath and grimaced with pain. I looked over at her boy—he was hunched against the wall looking at the ground.

Our nurse, Franca, gently took the woman's hand. "Emma," she said softly. "You know that Aunty Irene is here? She has built a home for sick people. It's a beautiful place and you won't have to worry about a thing. There will be nurses there to look after you and cook food for you. Joachim can get on with his studies and he can visit you any time. And Pastor Denis will be around to pray for you."

The woman's eyes remained shut. I looked over at her son for his response. His lips were quivering. Tears streamed down his cheeks. His three small brothers peered in the door and he waved them away.

In that moment, I had realised that although I had always tried to avoid hospitals, God had used my painful past experiences to encourage me to rescue others in similar circumstances. Yes, the devil had robbed me of my youth. And I had actually dwelt many times in the valley of the shadow of death: I had been tested by tropical diseases, latent ambushes and late night attacks. I was confident that I could call on the supernatural power and grace which I found in God to keep walking and, even better, to show others a way through.

Nurse Franca turned to me, "Emma says she would like to rest for a bit. But next week she would be very grateful to be transferred to Gloryland Junction."

On the day she arrived, her son carried her over to the bed and laid her thin body on a clean mattress—something she had never experienced before. "Rest well Mother," he whispered, pulling up a colourful new sheet.

As she lay in her bed, she glanced up at the walls which were painted with magnificent murals on every side: wonderful chocolate-skinned angels floating up to heaven, escorting smiling patients, while the earth spun blue-green in space. The local hospitals are places of hopelessness, where victims pray for God to take them quickly. In contrast, Gloryland Junction is a place of hope; God's hand is on every patient in every bed.

Gloryland Junction serves as an oasis of hope for those infected with HIV/AIDS and those with tuberculosis. All patients receive round-the-clock care and ARVs (antiretroviral drugs), which are used to hold off HIV. Gloryland is the only residential AIDS hospice in all of Uganda . . . an amazing facility for AIDS patients who have been discharged from hospitals and sent home to villages to die . . . Miraculously, many lived.

48

WHERE NEED ABOUNDS

KITGUM, 2006

THE CHILDREN who lived in the Amida IDP camp sur-rounded us, shaking our hands. One small girl grasped my hand and pulled me into the confusion of mud huts nestled in this camp. In one of the narrow alleyways between the huts, we found her grandmother beside a small heap of fermenting millet. She had tears in her eyes as she shook her head and waved her arms.

"These rations . . . they are too little. I have to make brew so that we can buy food. All my sons are dead. Now I am the only one alive to care for all these—" she shook her head in despair, and then covered her face. Beside her, a young girl sat with a naked toddler asleep on her lap. She brushed away flies and spread her ragged skirt over his scrawny body.

A thin 10-year-old boy emerged from a hut. "*Ja-ja* (grandma) is ashamed that you found her brewing."

"It's okay," I said softly, understanding the need to do whatever was necessary to feed your family. "How many of you are there?"

"Nine," he replied.

I imagined the condition of these children: runny noses, ring-worm, swollen bellies. I longed to dunk them all in a sudsy bath, give them a meal and some medicine.

The grandmother began to weep, grieving for the children she could not care for. The boy patted her shoulder. "She gets too sad. My father died, then her other son, then our mothers. We are all she has left." He pointed to the hills. "We have my father's good farmland, but the soldiers won't let us go back to dig."

"Do you go to school?" I asked.

He shook his head. "We did go to school in that far village, but one day the army told us to leave and come here to the camp. As you can see, it is not good."

"Your English is very good," I said to him.

"Of course," he said. "I am the eldest man in my family and I have a lot of responsibility."

"Would you like to go to our school?" I asked.

He stared at me.

"We are building a new school across the road. It's nearly finished. We have built it for people like you."

I stroked the grandmother's white hair. "Jesus loves you," I told her. "He understands your sadness and He sent us to stop the devil's work and build a day care school for your children. We will give them food and medicine and free school, and teach them all about Jesus. He is the one who will make all this happen. Isn't that good news?"

Her wizened face lit up and she clasped my hand tightly in hers, crying "*apwoyo, apwoyo*" (thank you, thank you).

I took the boy's hand. "Let's go and see your new school."

As we walked through the camp, we passed a noisy, smoky grinding mill. A few mothers queued outside with baskets of pink-stained maize. My visiting nurse, Chris, remarked, "That is seed maize. Look, it still has the pink insecticide on it. It's for planting, not for eating. That could kill them."

The grinding mill operator shrugged. "What can they do? They were given seed maize as a gift, but there was no rain. It's not planting season and there is no other food for the children, so the mothers are washing it as best they can."

I shook my head and muttered a prayer, "Almighty God, bring justice for these people. Overturn all obstructions and release them back to their lands."

With my motley crew in tow, I crossed the dirt road and trudged half a kilometre through prickly scrub to check on the progress of our newest school. During my recent absence in Australia, I had imagined our graduated building students loyally toiling under the hot January sun to complete eight classrooms. But I had not factored in Christmas and New Year holidays, attending to family crises, creating their own income, generating brick kilns and repairing their own houses. Thus, standing in the searing heat on the edge of five thorny acres, I was disappointed to find neither shade nor structure above ground level.

The builders rose from their resting places under some mango trees. "Welcome back from Australia," they chorused.

"What happened?" I gestured towards the non-existent buildings, then to the children. "Where are their classrooms? They need to start school."

The supervisor, Francis, began mumbling.

I shook my head, "Francis, how many men have you got here?"

"Thirteen masons and eight porters."

"How many pillars to hold up the roof?" I asked.

One young apprentice, Peter Rackara, who had graduated from primary school and was now helping to build the new school in Amida, caught my drift.

"Sixty-four, Aunty," he said.

With wisdom from heaven, I directed, "Okay, that's eight pillars each for eight of the masons. And five extra masons to build partition walls. Are you strong? Can you do it?" I granny-punched one of the youths on his arm. "Have you got muscles?"

The young builders were smiling.

"How long to do one pillar?" I asked.

"One and a half days."

"I can build one every day," another boasted.

"Okay, every mason grab the best porter you can find and see if your team can finish your quota of eight pillars in two weeks. Francis, employ another five porters from the IDP camp to help with the partition walls. We'll bring in our carpenters to start making the trusses. Then all you builders can lay the floor while they are putting up the roof." I looked at the children. "Your school should be ready in a month." And it was!

A month later, as we drove through the grass to the finished classrooms, children emerged from the bush. Some came in their Sunday best, others in rags and a few were naked. Our teachers, who had been selected for their singing and storytelling skills, soon settled the children in classes. A visiting photographer captured poignant moments: a small girl opening her treasured tin pencil box holding tiny stubs of pencils; hundreds of children seated on the floor clapping and singing boisterously.

As we drove away, a tiny boy grinned broadly and waved his scrap of paper at us. He shouted with all his strength, "Aunty Irene. See, I started schooling today!"

Several days later we exchanged the children's rags for red T-shirts.

On the day Childcare Amida Primary School opened, the children were barely recognisable as the same wretched children who used to sit on faeces-littered ground every Tuesday when we visited to sing and preach. It had been a challenging experience, and not for the faint-hearted. Unwashed, hungry, shoving and pushing like irritated rats in a cage, it would take twenty minutes of singing to God before the children settled. I would stand at the side and study them, wondering how on earth we could bring some order back to their lives. Without food, without water, without medicine, without school, they were condemned to live like feral animals. Man's greed and evil ways may force people to live in subhuman conditions, but God surely sees their trouble and grief—and He is especially concerned for orphans and widows.

In six months of miracles, God had enabled us to build a sixteen-room school across the road from Amida IDP camp. With level playing fields, two water boreholes, a kitchen and medical clinic, it met every urgent and growing need of the children.

The new school was six kilometres from the school at the project site and I would visit the classrooms weekly to encourage our teachers, who I felt were somewhat isolated. Although we started without chairs or benches, I would watch these shining-faced children singing rhymes, counting numbers and listening to stories. Seated on a hard, cold, concrete floor, these children were keen to learn and their eyes and smiles reflected their gratitude.

"Heads, shoulders, knees and toes," one energetic teacher sang as the children eagerly followed her lead. As they practised English, I could see illiteracy and poverty leaving the community. I dared to dream of a new generation of young men and women shaping their own future. As I gazed out over the sea of faces I murmured, "Thank You Papa God, for this miracle."

In 2007 we opened our third primary school at Padibe IDP camp, twenty-five kilometres north of Kitgum, and a fourth opened in Palabek forty kilometres northeast of Kitgum in 2013.

49

RESTORING DIGNITY

KITGUM, 2006

EARLIER IN THEIR young lives they had been mercenaries and sex slaves, but in 2006 they were fine men and women and new graduates of our vocational training centre.

On graduation day the assembly hall was filled with eager faces. Pastor Alfred, headmaster of the school, smiled broadly and addressed the students.

He took a moment, looked around the crowd and began, "We started four years ago with 300 destitute youth. Now you graduates are pioneers of this school. You have completed your final exams and with excellent results—the highest in the district. You have even built many of the classrooms for primary and technical students. You have left behind a legacy for the next generation of students. Your reputation as disciplined students is envied across the district. We have equipped you both technically and spiritually. Guard carefully what we have put in your soul. How tragic it would be if you became very rich and gained the world, but lost your soul."

Next, David Livingstone, our project manager, shook Alfred's hand and took the microphone.

"When I look at you fine young people, the next generation of business people in Uganda, I can say, 'Surely God had a good plan.' I am proud of you. You are sanctified, qualified pioneers of a new Uganda. Kony seized many of you by force and drilled into you his beliefs, but God rescued you. Guard God's word and God's love and begin to walk in the paths which He has laid out for you."

I looked over at the assembled youth and quietly whispered a thank you to God, as I was seeing His word come about. Years earlier, I had claimed Zechariah 9 for this project, where God talks about setting prisoners free and raising up sons against the enemy. I thought about the final verses as I studied the faces of these young men and women who now shone: "The LORD their God will save His people on that day as a shepherd saves his flock. They will sparkle in His land like jewels in a crown. How attractive and beautiful they will be! Grain will make the young men thrive, and new wine the young women" (Zech. 9:16-17 NIV).

But this success hadn't come without struggles and heart-ache. As the formalities continued, my mind drifted back over the years. I remembered my husband standing next to me at our Christmas farewell party in 1991, laughing and joking on home video about the sacrifices he had made in order to go to Uganda, and who now lived a different life back in Australia. I remembered the many fear-filled nights in my caravan in the deserted school grounds, surrounded by war, the midnight attacks by men in khaki, the shame of having my staff challenge me, and the day of terror when our school children were stampeded by gun-waving police who closed the school down for a month.

I thought about my growing confidence in God as He protected me and gave me His grace to continue the work. At times we had sown in tears, but on this day, as I watched our graduating students receive their certificates, their eyes shining and smiles wide, we reaped with much joy.

❖ ❖ ❖

Many of our youth had lived in congested IDP camps, where promiscuity was a common escape from the stress of poor living conditions. They had become like sewer rats. But the Lord showed me these young men and women through his eyes—His beautiful creations, many bruised, and many wounded, standing precariously on the precipice of adulthood. They could so easily fall and be lost forever. Many of them faced an uncertain future, clouded with the responsibility of looking after their younger siblings. Moreover, starvation and unemployment added to their woes. Their senses were dulled and they were numb. It was a scourge that needed to be addressed.

On a blisteringly hot Saturday in 2006, we held a day-long seminar punctuated by energetic praise and worship and a message from our pastor about healthy boy–girl relationships.

After the word and a communal lunch of meat and cabbage, the girls were summoned to the guesthouse to be fitted with princess gowns, and the boys, new white shirts. Each received a Gideon Bible. As they re-entered the hall the audience gasped. Despite feeling a little overwhelmed—exchanging their dirty, ragged and torn clothes for beautiful new ones—they were transformed. No longer staring hopelessly at the ground, feeling too miserable to make eye contact, these teenagers held their heads high as the pastor read God's word to them about their bodies being temples of God's Holy Spirit and remaining celibate until Papa God gives them away in marriage.

As the sunset washed the clouds luminous pink, the teenagers spilt out of the hall, their faces radiant. The girls were all encouraged to wear their princess dresses every Sunday as they had a date with the King of Kings.

That night I fell into bed smiling. This commission from my Captain had been fulfilled and I would sleep well.

I awoke to the news we had all been waiting for.

50

THE BEGINNING
OF THE END

KITGUM, 2006

AT FIRST LIGHT, I tuned my radio to the BBC as an announcement was being made. Peace talks between the LRA and the Ugandan government had commenced. We were overjoyed.

After several false starts, finally in 2006 the government of Uganda and the LRA met in Juba, the capital of southern Sudan to sign a Cessation of Hostilities agreement, which meant an end to the brutality that had brought this country to its knees and displaced more than 1.5 million people. For some, the announcement meant a return to their ancestral land to rebuild their disrupted lives. For others the news wouldn't change anything: these were the people who because of their age, disability or a lack of resources wouldn't be going anywhere. They would be permanent residents of the IDP camps.

In 1987, Joseph Kony and his "army" of disgruntled youth had taken to the bush to fight the government. So began a twenty-year campaign of terror against the Acholi people of northern Uganda. During this time Kony and his army killed, mutilated, maimed and abducted close to 66,000 young men and women aged between 14 and 30. Young men were turned into sadistic killers and young women were raped and turned into child brides for rebel commanders. Thousands of civilians: children, parents and grandparents were sadistically murdered and tortured while the rest of the world looked away.

With only forty-eight hours' notice, villagers had been herded into IDP camps which became their home for the next eight years. In these camps many contracted fatal diseases due to lack of water, medicine, food and sanitation. The fabric of this once hospitable, sociable, self-sufficient community had been torn to shreds.

Even though it was now time for the Acholi to return to their villages, their lives had changed forever. Eight years of refugee-camp life had destroyed the social structure of a once-proud tribe, famous for their self-discipline, generous hospitality and respect for elders. Many fathers had either been killed or were constantly drunk, trying to block out the horror of their existence. Many older sons had been conscripted into either the Ugandan army or the LRA. If they survived, they came out unwilling to return to farming. Facing a hopeless future they, too, sought oblivion in the local brew or brawling.

Teenage girls considered selling themselves to try and snare a husband, even becoming co-wives due to the shortage of men. By doing this they often signed their own death warrant to AIDS. This left mothers and grandmothers with the intolerable burden of returning to build a house on their land (if it still existed), without food supplies and with young children in tow. All stocks of seed and animals had been lost during the war. They had nothing.

Before they could return to their land, the UN decided to register everyone. For one full week, there was no productive work in Uganda. The school grounds were silent and the market stalls empty. Roads were crowded with queues of people walking to register, while in camps, teachers, builders and villagers sat idly waiting for the officials to set up tables to fingerprint and record every human being. With many relatives almost starving, people were desperate to be registered for UN food rations.

While the end to the war was celebrated, it brought with it significant problems for all the child-led families like Moses'.

Throughout the war years, Moses had helped his mother dig during daylight, then at nightfall had walked several kilometres to town to sleep with thousands of the "night commuter" children. One night, as he walked with his two brothers and many other children along the narrow track, there was a rustling in the elephant grass. Rebels brandishing machetes leapt out and bludgeoned one boy to death in front of all the children. Moses and his brother Regan fled home to tell their mother. Later that night, as she was settling them down to sleep, she heard a noise and looked out into the black night. Her eyes filled with horror to see rebels running into her compound. One steely eyed youth took aim, then shot her dead in a round of clipped gunshots. The two little boys fell to the ground, paralysed with fear, as the rebels continued their killing spree. Now orphaned, Moses moved his siblings away from his village into a leaking, abandoned hut near Padibe IDP camp.

When the war ended and camps disbanded, aid agencies stopped distributing food, leaving these children hungry at weekends and during school holidays. Authorities began demolishing huts in the camps, forcing people to return to their land. But how was an 11-year-old with four dependants going to resume a normal life without even any shelter?

Not content to let such children suffer any more, we enlisted the support of churches and friends from around the world, then set about building them their own brick homes on their land. We gave each family three goats and three chickens, and a paraffin lamp to enable them to study at night.

51

LOVE DEFEATS DESPAIR

KITGUM, 2007

I HAD LEARNT to cope with sexual abuse as a child, my mother's death, two failed marriages, and over a decade of war and instability, but now out of the blue I found myself depressed. I had just arrived back from my annual holiday in Australia. The trip had been fruitful and I had enjoyed catching up with family and friends. But as we touched down at Entebbe Airport, I felt a wave of despair envelop me. I despaired at the hopeless poverty that surrounded me. Moreover, I felt crushed beneath the responsibility of thousands of needy children.

Driving through Kitgum Town, I noticed the mounds of rubbish strewn everywhere and the seemingly hopeless state of the community. It was overwhelming. I wondered how I would cope with the year ahead and all the sickness and poverty that needed to be addressed.

We arrived in Kitgum late in the afternoon as the crimson-coloured sun set the clouds ablaze. On any normal day, I would have been captivated by the sight, but on this day I was wrapped up in my thoughts. Hauling my suitcase out of the trunk and pulling out the handle, I began to amble towards my room, when I head little voices calling, "Aunty Irene . . . Aunty Irene."

A few moments later, some of our staff emerged from a house that was under construction. I spotted John Ochola, who hugged me with arms that ended in stumps.

"Welcome back Aunty! See my friends are building me a house. The road grader demolished mine, so now they are re-building it for me."

Each builder shook my hand and smiled a huge welcome.

Arriving at my room, I tentatively unlocked the door. I had swapped my beleaguered caravan—which had become a target for thugs and termites—for a large room on top of the guest quarters. It had beautiful jarrah floorboards, a cathedral ceiling and a verandah. But on this day, I only noticed the flaws. As I stood surveying the cobwebs, ash and dust swathing the rooms, eight of my resident girls bustled past me with brooms and basins of water. Singing as they dusted and swept and mopped, I felt convicted. I had come home from my annual holiday to a lovely welcome. Why was I complaining?

David Owor, our concierge, hovered nearby. He had arrived at 7.00 a.m. that morning to ensure that I had a cup of tea on arrival. He proudly presented me with a meal of rice. I sat on the verandah, which overlooked an ancient tamarind tree, and sipped my tea while the sun set amidst a glorious burst of colour and listened to the children who were drumming and singing worship songs. Again, I sighed, "Thank You God. These people are teaching me to value human beings above all else. They may not have material things, but they have rich communion with each other."

The next morning I awoke to the sound of hundreds of vil-lagers singing in our school hall—Sunday church had begun. Beloved local church pastor Walter Otim, who had built up a huge following from his nightly radio programme, was preach-ing a very humorous message. Feeling jetlagged and irritable, I looked around at the laughing congregation. I didn't feel like joining them.

God spoke to me: "Lighten up Irene, this laughter is bringing them healing. You look at life from the wrong aspect. You look for perfection, and when you don't find it you are disappointed. These people begin at survival, so anything more is a bonus which they celebrate and thank Me for. Try and learn from them."

Moments later, Pastor Walter invited people to come and follow Jesus. Villagers began moving to the front and knelt on the floor—weathered old women leaning on walking sticks, mothers with babies on their backs, gaunt youth in tattered shirts. Pastors prayed over each one, as hands were raised heavenwards and tears flowed.

Before closing, Pastor Denis announced, "We have a baby to dedicate."

A young woman brought her infant forward.

"Unfortunately his father died recently. But God will help you to raise him. What is his name?" he asked.

"*Oweka* (Abandoned)," the mother said. A murmur went through the congregation. She added quickly, "Denis Oweka. I will call him Denis Oweka." Still the congregation murmured.

One grandmother stood up. "You cannot call him Oweka. He is not abandoned," she objected. "You should call him Denis *Rwot-Omiya* (God's gift)."

Pastor Denis nodded. "He is God's gift to our church family. We will help you raise him."

I silently thanked God for teaching me the value of human life. The people I had been working with for the past sixteen years did not have running water, clean homes or sufficient food. But observing this moment and recalling destitute children eating sloppy porridge from a shared bowl, or villagers offering precious water to each other and then offering to help bear the burden of carrying loads of firewood was a humbling reminder of the value and respect they had for each other.

Many of my white visitors found the unconditional love given by Africans irresistible. The Acholi motto is, "Never offend, never reject anyone." That is why people often kneel while serving water or food and always respond to a cry for help. It's rude to ask anyone if they would like food. Rather, extra places are always set for any passing visitor. There is no system of borrowing or lending and expecting it back. They heed God's advice and give without expecting anything in return. If someone asks for your cloak, give him your shirt as well.

These people were teaching me a thing or two about living according to God's original plan. In turn, I would offer practical support in restoring the poorest of the poor to God's original plan—human dignity.

52

EASTER TIME

KITGUM, 2007

IT WAS GOOD FRIDAY in early 2007. I woke early and gulped in breaths of cool fresh air as I walked to the post office. The sun, as huge as a dinner plate, began to ascend above the mountains of Sudan. Fiery gold, it slowly rose. I was once again charged and humbled by its phenomenal energy. God is a consuming fire. Just as we cannot gaze at the sun, we cannot see God in all His glory. Tears filled my eyes as I experienced His omnipotent presence, then all at once thought how blessed I was to be stripped of material comforts these past years, enabling me to taste the fullness of my creator in that simple moment, and in all the miracles I had witnessed over the years since arriving in Kitgum.

There were no chocolate eggs to be had in Kitgum. Instead, God's Holy Spirit gave me something special. In the mail were two precious Easter cards. One was a booklet entitled *From Gethsemane to Galilee* containing paintings of Jesus. As I walked back from the post office, I put my earphones in and tuned in to our radio station, which was playing well-known hymns.

The Holy Spirit said, "Irene, go up the hill to the radio station and read to the listeners from Matthew."

I baulked. "No way, I can't climb that hill on an empty stomach. I need breakfast."

"Go on, yes you can," He urged.

I clambered up the rocky hill, pebbles skittering downwards beneath my feet. It was 7 a.m. and already the sun was blisteringly hot.

The radio presenter was surprised to see me and my flushed face.

"Can I read the Easter story?" I asked.

He nodded, turned down the music and announced, "We have a special visitor this morning. Aunty Irene has climbed the hill to bring us the Easter story."

After reading from Matthew's Gospel I continued, "Good Friday! Two thousand years ago, the most important event in the history of the world took place. God became man and then suffered and died for us so that the devil has no hold on us, no legal right to our lives. Do you want to kneel before Jesus right now? Tell Him you love Him and that you want Him to take control of your life and put some sanity back into it. Just close your eyes and repeat this prayer . . ."

As I carefully inched my way back down the hill, I felt elated. Over breakfast, God continued speaking to me. "Irene," He said, "you can create your own celebration." I looked into my cold millet porridge and doubted it. "Here's the plan," He continued. "Celebrate Easter Sunday by giving ten radios and twenty Bibles away as prizes. At 3 p.m. on Sunday, announce ten locations over the radio. The first people to reach the spot and say the password will win. The password should be, 'There is power in the blood of Jesus'."

Gerald Omal, our Peace Radio technician made a great advert, emphasising the special password, then sandwiched it in between Darlene Zschech and Ron Kenoly singing "Jesus is Alive." Soon, the whole district was abuzz with excitement waiting for Easter Sunday to arrive.

On the Saturday, I was stiff and achy; I crawled out of bed. My calves were tight from hill climbing, but I knew I needed my morning exercise. As the sun rose, a hot, dusty wind gained strength. I paused, as I often did, when bright-eyed children ran squealing from their mud huts to grasp the hand of their white grandma.

Back inside the house it was already hot. I imagined the surf at Narrabeen Beach and the warm sand between my toes; then tucked into my sloppy porridge, wiped the sweat off my brow and wondered how I was going to enjoy my holiday. The big tamarind tree outside was being buffeted by the wind, its green leaves shimmering. Cautiously, I opened a window, pulled up a deckchair and sat down. As the tree filtered the dust and heat, a wild fresh breeze flapped my curtains. I closed my eyes and dreamt. Was that the flap of a canvas sail I felt? The balmy air relaxed my body and caressed my face. I felt my fingers trailing through sparkling blue waters and the wind carrying my yacht swiftly on its journey towards heaven's safe harbour. Did I feel gentle sea spray? Occasional tiny showers cooled my face. I felt refreshed. Then I remembered the thirty bats resident in that tree. Ugh! Bat urine! I laughed, stretched out in my chair and read Rick Renner's *Sparkling Gems from the Greek*, a revolutionary feast for my spirit and soul.

Easter Sunday arrived and I read Luke 24 over the airwaves, then walked to church, which was packed with excited villagers in vibrant cottons.

Afterwards I gathered twenty young men for lunch and, between mouthfuls of beans and chilli sauce, supervised a trial run of mobs pushing and shoving. Africans are great at improvising and really enjoy acting.

"I won. Give me the prize." A youth wrenched the radio.

Another grabbed it back and held it over his head.

"No!" he screamed, "I was first. What is the password? . . . There's power in the blood of God!"

"Aha. Wrong!" said another. "There is power in the blood of Jesus," he said raising his voice. "I am the winner!"

There was much laughter as each one had their turn at handling "the mob." Then, with military precision, each was dispatched to his secret location to await the countdown. At 2:59 and 50 seconds, the radio announcer began to count: 10 . . . 9 . . . 8 . . . 7 . . . 6 . . . 5 . . . 4 . . . 3 . . . 2 . . . 1 . . . and then the ten secret locations were announced.

Soldiers commandeered bicycles and pedalled to win radios. Mothers with babies on their backs left their vegetables and ran to the locations. Students put down their books and sauntered to different spots. Greeted with a sea of blank faces, they repeated the password until they found one of our men.

My men returned with many amusing stories, which made my Easter a happy one and made up for the lack of chocolate eggs and being apart from my family.

◈ ◈ ◈

On one of my visits to Kampala, I met George Lubega. I had been invited to preach one Sunday morning at a large church in the city and George was singing. Afterwards he shared his story with me.

George was a creative little boy who lived in a loving home with his mother Dorine and brother Gilbert until his mother's slow and painful death from AIDS in 1994. While 5-year-old Gilbert was taken by an aunt, 10-year-old George was at first taken in by his polygamous father. At the age of 12, however, his father threw him out and he was forced to live on the streets, scrounging food from dustbins, smoking *ganja* (marijuana), sniffing petrol and pickpocketing.

In 2002, George was found half dead on the streets and admitted to hospital. Sometime after he was discharged, he and his friend Dan visited Miracle Centre Cathedral—a thriving Pentecostal church in Kampala—and George gave his life to Jesus. He was accepted, loved and encouraged to join the choir, as he was a gifted singer. And it was here that we met.

George and I became good friends and I encouraged him to pursue his dream of singing professionally. In 2008, he fasted for forty days, and then wrote his first song "Ganjaman." It was based on his experiences living as a street child and in Kampala ghettos. His song hit the top of the charts in the first week and stayed there for six months.

George, whose stage name is Exodus, has gone on to become one of Uganda's bestselling gospel recording artists. Youth in northern Uganda have been particularly inspired by George's strong Christian values. They have seen the power of God at work in a former street kid.

He now also works with CKS as an artistic director and peace ambassador, and lives at the Rubaga house in Kampala.

53

A CERTAIN FUTURE

KITGUM, 2008

AS I STEPPED ACROSS mud drains full of slimy water and garbage in one of the IDP camps near Kitgum Town, and looked into the surly faces of idle youths playing cards, squatting in the shade beside their mud huts, I recalled the words of a United Nations Development Programme report: "Northern Uganda's displacement crisis is still one of the world's worst—with more than a million people still crammed into squalid camps."

Since the peace talks had commenced, families had started to leave the IDP camps and migrate back to their land, but after eight years it wasn't that easy. Land boundaries were unclear and were far from schools, water and medical care.

It was particularly difficult for youths making the transition from camp life to farmland. They missed the camp health centres and the recreational spots such as bars and video halls. Many of them had few memories and little experience with rural life. The work on the land was much harder than they were used to and they were separated from their friends. A statistic that reminded me of their plight was that eighty percent of local Kitgum children and young adults had been abducted by rebels. Some had been forced to kill fellow villagers and had been brutalised for years before they were able to escape. Many of the long-time servers in the LRA would be shunned and unwelcome in their communities. Alienated from a community they used to be part of, many would drift back to market centres and form social bonds with groups of ex-abductees. My heart went out to this generation of lost young men.

"*Kop ango*?" I greeted them.

They looked up and grinned. They knew who I was. Everyone has a cousin, brother or sister who is a pupil in one of our schools.

"Does anyone speak English?" I asked the group.

One young man stood up and shook my hand.

"How is life here?" I asked them.

They shrugged and looked down.

I continued, "Anyone want to learn building or carpentry? Then when you go back to your village you can build yourself a good house or a chicken shed." I asked them if they had thought about joining our vocational training school, sharing with them the story of our headmaster who had been just like them.

"There are sponsorships when you have no money and you will get breakfast and lunch for free." I left them discussing their future options and continued strolling through the camp.

When the new term began at the beginning of 2008, we had more than 1,000 young people enrol to learn a trade. I peered through the crowd to see if I could spot some of the young men I had spoken with. Several of our new boys waved at me. Others, who had already been through a year of vocational training, wheeled in their new bikes, bought with money they had earned during the holidays as they worked roofing buildings, framing doors and building furniture.

That year, we built a new three-storey building, complete with library on top—an extension to our existing vocational training centre. We fitted out our classrooms with new computers that had been donated by Crossroads.

With each passing day, I marvelled at God's goodness to us and the results we were seeing, as this once devastated community flourished, and a new generation of qualified teachers, doctors, accountants and mechanics emerged.

One afternoon, an old grandfather in our community grasped my hand in his leathery grip and shook it vigorously. His black, furrowed farmer's face broke into a smile, while his roomy eyes welled with tears. He had never dreamt that his 18-year-old grandson, the eldest of a large family of brothers and cousins, would now be in Kampala studying to be a doctor and planning a medical practice in Kitgum.

One of our girls, Josephine, had arrived at CKS in 1998. She had stumbled into the centre with ripped clothing, her face splattered with mud and tears. She had escaped a vicious beating by rebels and run to us for safety. I can remember looking at her and wondering what the future held for her. Shivering and in shock, she stuttered for months. After completing primary school, we sponsored her to study at high school. And then she completed two years of study in hospitality and catering.

Around the same time, a young man called Alfred appeared on our building site. He was gaunt with hunger and begged for work. We trained him in the basics of carpentry. As the years progressed, he was promoted to principal of the CKS vocational school and then to pastor of our community church.

Josephine and Alfred began dating, and then in February 2008 they married. A thousand friends and family gathered to celebrate this day. The project site was decorated with ribbons and bows as the young couple walked down the aisle. A *calabash* drum roll, followed by trombones, heralded the arrival of the bride. I sat in the front row wearing my Sunday best and beaming from ear to ear as Josephine slowly walked to the front. She looked so beautiful in white satin and diamanté, her eyes sparkling as she looked into the eyes of her bridegroom. After the couple had made their vows, they shared cake. Alfred served his wife as a sign of his loving care. At the end of the service, the guests were entertained by a rap song and dancing. It was a wonderful occasion.

Josephine and Alfred were just two of the many young people who arrived at CKS desperate and without hope, but now were able to look forward to a bright future.

54

VERY IMPORTANT PERSONS

KITGUM, 2010

THE INVITATION CAME unexpectedly. In June of 2009 I was honoured and humbled to be awarded Officer of the Order of Australia "for service to international relations, particularly through sustained aid for children affected by war and HIV/AIDS in northern Uganda," and this opened up all sorts of new doors for me.

Your attendance as a VIP guest is requested at a public meeting for His Excellency Yoweri K. Museveni, President of Uganda, to be held in Mucwini. The function begins at 8 a.m.

After a frantic search for an electric iron—the charcoal iron box can spoil your good clothes with black marks—I was dressed in my best suit and on my way to meet the President of Uganda. As John Paul drove us along the dusty, bumpy roads I wondered if I would have an opportunity to shake the President's hand.

Yoweri Kaguta Museveni became President of the Republic of Uganda on 29 January 1986 after leading the rebellion that subsequently led to the demise of the Milton Obote regime. He had been President of Uganda for twenty-four years and I was looking forward to finally meeting him.

An hour later, we arrived at the paddock, dotted with villagers dressed in the national colours—yellow T-shirts and bright red *kikois* (sarongs).

In my best shoes I hobbled across the spikey grass and was ushered to a chair under the shade of a plastic tarpaulin to wait for the President's arrival. For three hours, drums were pounded and dancers performed their energetic traditional dances. Numbed by the noise and the heat, and suffering with a bout of malaria, I dozed until the President arrived. I soon woke up and jumped to my feet when I heard my name being called.

"Irene Gleeson AO, please open the meeting with prayer."

Standing in the open field, squinting in the sun's glare, I took the microphone and thanked God for the leaders He had appointed over us. Then I asked God to have His hand on the proceedings.

I tottered back to my seat.

After several hours of speeches I was dozing again. My eyelids felt like lead weights.

John Paul elbowed me and whispered, "Mama, they are calling you."

Winding up his accolade, the Honourable Minister for Foreign Affairs, Henry Okello Oryem's voice cut through the haze, ". . . one of the largest learning institutions in Uganda. Your Excellency, I present to you Irene Gleeson AO. She has been working here tirelessly for the war-affected children in northern Uganda for the past eighteen years."

I stood to my feet, waved and smiled at the President, who was sitting in another marquee flanked by his security guards.

Then Oryem boomed through the microphone, "If you can be quick, you may shake hands with the President."

"Holy Spirit, help me," I murmured, trying to swallow a yawn as I stumbled across the grass, trying my best to look dignified as I walked.

Obviously military-trained, the President sat alert and bright-eyed—physically fit and robust for a man of his age. As he extended his hand, I bowed and then said, "I am honoured to meet you. Thank you for bringing peace to northern Uganda. Now we can get on with our work."

I fished in my handbag, and the security guards immediately looked alert.

I offered my business card, which the President put in his coat pocket.

"I would like to visit your office," I said.

He smiled brightly and replied, "I will call you."

I never heard from him again.

55

ON WITH THE TASK

MEETING THE PRESIDENT was exciting—but it was not time to rest on our laurels. God was already speaking to me about our next building project—a mortuary.

Since opening in 2005, we had filled Gloryland Junction with many needy patients from around the region, who without the hospice would have been forced to face an undignified death, often alone. We wanted to afford them dignity after death and to send them off in a manner fitting for a child of the King. We named the mortuary Heaven Express. Thankfully, there hasn't been too much of a demand for our mortuary, as we have sent home more patients than we have buried. But, like our hospice, the mortuary doesn't look sad or depressing. It is colourful and inviting—a glimpse of the glory that awaits us on the other side.

God had also spoken to me about the children. Mothers who lose their battle with AIDS often leave behind AIDS-infected children, which prompted us to open a children's ward at Gloryland Junction. These children, who vary in ages, attend the CKS nursery or school during the day, but sleep in the ward under the supervision of nurses who monitor their condition and give ARVs as necessary.

One such boy is Emmanuel. Both his parents had died of AIDS when he was 3 years old. Showing signs of infection himself—vomiting, diarrhoea and body rashes—he was shunned by his siblings and left on his own in a mud hut. When neighbours bought him to CKS he was severely traumatised. He had forgotten how to smile or talk. For six months he sat mute on his bed, tears running down his cheeks, his eyes hollow and sad. Each time his blood count showed that he needed ARVs he would lie exhausted for days on the cool cement floor, as the drugs fought the virus.

Over time, Emmanuel learnt to trust the nursing staff at CKS. On Sunday mornings he would walk cautiously into the community church and stand next to me looking up at me with his puppy-dog eyes. I would lift him onto my lap and try to coax a smile out of him. After six months of continuous love and care, a miracle happened. Emmanuel smiled.

In 2010, by this time a resident of the Gloryland children's ward, he was a 9-year-old boy able to enjoy life. His day, like many of the children in the hospice, began each morning at 7 a.m. when he would be woken by the laughter of the twenty other hospice children. He would make his bed, take his basin and wash near the water borehole. Donning his red T-shirt and navy trousers, he would carry his exercise book, pen and bowl and walk up a small hill to the school assembly where he would sit amongst thousands of other children, all boisterously singing.

When the 8.30 a.m. gong chimed, he would line up at his Primary 2 classroom. Lessons would continue until 10.30 a.m., when Emmanuel would queue up alongside his classmates for a bowl of maize porridge. More classes would follow until 12.30 p.m., when almost 5,000 students would queue for a lunch of beans and *posho*. During his lunchbreak, Emmanuel would often head to the library and immerse himself in picture books, or if he was feeling sick or had injured himself he would line up with other children at the school clinic. At 2 p.m. his classes would resume until 4 p.m. The overcrowded classrooms can get very hot in the afternoon hours, so teachers encourage singing, drawing or storytelling.

By 4.30 p.m. Emmanuel would be back with his friends at Gloryland Junction. He might wander up to watch some of our teenagers playing basketball or soccer on our designated fields. At 7 p.m. another basin would be filled to wash away the day's dust, then a meal of maize and vegetables would see all the children getting sleepy. Nurses would give out relevant medicines, and then it would be lights out on another day of loving care.

As often as I could, I wandered down to Gloryland Junction to spend time with Emmanuel and the other children. I always found Matron Franca dispensing loving care. As I walked through each ward—the men's, women's, teenagers' and children's wards, I could hear our radio station playing music and children outside running around laughing. The babies were smiling and growing plumper each day.

In 2010, we only lost five patients, who exited through our Heaven Express mortuary. Thirty hospice patients were discharged to resume farming and community life. Many of the patients who arrived looking emaciated, with eyes sunken in their sockets, were transformed after being given loving care, medicine, nutritious food and prayer.

❖ ❖ ❖

With my mind on the plight of our patients and all the work going on at the project site, I paid little attention to what was going on at home in Australia—that was until I got a Facebook message from my daughter, Shelley, in March 2011. She had been diagnosed with breast cancer.

The announcement brought back memories of my mother who had died from cancer. It also reminded me how far away from home I was at a time when my daughter needed me. I began pleading with God for her healing.

Several months later, I was back in Sydney. Hand in hand, Shelley and I prayed and believed for the lump to disappear. Before getting on my flight back to Africa, her father and I gave her a bracelet—a small reminder that I would always be with her in spirit.

Every morning when I woke I turned on my laptop and checked Facebook for any updates on her progress. She eventually underwent surgery to remove the lump, followed by nine months of chemotherapy.

If it weren't for Shelley's remarkable sense of humour in the face of such adversity, I might have gone back to Australia for good. But she is tough and resolute and has a keep-going attitude, no matter how bad things seem at times. Moreover, she had her own children to consider. I knew she would be okay. I had made a pact with God twenty years earlier and I trusted that my children were in safe hands.

56

FULL CIRCLE

USA, KITGUM AND AUSTRALIA, 2012

IN JANUARY OF 2012, I was sponsored to visit the USA, my father's homeland, to speak about the work of CKS. It was such an honour and I was treated like a veteran war hero.

As I told my story the response was astounding. My stories of God's faithfulness and protection inspired and challenged people from all walks of life—from business people to troubled women. I was amazed at the opportunities I was being given. At a dinner with students at Princeton University I explained that I had no degree and no social standing in the world's eyes, but despite this God had chosen to use me to impact a community. I visited Washington and then went on to Dallas to appear on Daystar TV (a Christian television network broadcasting globally).

In many churches, I was able to share the work God had done through this vessel and the hands of faithful supporters around the world. The trip was an important time for me. For many years I had felt rejected and abandoned and now I was being accepted and loved by so many. Furthermore, I had finally found peace with my identity. My name was Irene Hephzibah Gleeson—I was one part Australian, one part Ugandan and one part American, and most importantly, daughter of the King of Kings.

Despite the accolades, I managed to come back down to earth and return to soaring temperatures, dust storms and a diet of beans. I was accompanied by a film crew from Daystar TV who filmed a documentary on the work of CKS. This was the second documentary we had taken part in. Several years earlier, film-maker Grant Windle had produced a documentary called *Cinderella Children*. I felt so honoured to have these talented people telling our story.

❖   ❖   ❖

Months later, another special visitor arrived. The Prime Minister of Australia's Special Envoy for Africa, the Hon. Bob McMullan, travelled to Kitgum to report on the progress of this Australian grandmother who had spent twenty years of her life in war-torn Uganda and who had recently been awarded an AO (Officer of the Order of Australia). He was accompanied by Australian High Commissioner for Nairobi, Geoff Tooth, and The Ugandan Minister for Foreign Affairs, the Hon. Henry Okello Oryem.

On the day the visitors arrived at the CKS compound, they were greeted by CKS school children who performed a traditional dance for them. Seated in the vast assembly hall, the men faced 5,000 children, all buzzing with excitement at having these important visitors come all the way to see us. I watched the men's faces and noted that each one of them was visibly moved by the children singing the national anthem and Exodus performing his own composition about mothers losing their children to war.

Each of the dignitaries stepped onto the stage and paid their tribute to the work of CKS. I looked around at my staff who lined the back of the hall and smiled—all of them had a story of their own. Many of them were former child soldiers and scruffy children who gathered under the trees all those years earlier.

Today they were teachers, leaders, pastors, builders, carpenters, dressmakers, mechanics, welders . . . I took a moment to rejoice in God. In my mind's eye, I pictured all the angels in heaven standing in a long line forming a bridge with their hands as one by one, thousands of Ugandans marched through the angelic tunnel into the throne room for their appointment with the supreme ruler of all time—the King of Kings.

◈　◈　◈

In May of 2012, I went back to Australia. I had been wrestling with an irritating cough and extreme tiredness for more than twelve months. After being admitted to the respiratory ward at Royal Prince Alfred Hospital, Sydney, for suspected TB, I was given the diagnosis—stage IV oesophageal and pancreatic cancer.

The doctors told me I had only weeks to live and so a plan was put into place, which involved a beautiful pink palliative care ward and the strongest of painkillers. After a week of intensive radiotherapy and a week of intensive chemotherapy, I was exhausted, so I cancelled my schedule.

One afternoon I was lying in bed at my daughter Heidi's house feeling sorry for myself when a video appeared on Facebook. It was my 5,000 children in Uganda singing and praying for healing for their "white mama." A big white sign held high amongst the sea of red said, "Mama Irene, be healed in Jesus' name." Then I got mad at the devil and told him he was not going to dictate my calendar, so after much prayer and support from friends all over the world, I rebooked my flight to Uganda. On 16 July 2012, although feeling very fatigued, I took a step of faith and boarded my flight to Africa with my good friend, Jacky, a nurse.

Equipped with God's word and a few painkillers, I went about my work at CKS. It was tough at times. In the daylight hours

I got on with it—meeting with the teachers, writing and answering emails. At night, the terror often struck. After several weeks of being back in Africa, I had a particularly disturbing night. Struggling to breathe, I cried out to Jesus. I pictured myself holding His hand. And if that meant walking hand in hand through the pearly gates, I was ready. But it was not to be. Several days later Pastor Denis prayed for me, rebuking the spirit of death. Immediately I felt better.

57

THE WHEELS KEEP
TURNING

KITGUM, SYDNEY AND USA 2013

I WAS NOT GOING to let the cancer define me. Instead, I focused on yet another need in northern Uganda—the plight of young pregnant women. In 2012 I heard a statistic that shocked me: sixteen women die each day in Uganda from childbirth-related complications, mostly due to a lack of prenatal and postnatal care, forced early marriages, teenage pregnancies, primitive traditional practices and lack of access to medical services. Although we had a limited budget, I had another royal commission—to build a maternity centre. By 2013, one whole floor had been completed, but we needed finances. It was time to trust God again.

Trusting God for provision was easy—trusting God for victory over this cancer ravaging my body proved more challenging. I went back and forth to Australia for many doctors' appointments and each time the news was more alarming. I found myself back on that pendulum, swinging from faith to fear. On the good days, I could conquer the world; on the bad days I was telling my staff to plan my funeral.

I had been invited to speak in the USA in January 2013, but didn't know if I was going to be able to make it. Days before I was due to leave Australia I stayed with a friend in Sydney. Pain racked my body. Tiredness was overwhelming. After dinner, I excused myself, washed my face and headed off to an early bed. Throughout the night, demons wrestled with me. In the blackness, I heard the devil say, "Irene, you can't go to America, you're too sick, you'll die in a park and because you have no insurance, they will bury you in a pauper's grave." I contemplated the demonic whisperings and considered my options. Perhaps I should check myself into the pink palliative care ward in Sydney after all. The following morning, the day was crisp and clear—a vivid blue sky framed a bright yellow sun. I had a scripture in my heart and I was pain-free. The Lord had one last assignment for me.

On 17 January 2013, I was a guest of Daystar TV in Dallas on a show called *Children of War/Children of Hope*. Exodus, who was with me, performed and I spoke about my desire to build this maternity centre.

Daystar founder Marcus Lamb began the interview with a question: "Irene, how in the world did the Lord get you to Africa? Did He trick you, did He bribe you?"

I looked at him for a moment, paused and then responded, "He broke my heart for the children of Uganda. He weeps because so many of His beautiful creations don't achieve their full potential—because of poverty and because of war. I went there to redress the imbalance. God sent me where no-one would want to go in the middle of a war. I sold my beach house and we took our caravan to the north of Uganda, near the Sudan border, and put it under a tree. And the children would creep in during the day and I would teach them songs like 'Jesus Loves Me This I Know'."

I looked over at Marcus' face—his eyes were moist.

"Now the children have grown to 8,000 in three different schools. I have 450 members of staff—many of them former child soldiers and those who sat under the original tree. My little children who were 6 are now 26 years old. They are nurses, doctors, builders and teachers. They have a sense of purpose and a destiny. They keep the wheels running."

58

FROM THE HEART
OF A LIONESS

SYDNEY, SPRING 2013

A VISITOR TO CKS once commented to me: "These people are so happy. When I hear their stories of war and suffering, of loved ones they have lost, I expect to find them suicidal. But here I see them laughing, full of joy and even concern for my comfort. They are rebuilding their lives with energy. It's not a logical response to their situation. Are you really their fairy godmother, Irene?"

"Whoa! Not me!" I said, pretending to duck for cover in case lightning struck. "You are seeing God in action. It's all His healing. It is His Holy Spirit working in their lives."

I love Andrae Crouch's song (featured on our *Cinderella Children* DVD) "This is the Lord's Doing and It Is Marvellous!" In our weakness, God's strength shows up to perfect things.

For years I trudged through IDP camps, muttering about the heat and the dust and frustrations and dreaming of the beaches of Australia. Then I would see a small child struggling to carry a jerry can of water too heavy for him, or a grandmother carrying an orphaned toddler on her arthritic hip, and I would reach out and touch them. Sometimes I'd carry the jerry can for the child and pat their head, or I'd stroke the grandmother's shoulders. I always had a special purpose in this. A shepherd strokes his lambs to rub the scent of a human onto them and so keep the wolves away. God told me, "If you can stroke My suffering humanity, you will be rubbing the scent of Jesus, the master shepherd, on them and so keep any enemy away from them."

Over the years I have had the privilege of being a conduit for God's protective Holy Spirit. Many times I have felt the compassion of Jesus flowing through my hands to comfort a grieving mother or to hold a child covered in sores and flies. Many times, while I have held a feverish baby, they have fallen into a deep sleep. I have often looked at my hands and asked myself, "Why has God used me?"

Do you feel unloved? Unappreciated? Forgotten or abandoned? I know I did. I was rejected and abandoned by my father, abused by evil stepfathers and rejected by the community. I was an embarrassment in an unwelcoming world. The ghosts of my past continued to haunt me through my traumatic childhood. As a young mother, they robbed me of joy and oppressed me with exhaustion. Those who did love me, I rejected. Eventually this led me to search for inner peace—a quest that led me to the cross of Christ and the wounds He carried.

Did you know, dear reader, that your name is engraved on His palms, your name is written in His sacred blood. He bled and died for you. Yes, you. Your name has always been on His lips. He pleads for your protection and your wholeness. Just pray this simple prayer and you will find what you have always been searching for, as I did:

Dear God, thank You for Your gift of Salvation. Thank You for sending Your Son Jesus Christ to die for me. I acknowledge that I am a sinner and need You in my

*life. Please forgive me for all my wrongdoings and be-
come my God. As I accept Jesus Christ as my Lord and
Saviour I believe that I am now a Christian, a child of
God. In Jesus name. Amen.*

If you prayed that prayer for the first time, then I welcome you
into God's family.

AFTERWORD

ON 21 JULY 2013, Mama Irene Gleeson went to be with her beloved Saviour, after a long and courageous battle with oesophageal and pancreatic cancer, leaving behind an enduring legacy of love and hope in Kitgum. The organisation she created—the Irene Gleeson Foundation—stands as a permanent testimony and will continue her mission of caring for destitute children in northern Uganda. The children you have read about in these pages—and many more—have grown into adults and are now serving with IGF to help carve out a better future for the children who follow them. These children strive to honour their mama by carrying on the work of educating, feeding and providing medical support to thousands of needy children daily.

After the news of Irene's death was passed to the community by radio and word of mouth, many travelled from far and wide to mourn and honour Mama Irene. 26 July saw a flurry of activity on the compound of the Irene Gleeson Foundation. The entire community, both those associated with IGF and those not, offered a helping hand. Some brought extra chairs from home so that guests would have a place to sit. Others gave financial contributions in order to help cover costs and ensure everyone would be fed. There had been rumours about who might attend—some said that President Yoweri Museveni himself might even be there. On the day of Irene's memorial service, those who loved Irene most—all 10,000 of them—crowded onto the football pitch Irene had constructed years earlier. Foreign dignitaries and government representatives, parents and former students all crowded together to pay their respects. Two of Irene's African children gave stirring eulogies and encouraged all present to take Irene's example and carry it forth.

It is these people—Irene's African children—who are ensuring that the organisation and legacy remain strong. Irene always believed in training up and empowering her Ugandan employees, ensuring that the project would be sustainable beyond her involvement. One of Irene's first sons is now head of the business school and a youth pastor. Another of her children, who once slept on the streets, is now a midwife running prenatal training for mothers. A young man who came on board as an accountant's assistant is now the Executive Director. All are Ugandan and all have been trained by Irene herself for such a time as this.

And what a time it is! While we mourn the loss of Irene deeply, the organisation has never been more excited for where it is going. Irene charted a course and IGF as a global body is continuing that course. Irene had a dream of opening a school in every IDP camp in northern Uganda. This dream continued. On 15 July 2013, from her bed in Sydney, Irene was able to listen by phone to the official opening of IGF's fourth primary school near Palabek town. This was to be the last communication Irene had with her beloved Uganda.

Our four primary schools and our vocational school continue well, enabling thousands of children to reach their full potential. The IGF health programmes are expanding to include Irene's long-dreamt-of maternity and children's centre, which is currently under construction. IGF continues to address societal ills and promote reconciliation through our community church, discipleship programme and outreach, as well as through our community radio station Mighty Fire FM, which is reaching one million listeners with hope for the future.

Irene's dream of rescuing children is now our focus and vision. Her children are now our children, and we will take hold of what she has established and endeavour to take the organisation to the next level. Additional teachers, more textbooks, better-quality classrooms, health and nutrition—these are all improvements that our IGF family around the world is helping us provide.

Irene and her story will always be symbolic of this organisation: a white woman who sold all she had to give to the poor, and transcended cultural boundaries to become an Acholi leader. She had a foot in both worlds and acted as a bridge for generous, compassionate people to give what they could in order to provide a better life for desperate children in northern Uganda. IGF believes that even though Irene has gone, that bridge remains open and that many more family members from Australia, America and around the globe will start their own journey across it.

Sadly Irene is not around to see the release of this book. If she were here, she'd be urging you to respond to the needs of the children she loved so dearly. So if anything you have read in these pages has stirred your heart, please join us. Or, if you accepted Christ into your heart by praying the prayer at the end of the last chapter, please get in touch with us via our website www.irenegleesonfoundation.com.

We need prayer, volunteers and regular givers. If you would like to help Irene's continuing legacy, please consider rescuing a child from the shackles of poverty through child sponsorship. Our website and newsletters explain how to do this.

We know that we can only achieve Irene's vision together. Her mantle has been laid upon people all over the globe.

Wii wa obi poo piri pi kare weng Mego. We will always remember you, Mama.

—Irene Gleeson Foundation

FURTHER NOTES AND STORIES FROM IRENE

MOST OF OUR WORKERS have said over the years, "Mama, you rescued us, now sit and watch us rescue other needy children and bring them up as you did us."

In 1992 I began sitting under the shade of a mango tree and teaching the children songs I knew. I had no master-plan or vision statement, only a word from Papa God. Those same children, with food in their bellies, clean, washed, and educated, grew up to become my African sons and daughters. Many now work for us and head up our departments.

I have always believed that each one of God's children has a unique personality and purpose, and that it was my job to help them fulfil their potential.

Here are the stories of a few of them.

Walter

One Sunday morning I was walking to church in town, when I noticed a small boy sitting forlornly beside a mud hut. I called to him and invited him to church with me. He shook his head and gestured to his dirty, ragged clothing. I returned to my caravan and collected a shirt and shorts for him. He told me his name was Walter and proudly escorted me to church.

The following day, he turned up at the project site, eager for school. For the next few evenings, Walter lingered around the site. He was obviously hungry, so he joined the dormitory children for their evening meal. Then, all of a sudden his visits stopped.

As I passed by his hut one day, my heart leapt to see him washing clothes in a basin. My joy was short-lived when an older woman ran at me waving a stick and scowling. A neighbour intervened, explaining that I was not to steal the child because his aunt had brought him from the village to house-sit while she did her gardening. If I interfered she would send Walter back to the village where he would probably be abducted by rebels.

However, hungry and lonely, Walter could not resist joining us each day. When his aunt resolved to carry out her threat, the neighbours intervened and convinced her to let the boy join our dormitory.

From the outset, Walter showed himself to be a leader, gathering the children for evening worship, rallying the boys for football and becoming class prefect.

He graduated from the Childcare primary school, and we sponsored him to study mechanics in Kampala. This meant running the rebel gauntlet by bus or truck forty times during the five years he was studying. He survived many ambushes by leaping from the windows and fleeing into the bush, while friends lay dead at the side of the road.

One day, he was travelling on the back of a utility truck when the driver, fearing rebels, jumped from the truck and left it unmanned, careering down a hill. Walter toppled overboard, but was dragged for several kilometres with one leg hooked onto the tray. Later he was found unconscious and carried to a local hospital, where he remained unidentified and in a coma for two weeks. Back at the project site, we assumed he had reached his studies in Kampala safely until we heard the news and began some serious prayer.

With his leg badly smashed, it seemed as though his footballing days were over. However, God did a miracle, the plaster was removed after only one month and he returned in good health, this time with a friend—a dog named Billy.

Billy was the runt of the litter. His coat of tawny gold hung in folds down his bony back. One by one his siblings were chosen as potential guard dogs, while he cowered in his pen, his nose snivelling underneath sad, brown eyes. Walter decided he should come and live with us in Kitgum, so he brought him home on the bus. Billy was stuffed into a cardboard box labelled "Bibles" and taken on board with Walter's other belongings. He slept most of the way but, nearing Kitgum, Billy began whimpering, so Walter nursed the box for ten minutes and then he put it on the floor of the aisle.

That's when all hell broke loose. Two vehicles in front, a truck carrying produce and families was hit by a bomb and rolled over. The next truck swerved sideways to avoid it. As people leapt from the tray, rebel soldiers ran at them, firing AK-47s. Walter looked out of the back window of the bus to see rebels charging down the road behind. Inside the bus it was pandemonium, as passengers stampeded towards the door. Walter cringed as he saw the box crushed beneath their trampling feet. He punched the window out and half-climbed, half-fell onto the road as rebels stormed into the bus, shooting, looting and terrorising passengers. Many were killed, many maimed.

Nursing a sprained ankle, Walter limped through the bush. When he eventually arrived at our project site, muddied, but safe, we were overjoyed to see that God had protected him. But what had happened to Billy?

Later that afternoon, a soldier drove the bus into town with the injured on board. Walter sent a note with a friend asking him to collect his tin trunk of belongings. "Jimmy," he added in the note, "if you find a squashed cardboard box with a dead puppy inside, just dispose of it."

Sure enough, Jimmy found the tin trunk. And the crushed box marked "Bibles." As he opened it up, two big brown eyes and a sloppy wet tongue greeted him. Billy became the school children's much-loved companion.

Walter went on to become a CKS staff leader with many responsibilities. He became the head of the CKS mechanics division, supervising fifteen mechanics and drivers and deployment of the trucks. On Saturday nights he was the DJ on our FM radio, hosting "The Dance Party Show." On Sunday mornings he would MC at our community church. Every afternoon, he mobilised CKS basketball teams, which drew youth from all over the Kitgum district. Every evening, he attended to the needs of the dormitory children as house-father. He grew into a bear-sized man and has always been generous with his bear hugs.

Charles

Charles's parents had been killed in the war and, together with his sister, he worked hard to survive, cultivating a few acres that would supply them with food and a little extra cash to pay for school fees, soap, salt and sugar. His story was like so many of our children.

One morning Charles was digging in the hot sun, collecting sweet potatoes, when khaki-clad rebels with cartridge belts over their shoulders surrounded him. They prodded him with their guns until he dropped his hoe. Then they tied him up with rope and led him away. Thus began the nightmare that this sensitive, intelligent boy would never forget.

By day, he was roped together with a hundred other youngsters, forced to keep moving. They stumbled barefoot through the scrub carrying heavy loads of food and stolen goods. At night, while still tied up, he slept fitfully on damp ground, shivering with the cold. He was photographed and recorded and told that if he tried to escape, he would be hunted down and killed. The soldiers kept driving them towards Sudan where they would undergo six months of indoctrination and mercenary training. Each night, Charles crouched in the bush trying to pray and recall the songs taught to him at CKS.

Then in the moonlight one night, something glinted on the ground. It was a razor blade. Charles picked it up and hid it carefully in his waistband, waiting for his opportunity. Before dawn, he managed to cut the rope from round his waist and run for his life into the bush. Bullets whistled past him.

When he finally stopped running, all was silent except for the pounding of his heart. Eventually he made it back to the project site, but he was severely traumatised. For several days he sat dejectedly at our compound gate while all the other children jostled around him. He didn't move or talk. His eyes were bloodshot red and blank. He had seen too much. With his arms wrapped tightly around his legs, his face was set like flint into the distance. He was immersed in his own private pain.

Over time, the love of Jesus and the comfort of the Holy Spirit became like soothing ointment for his broken heart and mind. Charles grew stronger, both physically and spiritually. He eventually went on to university and now works for the Ugandan government. He was with CKS for ten years, where he met and married our worship leader, Concy.

Christopher

In 2002, at the age of 16, Christopher was caring for his younger brothers and sisters while his mother was in hospital recovering from a goitre operation. Late one night, the children heard the sound of rebels battering down their neighbours' doors. Frightened, the children ran and cowered in the bush. The rebels advanced, slashing the grass around them with their machetes and hoes. Christopher watched in horror as his 12-year-old brother, Godfrey, was pulled from his hiding place. They were about to pounce on his younger siblings when Christopher stood up and surrendered. The rebels tore his shirt and tied his arms behind his back. Leaving the smaller children behind, still hiding and terrified, Christopher was shoved towards a line of other prisoners and roped to them.

After marching several kilometres, the night exploded around them in fireballs and whizzing bullets as the Ugandan army pursued them. His face on the ground, Christopher wept tears into the dust as his friends shrieked with pain, their limbs lacerated by ammunition. When the battle abated, the rebel kicked through the prisoners' bodies to find out who had survived. Christopher and his brother were the only ones who had.

"I was led to the body of a dead soldier and told to take off his gumboots," he said. "He was about my age. His face was peaceful, but his legs were mangled. I took off his boots and put them on. Inside I was crying. We walked and walked and walked. We were on our way to Sudan. The soldiers made me carry a B-10 gun—it weighed more than 50 kilograms. My shoulders hurt, but they told me I would be shot if I put it down or complained. We were always on the move, especially at night, just sleeping and hiding for hours in the daytime. We had nothing to eat, so we would pick and eat roots from the ground. I could hardly bear the pain in my shoulder and back. Even now, I suffer with it. I can remember crying, 'God, I am not born to be a soldier. I'm missing my family. Please let me and Godfrey go home.'

"A few days later, the rebel soldiers were gathered around a boy on the ground. They were laughing and shouting like demons: 'Come and see, brothers, this is what will happen to you if you try to escape.' Ten rebels were kicking and beating the young boy with heavy canes. They rolled him over and I saw the boy's face. It was Godfrey—my little brother! He couldn't move or speak for days. He never tried to escape again. As far as I know he is still with the LRA . . . maybe in the Congo (or even dead). But I keep praying for him.

"After thirty days of walking I was desperate. One morning I woke up and said to myself, 'Today is my day! I am leaving these people. If I die by the bullet, so be it.'"

Christopher continued walking until he saw his chance and dropped to the back of the line and veered off onto a side track. When no-one was looking, he crouched down in the bushes and let the gun roll off his shoulder. Moments later, he stood up and ran as hard and as fast as he could.

Eventually he arrived in his district at a *samba* where an old man was digging. The man was terrified and thought he was going to kill him. If the man called for help, the rebels would catch him. He fell on his knees and begged for mercy. The farmer took pity on him. He fed him, washed him and took him to see his father. Knowing that Christopher's life was in danger, his father took him to Kitgum where he joined the other night commuters. He slept under a bamboo table, ever watchful for approaching rebels.

A short time later, Christopher turned up at CKS and asked to be admitted into our vocational programme. Over time, with the help of our staff, prayer and being given basics like food and water, he grew strong and completed a three-year certificate in building, then a craft course. Although he is a qualified builder, he assists many of our teams, and is a worship leader and musician at our community church.

Prisca

Early one morning in the middle of the war, I was on my way to town to buy food for the children. Under tables on shopfront verandahs were children who had slept rough the previous night and who were just waking up. They were gathering their little bundles of belongings ready to head back to their villages. These were the night commuters and Prisca was one of them. I stopped and asked her if she was okay. She told me that she was 11 and that she was sleeping in town because her dad had chased her away from home. I later learnt that he was a drug addict and wanted her, his youngest daughter, to get married. I could tell that Prisca was naturally intelligent, but because of the war and because she was a girl, formal education was not an option. Normally she would have been expected to just get married and have children. But that was not what she wanted.

Prisca's story broke my heart. I could see so much potential in her. So I invited her to move into the girls' dormitory at CKS as my daughter. Prisca readily accepted and was enrolled in the CKS primary school.

After three years, Prisca finished primary school at the top of her class and I sponsored her to go on to secondary school. She was a brilliant student and was keen to keep studying. CKS sponsored her to go on to train as a midwife.

Editor's note: Eventually Prisca got a job as a midwife in a local hospital and is now awaiting the completion of a CKS maternity centre so she can use her skills supporting her Mama Irene's legacy.

Everest

Twenty years ago, a small scrawny boy by the name of Everest gathered with other children for Aunty Irene's school under the mango tree. He watched intently as I turned the pages of the picture books. He, like many others, smiled and giggled as he viewed the cartoon animals wearing clothes.

"Oh yes," I would tell them, "Australian animals always wear clothes." Little by little, they learnt to sing songs about Jesus in halting English and try to mimic my silly actions.

Everest was an outstanding student. CKS sponsored him to train him in carpentry—a skill that would develop his sense of scale, but almost cost him his life. Studying at technical college, twenty kilometres from Kitgum Town, their college was targeted by rebels several times.

One dark evening in the playground, rebels were abducting children under 14 and tying them with rope. Everest and his 16-year-old friends were considered too old for the brutal indoctrination, so, at gunpoint, they were forced to lay face down on their dormitory floor while rebels prepared to throw hand grenades into their midst. But God intervened. A baby started crying outdoors, which alerted some slumbering army guards. Gunfire zapped across the night sky. Students and rebels fled in all directions. Everest's life was saved for a higher purpose.

As one who always loved and appreciated art, his sketches caught my attention. So I arranged for CKS to sponsor him to attend Michelangelo College of Creative Art in Kisubi for several years, where his talent was honed.

A large proportion of the CKS Community Church congregation are illiterate villagers. Everest brought the Bible to life on the walls of our church. In 2010, he painted the crucifixion scene which has caused many to fall to the ground weeping. Some have risen to their feet, healed and delivered. And one of his paintings now hangs on the wall of gospel singer Andrae Crouch's house.

Vincent

Fifteen years ago, a young boy sat listening attentively in our classroom. He did well in his exams and we sponsored him to go on to a nearby high school, where again he excelled. Deciding to study medicine, Vincent applied to Gulu University. During his holidays he worked tirelessly in our AIDS hospice.

One afternoon I asked him more about his story. He told me he was quite young when the rebels visited his compound. While he hid in the long grass, the rebels abducted members of his family and killed others. From that day forward, Vincent was alone.

In spite of his past pain, this quiet, studious and sensitive young man went on to become a top student in Gulu University. UNESCO then chose him to study medicine in Algeria. When asked about his pain, his response is: "Life is not about what happened to me in the past. Living is what I can do for my people in the present. My past is already gone, my present is where I live, my future is in the hands of God and He plans the best for me."

When Vincent completes his studies he hopes to return to the project and work as a doctor.

Rose

On a hot, dusty Sunday morning I was walking to church and saw a young girl walking towards me. Her tiny frame was struggling under the weight of a huge saucepan of water she was carrying on her head. She looked troubled. Curious as to why a young girl would be carrying such a heavy burden, I followed her home. I soon discovered that this girl's life was marred by abuse and neglect, so I asked her family if she could come and live in our girls' dormitory and study with us. They reluctantly agreed and Rose Akwo joined the CKS school at the age of 12.

She was a committed student and keen to learn. After completing her primary education, she joined our vocational training programme and learnt the skill of tailoring. I could see Rose had a natural eye for fashion and design, so I sponsored her to further her studies.

In 2007, Rose joined our teaching staff at the vocational training centre, where she worked for five years. In 2012 she opened her own tailoring shop in town, which often supplies our school children with their red shirts and skirts. My mission has been to develop the potential in each of our students. Rose told me she plans to be the top business entrepreneur in town. I believe she will do it.

BIBLIOGRAPHY

BBC News Africa. "Uganda Profile," http://www.bbc.co.uk/news/world-africa-14107906 (accessed 28 October 2013).

Department of Disaster Preparedness and Refugees. "Northern Uganda Internally Displaced Persons Profiling Study" (2005) http://www.fafo.no/ais/africa/uganda/IDP_uganda_2005.pdf (accessed 31 October 2013).

Gleeson, Irene. *Dance of the Tragic Heroines* (Hephzibah House, 2011).

Harlacher, Thomas. Traditional Ways of Coping with Consequences of Traumatic Stress in Acholiland: Northern Uganda ethnography from a Western psychological perspective (Switzerland: University of Freiburg, 2009).

Kapuscinski, Ryszard. *The Shadow of the Sun: My African Life* (trans. Klara Glowczewska; London: Penguin Books, 2002).

Moubarak, Alexa. "The Lord's Resistance Army: Enslaving the Children of Africa" (March 2010) http://ihscslnews.org/view_article.php?id=263 (accessed 28 April 2014).

Patel, Sheetal, et al. "Comparison of HIV-related vulnerabilities between former child soldiers and children never abducted by the LRA in northern Uganda" (2013) http://www.ncbi.nlm.nih.gov/pmc/articles/PMC3751706/ (accessed 31 October 2013).

Republic of Uganda Ministry of Health. "Health and mortality survey among internally displaced persons in Gulu, Kitgum and Pader districts, northern Uganda" (2005) http://www.who.int/hac/crises/uga/sitreps/Ugandamortsurvey.pdf (accessed 7 November 2013).

Rujumba, Joseph and Japheth Kwiringira, "Interface of culture, insecurity and HIV and AIDS: Lessons from displaced communities in Pader District, northern Uganda" (2010) http://www.conflictandhealth.com/content/4/1/18 (accessed 31 October 2013).

Sara, Sally. *Gogo Mama* (Australia: Pan Macmillan, 2007).

Uganda AIDS Commission. "Global Aids Response Progress Report: Country Progress Report Uganda" (2012) http://www.unaids.org/en/dataanalysis/knowyourresponse/countryprogress reports/2012countries/ce_UG_Narrative_Report[1].pdf (accessed 31 October 2013).

UNICEF. "Strengthening Birth Registration in Africa: Opportunities and Partnerships" http://www.unicef.org/esaro/Technical_paper_low_res_.pdf (accessed 30 October 2013).

UNICEF. Survey of War-Affected Youth (SWAY)

Women's Commission for Refugee Women and Children. "Resilience in the Darkness: An Update on Child Adolescent Night Commuters in Northern Uganda" (2005) http://womensrefugeecommission.org/resources/children-and-youth/453-resilience-in-the-darkness-an-update-on-child-and-adolescent-night-commuters-in-northern-uganda/file (accessed 30 October 2013).

Irene's work in the north of Uganda continues.

*To support Irene's ministry through child sponsorship
or by making a tax-deductible donation,
please visit:*

www.irenegleesonfoundation.com

Or you can purchase a variety of products
including crafts, music and media.